Drupal Web Services

Integrate social and multimedia web services and
applications with your Drupal website

Trevor James

PUBLISHING

BIRMINGHAM - MUMBAI

Drupal Web Services

First published: November 2010

Production Reference: 1161110

Published by Packt Publishing Ltd.
32 Lincoln Road,
Olton
Birmingham, B27 6PA, UK.

ISBN 978-1-849510-98-1

www.packtpub.com

Cover Image by Javier Barria (jbarriac@yahoo.com)

Credits

Author
Trevor James

Reviewers
John K Murphy

Michael L. Ruoss

Acquisition Editor
Steven Wilding

Development Editors
Akash Johari

Meeta Rajani

Technical Editors
Ajay Shanker

Mohd. Sahil

Copy Editor
Lakshmi Menon

Indexers
Hemangini Bari

Monica Ajmera Mehta

Rekha Nair

Editorial Team Leader
Aanchal Kumar

Project Team Leader
Lata Basantani

Project Coordinator
Zainab Bagasrawala

Proofreaders
Aaron Nash

Denise Dresner

Graphics
Nilesh Mohite

Production Coordinator
Kruthika Bangera

Cover Work
Kruthika Bangera

About the author

Trevor James is a Drupal consultant and web developer based in Middletown, MD, USA. Trevor has been designing websites for 14 years using a combination of HTML, XHTML, CSS, and ColdFusion, and has been using Drupal intensively for over 3 years. Trevor's focus is on building web portals for higher education, public education (K-12), non-profit, medical systems, and small business environments.

He is interested in best methods of integrating web services with Drupal sites, Drupal site performance, and using CCK, Views, and Panels to develop frontend interfaces to support data intensive websites. He loves teaching people about Drupal and and also about how to use this excellent open source content management framework.

Trevor has designed and developed websites for non-profit, education, medical-based systems, and small business organizations. He is currently working on a number of Drupal-related projects.

Trevor co-authored the Packt title *Drupal 6 Performance Tips*, published in February, 2010. For more on this title visit:

```
https://www.packtpub.com/drupal-6-performance-tips-to-maximize-and-
optimize-your-framework/book
```

Trevor created an 11+ hour video tutorial series titled *Introduction to Drupal 6* for VTC (Virtual Training Company) in 2009. The video is available via the VTC website at:

```
http://www.vtc.com/products/Introduction-To-Drupal-6-Tutorials.htm
```

Table of Contents

The book is dedicated to my wife Veronica and our daughters Clare and Francesca.

About the reviewers

John K Murphy is a software industry veteran with more than 25 years experience as a programmer and database administrator. A graduate of the University of West Virginia, he began writing computer games in the 1980s before pursuing a career as a computer consultant. Over the years, John has enjoyed developing software in most major programming languages while striving to keep current with new technologies.

In his spare time, John enjoys scuba diving, skydiving, and piloting small planes. He lives with his wife and two children in Pittsburgh, Pennsylvania.

Michael Ruoss is founder of and senior developer at UFirst Group. He holds a Master's Degree in Computer Science from Swiss Federal Institute of Technology in Zurich. After his studies, he worked for Optaros for two years as a developer/consultant. In 2010, he founded UFirst Group, a company doing system integrations based on open source frameworks.

During the past years, working for Optaros and UFirst Group, Michael Ruoss gained much experience in the integration of Drupal, Magento, Alfresco, and other CMS and eCommerce solutions. Michael also maintains two Drupal community modules, the *SEO Compliance Checker*, and the *Overlay Gallery*.

Susan Morrison and Ryan Wexler of Medical Business Systems were instrumental in testing and implementing many of the social application service integrations documented in this book. While writing the book, I worked closely with them on a redesign of the MBS website and integrated Twitter, Facebook, and LinkedIn with their new site. They taught me a great deal about these integrations from the end user and website manager perspectives.

Last but certainly not least, thanks to my friend and colleague Will McGrouther. Will is an expert on social web applications and the many discussions we had over the course of this book's roadmap inspired the text in many ways.

I look forward to working with you all in the near future. Drupal on!

Acknowledgements

Without the love and support of my wife Veronica and our twin daughters Clare and Francesca, this book would not have seen the light of day. I cannot express enough love and grace to the three of you for your encouragement and enthusiasm for my writing career.

Thanks (again!) to my father-in-law Tony Gornik for offering his residence in Hershey, PA as writing space on weekends.

Many thanks to the entire Packt editorial, project, marketing, and production teams for inviting me to work on this project and for continuing to publish exceptional titles on Drupal and open source applications. Many thanks to Steven Wilding, Packt Acquisition Editor, for serving as the lead editor on this title. Steven's encouragement and wisdom kept me on task with this book.

Thanks to Zainab Bagasrawala, Project Coordinator; Poorvi Nair, Project Coordinator; Akash Johari, Development Editor; Meeta Rajani, Development Editor; Lata Basantani, Projects Team Leader; Mohd Sahil, Technical Editor; and Patricia Weir, for keeping the project on track and for guiding the construction of this title.

A special thanks to Radha Iyer, Marketing Research Executive at Packt. I've worked closely with Radha on all aspects of marketing my first book, as well as having the opportunity to write multiple book reviews for Packt under Radha's guidance and vision. I am always impressed with Radha's ability to locate new marketing opportunities and applications to help increase knowledge about Drupal and open source.

Thank you to Jim Mason and Eric Condren for their help and knowledge using Drupal and CiviCRM at Frederick County Public Schools on multiple projects.

Preface

Drupal is a rich and dynamic open source content management system that can feed content into its framework from other web applications including Facebook, Flickr, Google, Twitter, and more, using standard communication protocols called web services. You may be aware that content can be driven to your Drupal site from different web applications, but when you think of experimenting with this, you can get bogged down due to limited knowledge of web services.

This book offers a practical hands-on guide to integrating web services with your Drupal website. It will compel you to learn more and more about web services and use them to easily share data and content resources between different applications and machines. This book also covers the usage of each web service for different purposes. It provides step-by-step instructions on integrating web services and web applications with your Drupal-powered website.

Drupal Web Services will show you how to work with all kinds of web services and Drupal. The book shows you how to integrate Flickr.com and Amazon.com content into your site; add multimedia and video to your site using video services including CDN2 and Kaltura. You will learn how to prevent spam using CAPTCHA, reCAPTCHA, and Mollom. You will also learn to explore the different types of web services Drupal offers and can integrate with using the Services module and XML-RPC. Next, you will learn to push content from Google documents, deploying this text and image-based content as Drupal nodes.

Next, you'll integrate your site with Twitter, Facebook, and LinkedIn and show how to post content from Drupal to these social networking applications automatically. At the end, you will learn about authentication methods for integrating web services with Drupal.

What this book covers

Chapter 1, About Drupal Web Services, focuses on web services from an introductory standpoint and defines what web services are and how they work with Drupal 6.

Chapter 2, Consuming Web Services in Drupal, turns to a discussion of how our Drupal site can act as a web services consumer. We discuss and show examples of using SOAP. We also install, configure, and use the FedEx Shipping Quotes module to get real-time shipping quotes in our Ubercart site.

Chapter 3, Drupal and Flickr, focuses on installing and configuring the Flickr module to communicate with the Flickr web service and display dynamic Flickr photo galleries on our Drupal site.

Chapter 4, Drupal and Amazon, focuses on installing and configuring both the Amazon and the Amazon Store modules to communicate with our Amazon associate account and practice filtering in specific Amazon products including books, CDs, DVDs, and other items into our Drupal nodes.

Chapter 5, Drupal and Multimedia Web Services, focuses on other types of multimedia including video and how we can integrate our Drupal site with two popular video hosting services, CDN2, and Kaltura.

Chapter 6, Drupal Web Services the Easy Way: The Services Module, focuses on installing and enabling the Services module and explore what the Services module offers our Drupal site(s).

Chapter 7, Drupal Spam and Web Services, focuses on installing and using various modules including CAPTCHA, reCAPTCHA, and Mollom to integrate our Drupal website with spam prevention web services.

Chapter 8, Using XML-RPC, looks in more detail at how Drupal uses the XML-RPC protocol and how this protocol can help integrate your Drupal site with external web service-based applications and servers. We'll deploy content from a Google Documents account to our Drupal site.

Chapter 9, Twitter and Drupal, focuses on installing and enabling a few Twitter-based modules to allow for integration with the Twitter web service API.

Chapter 10, LinkedIn and Drupal, focuses on exploring methods of integrating the popular professional social networking application LinkedIn with our Drupal site.

Chapter 11, Facebook and Drupal, focuses on exploring methods of integrating Drupal with the popular social networking web application Facebook.

Chapter 12, Authentication Services, focuses on exploring methods various web service authentication methods and protocols for use with your Drupal site including OpenID and OAuth.

Appendix A, Modules used in the Book, summarizes the contributed modules we've used in the book and present a listing of modules that allow for integration between Drupal and web service applications and servers.

What you need for this book

The book assumes you have a working installation of Drupal 6.19 (latest Drupal 6 version at time of this book's release). If you need to install Drupal, you can do this by first setting up a localhost development environment on your computer. First, you will need to install a LAMP stack on your computer (Apache web server, MySQL, and PHP. You will also need to install the latest version of Drupal 6. Drupal can be downloaded at: `http://drupal.org/`.

For an easy to install Drupal package that includes the entire suite of Apache, MySQL, and PHP, you can download the Acquia Stack Installer. This will install the entire LAMP and Drupal application stack on your computer. The Acquia Stack Installer can be downloaded at: `http://acquia.com/downloads`.

The book installs and runs Drupal on a Windows PC but you can easily run the Acquia Stack Installer on a Mac or Linux computer.

For detailed instructions on installing the Acquia Stack go to: `http://acquia.com/documentation/acquia-drupal-stack`.

Who this book is for

If you are a Drupal user, webmaster, or Drupal site administrator who wants to integrate Flickr, Facebook, Twitter, Amazon, LinkedIn, Kaltura, and Mollom with your Drupal site then this book will be a good addition to your Drupal library.

You do not need to have programming experience to use this book. Drupal web services is written for anyone who works with Drupal on a daily basis.

Conventions

In this book, you will find a number of styles of text that distinguish between different kinds of information. Here are some examples of these styles, and an explanation of their meaning.

Code words in text are shown as follows: "We can include other contexts through the use of the include directive."

A block of code is set as follows:

```
<?xml version="1.0"?>
<methodCall>
<methodName>examples.getBlogName</methodName>
<params>
```

New terms and **important words** are shown in bold. Words that you see on the screen, in menus or dialog boxes for example, appear in the text like this: "clicking the **Next** button moves you to the next screen".

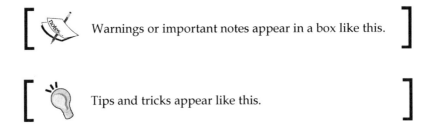

Warnings or important notes appear in a box like this.

Tips and tricks appear like this.

Reader feedback

Feedback from our readers is always welcome. Let us know what you think about this book—what you liked or may have disliked. Reader feedback is important for us to develop titles that you really get the most out of.

To send us general feedback, simply send an e-mail to feedback@packtpub.com, and mention the book title via the subject of your message.

If there is a book that you need and would like to see us publish, please send us a note in the **SUGGEST A TITLE** form on www.packtpub.com or e-mail suggest@packtpub.com.

If there is a topic that you have expertise in and you are interested in either writing or contributing to a book on, see our author guide on www.packtpub.com/authors.

Customer support

Now that you are the proud owner of a Packt book, we have a number of things to help you to get the most from your purchase.

> **Downloading the example code for this book**
> You can download the example code files for all Packt books you have purchased from your account at http://www.PacktPub.com. If you purchased this book elsewhere, you can visit http://www.PacktPub.com/support and register to have the files e-mailed directly to you.

Errata

Although we have taken every care to ensure the accuracy of our content, mistakes do happen. If you find a mistake in one of our books — maybe a mistake in the text or the code — we would be grateful if you would report this to us. By doing so, you can save other readers from frustration and help us improve subsequent versions of this book. If you find any errata, please report them by visiting http://www.packtpub.com/support, selecting your book, clicking on the **let us know** link, and entering the details of your errata. Once your errata are verified, your submission will be accepted and the errata will be uploaded on our website, or added to any list of existing errata, under the Errata section of that title. Any existing errata can be viewed by selecting your title from http://www.packtpub.com/support.

Piracy

Piracy of copyright material on the Internet is an ongoing problem across all media. At Packt, we take the protection of our copyright and licenses very seriously. If you come across any illegal copies of our works, in any form, on the Internet, please provide us with the location address or website name immediately so that we can pursue a remedy.

Please contact us at copyright@packtpub.com with a link to the suspected pirated material.

We appreciate your help in protecting our authors, and our ability to bring you valuable content.

Questions

You can contact us at questions@packtpub.com if you are having a problem with any aspect of the book, and we will do our best to address it.

About Drupal Web Services

1

Besides its core content management functionality, Drupal can also feed content into its framework from other web applications, including Flickr, Twitter, Google, Amazon, Facebook, Mollom, and many more. This communication between Drupal and other web portals is what makes Drupal a feature-rich content management framework capable of supporting multiple methods of feeding content into its database and site structure. For example, as a Drupal developer, you can feed content into your Drupal site using aggregation or RSS feeds. The Drupal FeedAPI (Application Programming Interface) module allows you to take RSS or XML URLs from external websites and add these feeds to your Drupal site. This is one robust method of getting content from other web applications and sites.

How do we take content from all of these different web applications and share the content with a Drupal site? This is becoming highly important now due to the wealth of rich content management applications that are both on the market and also available in the open source community. For example, how can we take all of the images we upload to our Flickr site and share those images with users on our Drupal site? In this book, we'll look in detail at the Drupal Services module, a contributed module that helps you to speed up your connections to web services. This module will allow us to integrate your Drupal site with external applications by using interfaces, such as XMLRPC, JSON, JSON-RPC, REST, SOAP, and AMF. These interfaces will allow your Drupal site to interact with and provide web services.

In this chapter, you will learn the basics of web services and Drupal, including:

- What are web services and why are web services useful?
- Why do we use web services in Drupal?
- How does Drupal 6 use web services?
- Standards compliance when using web services in Drupal
- Drupal as a service consumer and as a service provider

Let's begin our discussion of what web services are and how they work with Drupal. To get started, we need to define some of the larger concepts and the Drupal concepts that we'll be talking about.

What are web services?

In order for our Drupal site to communicate and interact with other web applications, such as Flickr, Amazon, Mollom, or Twitter, we need to use standard communication protocols in the web development world called web services. Web service protocols will allow applications that reside on external websites and servers to interact and communicate with our Drupal website that is running on our own server. Web services will also allow our Drupal site to pass along content and data to external web applications existing on remote servers.

When we define web services, we need to point out that this type of communication provides for interoperability. This means that a web service communication can happen between two completely different environments but still work because we use standard protocols to make it happen.

Web services allow us to call another application on a remote server. A good analogy to this is using your cell phone to call a friend or colleague. You have one type of cell phone using one type of cell phone service. You call your colleague's cell phone. They have another type of cell with a different service provider, but the call goes through and is successful because the two services communicate with each other using standard cell phone communication protocols.

The web service call happens through coded protocols that are translated into a language and standard protocol that both computers can understand. Generally, this is done by using the XML language to translate the programmed request into the other external applications. Web applications have a standard in which they can usually read XML files. XML is a text-based format, so nearly all computer systems and applications can work with the XML format.

The web services protocol also uses a concept called remoting or **Remote Procedure Calling (RPC)** that allows one application to initiate or "call" a function inside of an application on a remote server. Our Drupal site can communicate with an application on a remote server and call a function in that application. For example, we might want to make our Drupal website call and interact with our Flickr photo gallery, or we may want to take all of our Drupal home page content and push it over to our Facebook account. We can do both of these actions using the web service protocols.

The computer that contains the application—that we will communicate with—can be anywhere in the world. It could be sitting on a server in the US, Europe, Asia, South America, or somewhere else.

XML and web services

As mentioned above, the base foundation for web services is a protocol or code called XML. For our Drupal site residing on our server, to talk and interact with a website or application on another server, we need to use XML, which is a language commonly understood between different applications. Our site and server understands XML as does the application we want to communicate with. We can do this over the standard HTTP protocol for website communication, as HTTP is the most standard protocol for Internet communication. The reason we use XML for communication between the applications and the sites is because XML replaces the proprietary function (whether the function is in RPC or another programming language or interface) and formats it into the standard XML code format. This allows applications to understand each other easily.

An analogy to this is: if we have two people, one from Germany and the other from France, speaking to one another, and neither person knows the other's language but both of them know English, then they must speak in English, as it's a language they both understand and can easily communicate in. It's a similar situation when XML is used to translate a web service's function into a commonly understood format.

So first we need to send the function call to a remote application. Our calling application or website creates the XML document that will represent the programmed function we want to execute. The XML is then transmitted over HTTP to the remote application and it can then be interpreted and understood by the remote application. The remote application then executes the function based on the XML formatting.

Some examples of web service's methods are **SOAP (Simple Object Access Protocol)**, **UDDI (Universal Description, Discovery and Integration)**, **WSDL (Web Services Description Language)**, **XML-RPC (XML Remote Procedure Call)**, **JSON (JavaScript Object Notation)**, **JSON-RPC**, **REST (Representational State Transfer)**, and **AMF (Action Message Format)**. We are not going to look at these interfaces in detail now but we will explore how they work with Drupal later in this book when we take a more detailed look at how the Services module works. For now, it's helpful for us to understand that these protocols and platforms exist and that our Drupal site can provide web services to other applications via these multiple interfaces and platforms.

Here's a diagram that outlines a simple web service request and response. This is a request sent from our Drupal site (client) over HTTP to an external server to request data. The data exists on the server (remote) in the form of a **URI (Uniform Resource Identifier)** item. The response is sent back to our Drupal site through XML.

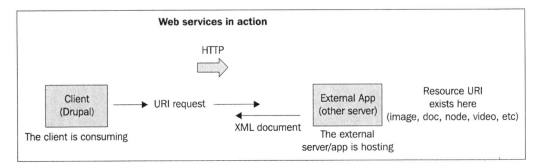

The REST protocol

Let's look briefly at one web service protocol and technology, and define it. As mentioned before, there are many technologies you can use to implement web services. REST (Representational State Transfer) is one such technology. The reason REST is a preferred technology within the web development and Drupal community is due to its flexibility and standards. REST allows us to do the following when we initiate a web service using its protocol:

- Use a standard method such as XML as our message format
- Send the message over standard protocol such as HTTP
- Provide or connect to specific resources where each resource (image, document, page, and node) is given a unique resource identifier (a URI)

We can take this concept and try it out on our Drupal site by writing some PHP code that makes an HTTP request to another web application resource. For example, we may want to make a call to a Picasa photo gallery and feed a select number and type of photos back to our Drupal site and display the photos in a Drupal node on our site. The request targets this specific resource by making a GET request to the URI of the resource. The application we are communicating with sends a response back to us in XML format. That XML can then be integrated into our Drupal site using a module, for example. The request might be made to a user's Flickr or Picasa photo gallery. The request gets returned to our Drupal site as XML and we parse this XML into our Drupal site and the user's photos or gallery then get displayed on our site.

This is just one protocol example. We'll discuss in detail about the other protocols in the later chapters.

 Greg Hines of pingVision provides a good introductory resource on REST and Drupal in the document titled RESTful Web Services and Drupal. The document is available on pingVision's website as a PDF download from: `http://pingvision.com/files/restful_web_services_and_drupal.pdf`

Standards compliance

As discussed in the REST protocol's example, web services and Drupal's use of web services follow specific standards. In order to maintain as much interoperability and flexibility as possible, all of the protocols used respond for the most part using XML as the standard response mechanism and format.

Additionally, all the communication between services, in our example between a client and a server, happens over HTTP (the standard web protocol). This is a uniform protocol that is used for transport and communication of the service. All transports take place uniformly using GET, POST, PUT, and DELETE requests, for example.

The HTTP requests are stateless, meaning that the request over HTTP happens once at one given moment and is isolated from all other activated requests. So the request stands alone. If it succeeds, it gets a response. If it fails, it gets no response from the server or application it's communicating with. The request can be repeated an infinite number of times.

Finally, all of the resources we try and access are those that we are sending to another application using a unique resource identifier (URI) to identify and define what they are. So images on our site have unique identifiers as well as those residing in another web application. Each of these unique identifiers allows for addresses or locations for each node or file in question. So each resource in a web service's communication has an address. Each resource has one URI and each address has one URI. Some examples of this would be the following locations on my Drupal site:

- `http://variantcube.com/`
- `http://variantcube.com/recommended-drupal-resources`
- `http://variantcube.com/node/68`
- `http://variantcube.com/search/node/podcast`
- `http://variantcube.com/rss.xml`

Another reason we want to be standards compliant, when writing or working with web services, is for simplicity. We do not need any special tools to program web services as long as we follow these standards. We can use the web application modules and PHP, and stick to these coding standards and protocols.

Why are web services useful?

Web services are useful for a number of reasons, especially when it comes to Drupal and Drupal's relationship and interaction with other web content management systems and applications. The web has a huge number of web applications, so web developers and content developers can pass their content to the web browsers and make it available to the web visitors. This is why the Internet is useful to us. We can go to a website and view the content. Whenever we do that, we're looking at content that is proprietary to a specific web application. In Drupal, our content is in the form of nodes, for example. We may want to share these nodes with other websites that are non-Drupal, such as a Wordpress-powered site.

Web services are useful because they present us with an architecture where a resource on a site (an image, textual content, such as a node ID or block ID, a video or audio file) is given a unique identifier. For example, in Drupal, every node has an ID. Every file you upload to a Drupal site also has a unique path to it.

This is extremely useful since all applications share this common semantic standard. We name things similarly on all of our web applications. We can then leverage this by writing code in PHP, for example, the one that calls these resources. The application server that houses the resource then responds to our request using an XML document.

Why use web services in Drupal?

With web services, we can take our Drupal content and share this content with other web applications and, essentially, with the web at large. Our content is no longer just our content and it is not specific to our Drupal website. It can be shared and integrated. Drupal's codebase is PHP-based and many of the popular web applications being used today, including Wordpress, Joomla!, and Flickr, are also PHP-based. So we have a common programming language we can work with and use to integrate these applications.

Here are some concrete examples. Perhaps your Human Resources Department wants to integrate its job postings and applications with another web application such as Monster.com. Web services can allow this to happen. Your office's payroll department may want to connect to its bank account in order to pass data from the payroll reports over to its bank reporting mechanism. Web services can allow this to happen. You may want to take all of the photos you upload to your Drupal site in image galleries built with the **Views** module, and take these photos and send them to Flickr so that they automatically show up in your Flickr account or on Flickr's public site. Web services can make this happen.

This leads to another advantage of using web services with Drupal and why we would choose to use Drupal in the first place. Instead of having to upload our photos twice—once to our Drupal site and then repeating the procedure to our Flickr site—web services allows us to upload the images to our Drupal site once and then automatically send that data over to Flickr without having to upload one (or even a batch of images) again. It saves us time and speeds up the entire process of generating web-based content.

Additionally, there may be applications we want to use in our Drupal site, for example applications where we want to consume content without having to code again. We can just reuse these applications using the web services protocols and get this application content into our Drupal site. So we can consume web services. Examples of this would be converting currency on our site, feeding weather reports and other weather data into our site, feeding natural disaster scientific data into our site from services that provide it, feeding language translation services, feeding music podcasts, and more. Instead of having to reprogram this type of content, we can grab it from another web application and show it automatically on our site using web services.

Simply put, this opens up a method of easily sharing data and content resources between applications and machines that are running on different platforms and architecture. We have opened up a gold mine of capabilities here because we can talk to applications that run different software from our Drupal site and on different computing platforms.

How Drupal uses web services

Drupal can use web services following any of the protocols mentioned earlier, including XML-RPC, REST, and SOAP. Drupal can consume web services by requesting data from other web applications using RSS and XML-formatted requests. As a web developer, you can write your own service code in Drupal using PHP. You can also use the **Services** module as well as other service-specific contributed modules to create these web service requests. In this next section, we're going to look at both these examples. First, we'll see how Drupal works as a service consumer, where basically it is a client requesting data from an external server.

We'll also look at how Drupal can provide services using the Services module, RSS, AMFPHP, and XML-RPC. All of these protocols will be explained in detail in the later chapters.

Drupal as a service consumer

Let's outline some brief examples of how Drupal consumes content and data from other web applications, including Mollom, Flickr, and Facebook. We're going to look at these applications in more detail later in the book, but we'll introduce them here and show some basic examples.

You can configure your Drupal site to consume various web services by using contributed Drupal modules for each specific task or application you are trying to consume. Drupal can consume services from applications that will help your website prevent spam, integrate photos, integrate taxonomy and tags, and enhance your Drupal free tagging and autotagging abilities, and integrate with applications such as Facebook and Twitter.

Mollom

Mollom is a web service that will help you to block spam on your Drupal site. It's a separate application that runs as a web service. Drupal can connect to the Mollom web service through a contributed module called Mollom. The contributed module project page is available at `http://drupal.org/project/mollom`.

Mollom will offer you CAPTCHA options for your Drupal site as well as prevent and block comment spam and Drupal node form spam, including any spam that might populate your nodes through content type forms, story, page, and forum forms. It will prevent user registration from being compromised and prevent fake users from signing up on your site.

The Mollom project was developed and is maintained by Drupal's founder, Dries Buytaert, and a team of developers very familiar with Drupal, so the integration between the two applications is seamless. Mollom is included in the Acquia Drupal packaged installation, so if you use Acquia Drupal you will already have the Mollom module and service integrated into your Drupal site. If you run a Drupal 6 installation independent of the Acquia package, you'll need to install the Mollom contributed module to make the service interaction work. You can read the entire Mollom client API documentation on the Mollom website at `http://mollom.com/files/mollom-client-api.pdf`.

The API documentation provides a huge amount of detail on how the service works, but simply put, it uses the XML-RPC interface. So as explained earlier in this chapter, Mollom uses Remote Procedure Call protocol, which itself uses XML to encode calls as its service mechanism. The Mollom API notes that any XML-RPC call to its service should follow the HTTP/1.0 standard. The documentation also mentions that any client (our Drupal site in our case) that makes a RPC call to the Mollom service needs to only make these requests from valid Mollom servers, and using a valid public and private key encryption for the specific website making the calls. This means that the communication is encrypted between your Drupal site and the Mollom application.

The RPC calls that Drupal makes to the Mollom application server are HTTP requests. These are the calls that your Drupal site makes back to Mollom:

- `mollom.getServerList` — this requests which Mollom servers can handle the call coming in from the Drupal site
- `mollom.checkContent` — this asks Mollom whether the request is legitimate
- `mollom.sendFeedback` — this tells the Mollom application that the spam message was indeed spam
- `mollom.getImageCaptcha` — this asks Mollom to generate an image CAPTCHA
- `mollom.getAudioCaptcha` — this asks Mollom to generate an audio CAPTCHA
- `mollom.checkCaptcha` — asks Mollom to verify the result of a CAPTCHA
- `mollom.getStatistics` — asks Mollom to send statistics
- `mollom.verifyKey` — asks Mollom to return a status value

These calls are routed from your Drupal site over to a Mollom server each time your Drupal site needs to check whether a specific content post is spam or not.

Another interesting concept here is that Mollom actually provides a higher availability backup server that a Drupal user can sign up for. This server would then kick in and work if the other Mollom application servers have failed. So Mollom also provides a fallback, but it will cost you to sign up for it. It's not a free service.

So you can see here that the Mollom-contributed module allows you, as a Drupal site manager, easy access to set up this web service. We'll look at the code and backend of this configuration in more detail later, but for now this introduces us to how a Drupal contributed module can allow our site connections to a web service.

Auto tagging

The **Auto Tagging**-contributed module allows you to auto-tag your site's content using a web services-based interface. The services interface provides you with the tag contexts to use to tag your content. This module allows for integration with the popular **OpenCalais** web service as well as the **tagthe.net** and **Yahoo! Terms Extraction** services. **OpenCalais** is a web service provided by *Thomson Reuters* that allows Drupal developers to access a huge variety of tagging and terms that are continuously updated and added to. It's basically a stockpile of tags and terms that you can utilize and integrate with your Drupal site content. You can use **Auto Tagging** module to make the connection to OpenCalais. More details about the **Auto Tagging** module are available on its Drupal.org project page at http://drupal. org/project/autotagging.

Also check OpenCalais project for other important details at http://www. opencalais.com/.

To utilize these web services, you first need to install and enable the **Auto Tagging** module on your Drupal site. Once enabled, and depending on the web service you decide to use, you will configure a category/vocabulary that will be populated with the terms from the service. For example, if you were going to integrate with OpenCalais, you would first create a taxonomy vocabulary for OpenCalais tags. You would associate this vocabulary with the content types you want to tag on your site. The services will read your content that you want to tag and then apply tags automatically based on the content of your node.

If you are using OpenCalais, you'll need to first create an API key with the OpenCalais application. Then you'll add this API key to your module configuration.

This is a great module to use if you are looking to auto-tag content on your site using common and popular tags that are being culled, based on other web content using these tag-based web services. It's another example of how you don't have to reinvent the wheel or the application when you are building your site. You do not need to create tags. You can simply use tags that have already been generated for popular web content.

Flickr and Flickr API

The Flick and Flickr API modules allow Drupal to consume and access photos that are posted on the Flickr website. In order to use this web service, with Drupal functioning as the consumer, we'll need to set up a Flickr API key so that we can use this key in our configuration in our Drupal site. You will become used to this process when setting up Drupal as a web service consumer. In order for your Drupal site to communicate with the web service and use its functionality, you'll need to sign up for API keys for many of these modules and configurations. We'll look at how the Flickr API works in much more detail in *Chapter 3, Drupal and Flickr*.

Apache Solr search integration

The Apache Solr Search Integration module takes your Drupal site and integrates it with the Apache Solr Search web service. There is more information about the Apache Solr project at `http://lucene.apache.org/solr/`.

You would use this module if you want to add a more robust and enhanced Search functionality to your Drupal site besides the core Drupal search module. The service provides many extra features and better performance than the core Drupal search. You can have specific searching on content authors, taxonomy, and CCK fields, for example. This is called faceted search (`http://en.wikipedia.org/wiki/Faceted_browser`).

The module provides XML files that you need to have installed in order to make the web services work. The module also depends on your Drupal core search framework being in place, so you can run both the core Drupal search and the Apache Solr search in tandem, or just run one or the other. But the core search needs to be installed. The Drupal.org website lists many related projects that you can integrate with this module and the web service.

Facebook

Drupal can connect to Facebook and also run Facebook-style applications using the abundance of recent Facebook applications and contributed modules available. These include:

- Drupal for Facebook (fb)
- Facebook Connect
- Canvas Page

The Drupal for Facebook module is actually a larger scale module that allows you to program applications that run on Facebook and/or on your Drupal site but provides Facebook mechanisms. You can code up applications that run on your Drupal site and consume Facebook data — these are Facebook Connect-style applications — using the standards that this web service provides.

Drupal as a service provider

Drupal provides web services using a variety of methods and protocols. Some of these protocols are supported by using core modules and code that provide RSS- and XML-based feeds; and contributed modules, including the Services module that supports various service protocols. Drupal also supports protocols including AMFPHP XML-RPC. We'll look at each of them briefly in this section,

Services module

The **Services** module is the latest and newest version of the web services-contributed Drupal module. The Services module is a standard solution that allows for the integration of external web applications with your Drupal site. This module supports service callbacks used with standard service protocols, such as JSON, JSON-RPC, REST, SOAP, AMF, and more. The Services module allows your Drupal site to communicate and provide web services via these multiple interfaces using the same callback programming. So the module provides a large amount of flexibility and standards that you can use when programming web services to work with your Drupal site.

We'll be discussing this module in detail in *Chapter 5, Drupal and Multimedia Web Services*, but here's a very brief introduction to what the module can do:

- Contains an API that allows other modules the ability to create web services
- Contains server API that allows modules to create servers such as REST and SOAP

- Includes test API and test pages
- Provides the ability to manage API keys easily
- File, Menu, Node, System, Taxonomy, User, and Views services included

As mentioned earlier, the Services module allows you to plug web services' API keys into its configuration so that you can set up a communication with various web service applications. An API key works similarly to a username, allowing you to access the applications securely by adding your specific API key or code. Many times an API key comes with a secret passcode that you will also add to the module's configuration. So when you sign up for a Twitter Developer's account to utilize and configure the Twitter module in Drupal, you'll be given an API key and secret code that you'll need to add to your module's configuration page. Many of the modules that we'll look at in this book use this method of API key and code.

The Services module provides a detailed handbook and documentation on Drupal. org at http://drupal.org/handbook/modules/services.

RSS

Drupal comes installed with core **RSS** functionality and support. Your main Drupal home page can have an RSS feed implemented on it if you post Story nodes to your home page. You can also create RSS feeds for any node or block in your Drupal site using the **Views** module to set up attached feeds. So, Drupal provides a very flexible environment for allowing other external web applications access to your content feeds. Many contributed modules also come installed with a default RSS feed. Using the core Drupal functionality for RSS feeds and also core modules such as Aggregator, you can post RSS feeds in RSS, RFF, or Atom format. These formats are all XML-based, again supporting and adhering to the web service standard.

In addition, each term on your Drupal site (using Taxonomy core module) displays an RSS feed. For example, on my site, I have a **Featured** term at this unique identifier at:

http://variantcube.com/taxonomy/term/4.

This term also has a feed attached to it at:

http://variantcube.com/taxonomy/term/4/0/feed.

This feed shows all of the nodes (node title and teaser) for any content tagged with the featured term. So, Drupal provides many ways for other applications to call for content. Other web apps can call our site and request these feeds and this feed's content. Drupal can also act as a client here and call feeds from other web applications using a module such as the FeedAPI module: http://drupal.org/project/feedapi.

AMFPHP

AMFPHP is an open source PHP-based implementation of the Action Message Format (AMF), which allows for ActionScript objects to be sent to server-based services. This allows for web client applications built in Flash, Flex, and AIR to communicate with PHP-based web applications such as Drupal. There is more introductory detail about AMFPHP on the AMFPHP website at `http://www.amfphp.org/`.

Drupal can use AMFPHP through a contributed module called AMFPHP. This module (`http://drupal.org/project/amfphp`) provides support for integrating the AMFPHP protocol with the Services module in Drupal. So this is a contributed module that allows for a bridge between AMFPHP and Services. In order to use this service and module, you need to have the Drupal Services module installed and you need to install AMFPHP (version 1.9 beta 2) on your server. With this in place, Drupal can act as an AMFPHP-based client and provide Drupal integration with Flash and Flex applications.

XML-RPC

Drupal supports the **XML-RPC** protocol natively. XML-Remote Procedure Call is one of the basic and simplest web service architectures. It uses XML to encode the function calls it makes and it makes these calls over HTTP. XML-RPC was created in 1998 by Dave Winer of UserLand Software. More about XML-RPC can be viewed on the main XML-RPC website at `http://www.xmlrpc.com/`.

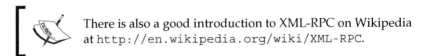

There is also a good introduction to XML-RPC on Wikipedia at `http://en.wikipedia.org/wiki/XML-RPC`.

In your Drupal site, you can view the main `xmlrpc.php` file, which is located in your root Drupal site folder. The code in this file looks like this:

```php
<?php
// $Id: xmlrpc.php,v 1.15 2005/12/10 19:26:47 dries Exp $
/**
 * @file
 * PHP page for handling incoming XML-RPC requests from clients.
 */
include_once './includes/bootstrap.inc';
drupal_bootstrap(DRUPAL_BOOTSTRAP_FULL);
include_once './includes/xmlrpc.inc';
include_once './includes/xmlrpcs.inc';
xmlrpc_server(module_invoke_all('xmlrpc'));
```

This PHP file provides the default core code for handling any XML-RPC request or call that is attempted on your site by an external web application. You will notice that it includes the Drupal bootstrap as well as two xmlrpc-specific include files that are located in your /includes core folder. It also invokes the xml_rpc server using a module_invoke_all.

In Drupal, the XML-RPC request is sent from a client (your Drupal site) to an external host or server. It's a similar type of call as the REST protocol explained earlier. If your Drupal site is acting as the server receiving the request from an external client, then your Drupal site provides the xmlrpc.php file to handle this incoming request. This file handles the incoming call. The incoming request will most likely be formatted in XML and look something like this:

```xml
<?xml version="1.0"?>
<methodCall>
  <methodName>examples.getBlogName</methodName>
  <params>
    <param>
        <value><i4>4</i4></value>
    </param>
  </params>
</methodCall>
```

This request is calling for a user blog on your Drupal site with the method call of .getBlogName. It's asking for a specific blog value of 4. This is just an example of the semantics of the code.

The response that is sent back from your Drupal site (client) to the remote server/application might look like this:

```xml
<?xml version="1.0"?>
<methodResponse>
  <params>
    <param>
        <value><string>Trevor's Blog</string></value>
    </param>
  </params>
</methodResponse>
```

For a very detailed introduction to XML-RPC, refer to *Chapter 19, XML-RPC*, of *"Pro Drupal Development"*, *John K. VanDyk*, *APress*. We will also return to a more detailed discussion of XML-RPC and how to write your own XML-RPC code in *Chapter 4*, *Drupal and Amazon*. For now, it's enough to understand that your Drupal site does support XML-RPC by default, using the `xmlrpc.php` file and code.

Summary

In this chapter, we've introduced the concepts and functionality of web services and how they interact with your Drupal site and applications. Here's a brief recap of what we learned in this chapter:

- We learned what web services are and how they work using a set of standard protocols, including HTTP, Uniform Resource Indicators, and the XML format.

- We discussed the various protocols and interfaces that web services take the form of when including the REST, SOAP, XML-RPC, and AMFPHP interfaces. We talked about how Drupal can integrate and use these protocols.

- We mapped out how a web service protocol works and functions, specifically looking at the REST protocol and also at XML-RPC, which comes native to your Drupal core install. Drupal supports web services in its core configuration using XML-RPC.

- We looked in detail at how Drupal uses web services, both as a consumer of services and a provider of services.

- As a consumer of web services, we looked at a number of contributed modules that Drupal uses to interface with web services when Drupal is the client in the client/server relationship. These include Mollom, Auto Tagging, Flickr, Apache Solr, and Facebook.

- We looked at how Drupal can serve as a web services provider by looking briefly at the Services module, RSS, AMFPHP, and XML-RPC.

- We looked in detail at some code examples of how Drupal uses XML-RPC, including the code for sending a call to another server or application, and for receiving the response back from the web service.

In *Chapter 2*, *Consuming Web Services in Drupal*, we will start taking a deeper and more detailed look at Drupal web services as we discuss how Drupal consumes web services using the SOAP client module. We'll also take a detailed look at the SOAP protocol.

2
Consuming Web Services in Drupal

In the previous chapter, we learned that our Drupal site can act as a web services client or a web services provider (or server). Drupal does this by integrating and using various types of web services code, including XML-RPC, REST, JSON, XML, and RSS. In this chapter, we're going to discuss how our Drupal site can act as a web services consumer. This means that we can take our Drupal site and add code to it in the form of a Drupal module, and make this module connect to an external server or application that provides a web service that we want to utilize and consume data from.

We're first going to look in detail at a protocol that Drupal can use to make this communication happen. This web services protocol is called **SOAP (Simple Object Access Protocol)**. We'll define SOAP and look at various implementations of SOAP with our Drupal site. We'll also look in detail at the two contributed Drupal modules that utilize SOAP for web service integration. The SOAP Client module is a developer's module and has a higher learning curve. It assumes you know how to write your own web services remote procedure call code and implement this code in a custom module. You can then use the SOAP Client module to enable your custom module to talk to an external web service and load its **WSDL (Web Service Description Language)**, for example.

WSDL is an XML-based document(s) that describes and outlines a web service and the model for interacting with this web service. The document specifies where the web service resides, and the types of operations the web service performs. This includes specifications defining the web service, port, or the endpoint where the service is located; the binding style; port type or interface; operations performed; and the message corresponding to this operation. For more on WSDL, see the definition at Wikipedia: `http://en.wikipedia.org/wiki/Web_Services_Description_Language`.

We'll also look in detail at a contributed module that has already been coded for us but provides a large amount of functionality, especially for Drupal sites running e-commerce using **Ubercart**. The module is the **FedEx Shipping Quotes** for **Ubercart** module and it allows our Drupal site to consume web services from the FedEx Shipping Services API. For example, this module allows your site visitors to get real time FedEx shipping quotes returned to them when they proceed to the checkout from their Ubercart order. With their products in their shopping cart, the site visitor can get shipping quotes immediately in their checkout screen and the quotes are up-to-date from the FedEx Web Services. Shoppers can then easily select the quote they want to use with their order, for example, FedEx Overnight shipping, and this will automatically add the shipping cost to their Ubercart order.

This module will give you a good practical and easy-to-use example of consuming web services in Drupal.

So to summarize, in this chapter we will:

- Define SOAP and determine how we can use SOAP with Drupal
- Use the **SOAP Client** module
- Use the **FedEx Shipping Quotes** module

Using SOAP

SOAP (Simple Object Access Protocol) is an object-access protocol that allows us to exchange information within our web services environment. The SOAP protocol is currently maintained by the XML Protocol Working Group of the World Wide Web Consortium (W3C). The current SOAP version is 1.2.

Like XML-RPC and REST, the SOAP protocol uses XML as its exchange format. SOAP is actually called a successor to the XML-RPC protocol, and offers more functionality and enhancement compared to XML-RPC. SOAP also follows a consistent and easy-to-use framework, similar to REST that keeps all of its messages formatted in XML, uses RPC (Remote Procedure Call) to make its function calls, and HTTP to transfer information. SOAP basically runs as a foundation for your web services interface and allows you to build up your web services environment on top of its protocol. This is why you run SOAP within your PHP environment because PHP is providing your foundational programming backend framework.

SOAP works by making a Remote Procedure Call to an application on an external server. In this chapter, we're going to look at an example of SOAP being used in a Drupal site to make a call from an Ubercart installation on your Drupal site to an external FedEx Shipping API to request shipping quotes for a customer's product that is in their shopping cart on the Drupal site. So, SOAP will enable this call to happen, and for Drupal to consume the resulting shipping quote.

The way the call works is that it is encoded in XML format by the SOAP client script. XML was chosen as the format to use for the messaging, as it's a standard markup language used by many major corporations and open source applications.

The XML is then sent over HTTP transport protocol to the external web application server. HTTP is a popular method of transporting the messages encoded by the SOAP client and server because HTTP is the common transport method used by many networks and firewalls. SOAP can also be used with HTTPS for any secure transactions, for example, when you are using Ubercart to pass client data over to the FedEx server API. These transactions should be kept secure so that SOAP supports this secure framework.

In our FedEx example, the FedEx server returns an XML-formatted document with shipping quote data based on the remote procedure call that was submitted by the Drupal client. This data gets integrated directly into our Ubercart installation using a contributed Ubercart FedEx API module that integrates with the SOAP protocol. We're going to look at both this Ubercart module and the Drupal-contributed **SOAP Client** module in this chapter.

Drupal uses two types of SOAP with its web services consumption. Drupal supports the PHP 5.x SOAP extension (through various downloaded package versions) and also the NuSOAP extension. NuSOAP is a not a SOAP extension but rather a set of PHP classes that allow for the creation and consumption of web services. You do not need to install any special PHP extensions if you run NuSOAP. NuSOAP does support the SOAP 1.1 specification and can generate WSDL documents. In this chapter, we're going to focus on using the PHP SOAP extension rather than NuSOAP, but you now know that there is another option for using SOAP with your server and site.

 For more on the history and functionality of SOAP, see the following articles: SOAP Wikipedia article (`http://en.wikipedia.org/wiki/SOAP`), SOAP specification and latest versions (`http://www.w3.org/TR/soap/`), using SOAP with PHP through Mac Developer Connection (`http://developer.apple.com/internet/webservices/soapphp.html`).

The SOAP message

The following is an example of what a SOAP message looks like in XML. You'll notice many similarities between this XML-formatted message and the XML-RPC version we looked at in the first chapter. I'm going to show you again what the XML-RPC message looked like by way of comparison and to point out some differences. Here's the XML-RPC:

```
<?xml version="1.0"?>
<methodCall>
  <methodName>examples.getBlogName</methodName>
  <params>
    <param>
        <value><i4>4</i4></value>
    </param>
  </params>
</methodCall>
```

Here is the SOAP message:

```
POST /InStock HTTP/1.1
Host: www.example.org
Content-Type: application/soap+xml; charset=utf-8
Content-Length: nnn

<?xml version="1.0"?>
<soap:Envelope
xmlns:soap="http://www.w3.org/2001/12/soap-envelope"
soap:encodingStyle="http://www.w3.org/2001/12/soap-encoding">

<soap:Body xmlns:m="http://www.example.org/stock">
  <m:GetShippingQuote>
    <m:ShippingType>FedEx Overnight</m:ShippingType>
  </m:GetShippingQuote>
</soap:Body/>

</soap:Envelope>
```

Notice here that the entire SOAP message is wrapped in an `Envelope`. The `Envelope` includes both `Header` and `Body` information. The `Body` includes the actual call (similar to the `methodCall` in the XML-RPC message). The call here is marked `<m:GetShippingQuote>`. The call then defines a specific shipping type from which it wants to retrieve data from. In this example, we're asking the FedEx server to return data for `FedEx Overnight`. Notice here that the XML format is basically the same as the XML-RPC, but uses different tags. Again, this shows the versatility and flexibility of web service protocols if they use a consistent format.

Enabling SOAP in PHP

Before using SOAP in PHP frameworks such as Drupal, we need to make sure the SOAP extension library is installed and enabled on our server. SOAP runs as a PHP extension. You can check your PHP info file, or click on your PHP version link in your Drupal status report to check your PHP configuration and see if SOAP is enabled. On many shared or dedicated servers, the extension should be auto enabled, so you'll see that SOAP is indeed enabled by default and you won't have to do anything special to get it working. However, in case the extension is not enabled, you'll need to enable it.

Go to your PHP info and locate the following text in your **Configure Command** area. You should look for this: **--enable-soap**.

This command shows you that SOAP is enabled. You can then scroll down on your info page and look for the specific SOAP extension section and you should see something that looks like the following screenshot:

This shows you that the **SOAP Client** and **SOAP Server** are both enabled in your PHP configuration, and various SOAP directives are also enabled and working.

Assuming that you have a SOAP package on your server, you can do the following to enable the SOAP extension. This may change depending on your PHP version, but I'll assume here that you are using PHP 5.2. If you are running a Fedora or CentOS Linux server and Apache, you can simply install the extension as long as you already have the SOAP package on your system, using your **Terminal** client and running the following command. Make sure you are logged into the server as the root admin user:

```
yum install php-soap
```

We're going to take a look at two examples of how you can use SOAP with your Drupal site to request data through a web services interaction, with an external server or application. First, we're going to install and use the contributed **SOAP Client** module and then we'll look at using the **FedEx Shipping Quotes API** module with an Ubercart installation on our Drupal site to request shipping quote information from the FedEx Developer's server.

Using the SOAP Client module

The **SOAP Client** module is a contributed Drupal module that adds a simple API framework to your Drupal site to allow for communication with either the PHP 5.x SOAP or NuSOAP extensions. This API will also allow for other contributed Drupal web services-based modules to access and integrate with external SOAP-based web servers. So, if you are trying to connect your Drupal site to a SOAP-based web service and consume its services, then this module is worth using.

I'm going to show you how to install and configure the module, and then we will use the module to connect to an external web application.

Installing and configuring the SOAP Client module

Go to the module's project page (`http://drupal.org/project/soapclient`) and download the latest version (**6.x-1.0-beta2**). This is the latest version of the module at the time of this book's publication. When you go about downloading the module, you may notice that there is a newer version of the module. Once downloaded to your desktop:

- Upload the module file to your site's /sites/all/modules folder.
- Visit your site's module configuration page and enable the module.
- Save your module configuration.

Once installed, you'll see a link to the SOAP Client's configuration page through your site's configuration menu (if you are using the Administration Menu module). See the following screen:

If you do not have the Administration Menu module installed, you can still navigate to the module's configuration page by first going to your main Drupal Administer page. The **SOAP Client** link is in the site's Configuration section.

Click on the **Configure** link first. If installed correctly and you have a SOAP Client library installed and enabled, the module should automatically notify you what library you are using. In this example and on my site, I see that the module has figured out that I have the Native SOAP extension for PHP 5 installed. If you have multiple SOAP extensions enabled on your server, you can specify which one you want to use with the **SOAP Client** module by selecting the **radio** button under the **Active SOAP Library** section. I'm going to leave this setting on **Auto Detect** because I want the module to automatically detect the extension on the server. See the following screenshot for an example of this.

The next section of the configuration contains fields that ask you to place a **Proxy Host**, **Proxy Port**, **Proxy User**, and **Proxy Password** information of the web service you are going to communicate with. So, here you would enter the web service application proxy host name, port, and your API username and password, if applicable, for the web service communication you are trying to configure. You may not need to use a proxy host for your integration, in which case you could safely ignore these fields.

Home > Administer > Site configuration

Configure SOAP Client   Configure   Test/Demo

Configure SOAPClient configuration

○ Current SOAP Client Library is **Native SOAP extension on PHP5**

Active SOAP Library:

○ SOAP Extension on PHP5

○ nuSOAP

◉ Auto detect (PHP5 SOAP first then nuSOAP)

Which SOAP library do you want to use? On PHP5, you may use the native SOAP extension, nuSOAP or PHP4 and later. Currently the **Native SOAP extension on PHP5** is activated.

Proxy Host:

Enter the IP address or host name of the proxy server between your Drupal server and the SOAP server, or leave blank if not applicable

Proxy Port:

Enter the IP port of the proxy server between your Drupal server and the SOAP server, or leave blank if not applicable

Proxy User:

Enter the user name for the proxy server between your Drupal server and the SOAP server, or leave blank if not applicable

Proxy Password:

Enter the password for the proxy server between your Drupal server and the SOAP server, or leave blank if not applicable

[Save configuration]   [Reset to defaults]

There is also a **Test/Demo** configuration button in the module settings as shown above. Click on this button and the following screen will appear:

Test SOAP Client   Configure   Test/Demo

Current SOAP Client Library is **Native SOAP extension on PHP5**

SOAP server endpoint URL: *

Enter the absolute endpoint URL of the SOAP Server service. If WSDL is being used, this will be the URL to retrieve the WSDL.

☑ Use WSDL?

Target Namespace:

If WSDL is not used, enter the target namespace URI here. Otherwise, leave it blank.

Use:

⊙ encoded

○ literal

Specify how the SOAP client serialise the message.

Style:

⊙ rpc

○ document

Specify the style of SOAP call.

SOAP Function: *

Enter the function name to be called.

Agruments:

This screen asks you to enter the **SOAP server endpoint URL**. This will be the absolute endpoint URL of the SOAP server service that you are communicating with. If the server is providing a WSDL to use, you would enter the WSDL URL here. There's also a checkbox to select if you are using WSDL.

You can also enter the target namespace URI in the **Target Namespace** field. You can specify how the SOAP Client (your site) will encode the message (either encoded or literal), and the style of the SOAP Remote Procedure Call (either RPC or document). We'll leave these set to their defaults, which are encoded for the URL, and RPC for the style of call.

Next, you'll enter the SOAP function that you want to call on the external application. Then you can add any specific arguments you want to add to the call.

We can use our FedEx Shipping Quote example to test the **SOAP Client** module. We'll use the **SOAP Client** module to test communication and integration with the FedEx Developer's API and web services in the next section of the chapter. The FedEx Web Services use WSDLs, so we can test these WSDLs with our SOAP Client.

Getting started with FedEx Web Services

To use Drupal with FedEx Web Services, you'll first need to familiarize yourself with the FedEx Developer Resource Center at FedEx.com (`http://fedex.com/us/ developer`), and also sign up for a developer's account. Once you have your account, you can log in to the Developer Resource Center and download specific WSDLs to use with your Drupal site integration. FedEx Web Services also provides the sample code that you can use.

If you use WSDLs with your test integration, with the SOAP Client, you'll need to locate the WSDL URL on the FedEx Web Service Server so that we can point to this in our SOAP server endpoint URL field. This is where we'll add the URL to the FedEx WSDL. You can also download the WSDL and upload it to your Drupal site/ server, and then add that URL to your SOAP Client configuration and test.

You can also get a developer test key to test your FedEx Web Service, and enter this API key's username and password in your SOAP Client configuration. To run your FedEx module integration in a real testing environment, you'll want to sign up for a FedEx Web Service Developer's account so that you can get the API credentials. We'll cover this in the following sections.

Using FedEx Shipping Quotes module

Let's take a detailed look at using a contributed Drupal module to consume web services from an external application using the SOAP protocol. This module integrates with Ubercart, which is one of the Drupal-based e-commerce modules. To follow along with the examples in this section of the chapter, you should have a Drupal site with the core Ubercart modules installed and enabled. I'll assume you already have Ubercart set up in testing mode with a few test products in your site that you can use for the examples in this section.

Here's an overview of the practical example we're going to walk through in this section. If you are running an e-commerce website using Drupal and Ubercart, you may want to gather shipping quotes in real time from a service such as FedEx. FedEx (as explained earlier in the chapter) provides web services through an API that you can communicate with and consume in your Drupal site. The example here will be to get shipping quotes for the products that your customers add to their Ubercart shopping cart. When they add the products, they will be able to get accurate and up-to-date shipping quotes from the FedEx service. FedEx will act as a service provider or server here, and your Drupal site will be consuming these services. Similar to the earlier section on using the SOAP Client module, you're going to need to sign up for a FedEx Developer account, so you can get an API key to use with the FedEx Shipping Quotes module.

The FedEx Shipping Quotes for Ubercart module is a contributed Drupal project module that allows your Drupal site to communicate with and consume web services from the FedEx Web Services API. This allows you to get shipping quotes directly from the FedEx servers. Your store customers and Drupal site visitors will be able to add a product to their cart and then select a FedEx shipping method (for example, overnight or second-day delivery) and retrieve the shipping quote for the respective method in real time from the FedEx API server. As a store administrator, you can select which FedEx shipping methods to use in your store and what types of packaging and pickup/dropoff to use. Shoppers will be able to click on a **Calculate Shipping Rate** button or add the shipping rate to be returned based on their shipping address information they have entered into the Ubercart shipping address form fieldset. The module requires you to have the SOAP extension enabled in your PHP 5.x installation. We have already confirmed that SOAP is enabled in our previous chapter section.

Let's get started. We'll first take a look at the FedEx Shipping Quotes module and how to install and enable it.

Installing and configuring the FedEx Shipping Quotes for Ubercart module

First, you will need to make sure that you have Ubercart and the Token modules installed and configured on your site. Once installed, you should add a few test products to your site that you can use for the examples. The latest version of Ubercart is 6.x-2.4. and the project page can be found at http://drupal.org/project/ubercart. The latest version of the **Token** module for Drupal 6 is 6.x-1.15, and the project page is obtained from http://drupal.org/project/token.

Once you have Ubercart installed, make sure that you enable the entire core Ubercart modules, including the Shipping and Shipping Quotes core modules.

Currently, the module is released for Drupal 6 and 5, and the latest Drupal 6.x version is 6.x-2.0. You can download the module from its project page available at `http://drupal.org/project/uc_fedex`. The module has been known as the `uc_fedex` module to Ubercart users.

It is recommended that you download the module from the Drupal project page. The module comes with the following files, including a `README.txt` file that contains installation instructions. The module folder includes the following folders:

- `translations`
- `wsdl-production`
- `wsdl-testing`

The `wsdl` folders contain the respective FedEx WSDLs for production environment transactions and for testing transactions. In this example, we'll be using the `wsdl-testing` folder, which contains the following files:

- `AddressValidationService_v2.wsdl`
- `RateService_v7.wsdl`
- `TrackService_v3.wsdl`
- `TrackService_v4.wsdl`

Finally, the `uc_fedex` folder contains the following code files that we'll be taking a closer look at:

- `uc_fedex.admin.inc`
- `uc_fedex.css`
- `uc_fedex.info`
- `uc_fedex.install`
- `uc_fedex.module`

For those of you familiar with Drupal module development, you'll notice that the module folder contains `.info`, `.css`, `.install`, and `.module` files. Let's open up the `README.txt` file and see what specific install instructions are for the module so that we can get it installed and working on our site. We'll then take a look at the module's code.

The `README` file explains that you need to have PHP 5 on your server and the SOAP extension enabled. Upload the module folder to your **/sites/all/modules** directory and unzip it. Then go to your Drupal site and enable the FedEx module on your main modules admin page. Save your module configuration.

Once enabled, you can get to the `uc_fedex` module's configuration page within your Drupal site by visiting **Store Administration | Configuration | Shipping quote settings | Quote Methods | FedEx**, or by going to `/admin/store/settings/quotes/methods/fedex` page.

The module's configuration page will load. It's broken up into the following sections: Credentials, Quote Types & Services, Dropoff and Pickup options, package types, and Markups. The FedEx Shipping Quote settings form will ask for the following credential information:

- **FedEx Web Services API User Key**
- **FedEx Web Services API Password**
- **FedEx Account #**
- **FedEx Meter #**
- **FedEx Server Role**

You can get this information by signing up for a FedEx Developer's account on the FedEx Developer's website at `http://fedex.com/us/developer/`.

To use the module, you'll need to sign up for an account to get an API User Key and password as well as the Account # and Meter # details. So let's head over to the **FedEx Developer Resource Center** page and sign up for a developer's account. Go to the developer resource URL, as mentioned before, and sign up for a developer's account.

Once signed up, you will receive your FedEx.com user ID, and then be prompted to start using the **FedEx Developer Resource Center**. Go ahead and proceed.

There should be a link to get started with the FedEx Web Services Technical Resources. You should get to this section of the FedEx site and proceed to the **Develop & Test Your Application** section to obtain a developer test key and account information.

As the module README states, in order for the module to work, you need these credentials. The first set of credentials you'll obtain will be for communication with the FedEx testing server. You need to test all transactions to the FedEx test server first before proceeding to production level quote requests. Also, note that your FedEx test account credentials will not be the same as your eventual FedEx production account credentials. This is important to note because you need to know that your company may get specific discounts from FedEx on their production account. These same discounts will not apply to your developer's testing account.

Go to the **Develop & Test Your Application** link, which will bring you to:

```
https://www.fedex.com/wpor/web/jsp/drclinks.jsp?links=techresources/
develop.html
```

Read the introductory material on that page and then click on the **Obtain Developer Test Key** button.

Bear in mind that, as you'll be integrating with the FedEx testing server, this server could experience unexpected downtime and go offline during your testing process. FedEx continuously tweaks and upgrades their testing API, so you should expect to receive communication errors at times because it is a web service and a testing environment. FedEx also posts detailed announcements about any offline status or other issues with both their testing and production web service environment on their main home page when you log in to your testing account. They will also send you e-mail notifications, alerting you to any maintenance they may be running on the test and production servers.

Click on the **Obtain Developer Test Key** button and complete all of the required forms and fields in the **Registration for FedEx Test System Access**. On the last Confirmation screen, you'll be given the following data:

- Developer Test Key
- Test Account Number
- Test Meter Number

- Test FedEx Office Integrator ID
- Test Client Product ID
- Test Client Product Version

Make sure to print out this confirmation screen for your records, and also note down your developer test credentials in a safe place. You will also receive e-mail confirmations of your test credentials from FedEx. The e-mail will contain your API password. Congratulations! You now have a test account configured, and we can now test it out using the `uc_fedex` module and get a better understanding of how SOAP web services work with our Drupal site.

Confirming your Ubercart store settings

Before we enter our test credentials into Drupal and start testing, we need to check one more basic setting in our Ubercart site. In order for this module to work successfully, you also need to make sure you have configured and set your main store address settings, as all shipping quote requests are going to use this store address as the main shipping origination address. So, to confirm that you have set the store address, go to your main **Store Administration | Configuration | Store Settings** page available at `/admin/store/settings/store/edit`.

Save your store settings configuration.

Entering your test credentials in the FedEx module configuration

Let's revisit the **Shipping quote settings** page of the FedEx module and enter our test credentials. The credentials section of the form looks like this:

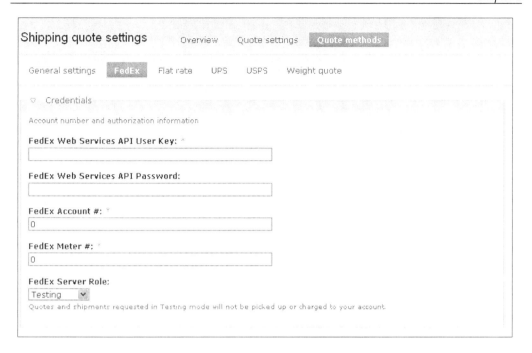

Enter the User Key, API Password, Account #, and Meter # that you received when you signed up for a test account. Also, make sure the **FedEx Server Role** is set to **Testing**. Make sure you enter your API Password that you received in the e-mail confirmation.

Once you have entered your credentials, go ahead and select the various **FedEx Services** you want to receive shipping quotes from. I'm going to stick with selecting the generic residential and commercial services, including **FedEx Ground**, **FedEx Home Delivery**, **FedEx Overnight**, **FedEx Priority Overnight**, **FedEx 2nd Day**, and **FedEx Express Saver**. Make sure the **FedEx Quote Type** is set to **List Prices**.

Choose your **FedEx Pickup/Dropoff Options**, **FedEx Package Type**, and also choose whether the destination address is a commercial or residential address. You can also choose to add any markups your store may require. The markup costs will be automatically applied to the shipping quote. Also, choose how the packages will be sent: either each product in its own package or multiple products in one package. Save your module configuration.

FedEx Pickup/Dropoff Options:

Dropoff at FedEx Business Service Center

Pickup/Dropoff options. It is assumed that all your packages are using the same method.

FedEx Package Type:

Your Packaging

Package Type. It is assumed that all your packages are using the same packaging.

Quote rates assuming destination is a:

○ Commercial address

◉ Residential address (extra fees)

☐ Add Insurance to shipping quote

When enabled, products are insured for their full value.

▽ Markups

Modifiers to the shipping weight and quoted rate

Rate Markup Type:

Percentage (%)

FedEx Shipping Rate Markup:

0

Markup FedEx shipping rate quote by dollar amount, percentage, or multiplier.

Weight Markup Type:

Percentage (%)

FedEx Shipping Weight Markup:

0

Markup FedEx shipping weight before quote by weight amount, percentage, or multiplier.

Number of Packages:

○ Each product in its own package

◉ All products in one package

Indicate whether each product is quoted as shipping separately or all in one package.

Save configuration   Reset to defaults

Finally, in our main **Shipping quote settings** in Ubercart, let's make sure we have checked the boxes next to the following:

- Log errors during checkout to watchdog
- Display debug information to administrators
- Prevent the customer from completing an order if a shipping quote is not selected

We're now ready to test our web service. We can add some products to our shopping cart in Ubercart and proceed to checkout. On our checkout page, we can request the FedEx shipping quotes and test our web services connection.

Also, make sure that you have selected the FedEx's **Shipping Method** as your default enabled shipping method for your Ubercart installation. Otherwise, the quote services will not work.

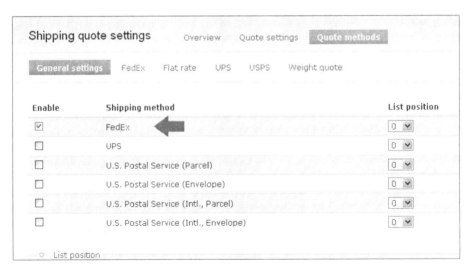

Testing the FedEx Web Service with our Drupal site

Let's go ahead and add a product to our shopping cart and then proceed to checkout. Make sure you have a **Payment Method** enabled for testing. Let's use the Test Gateway. On your checkout form, enter the delivery Information and the billing information. As soon as you fill in this delivery and billing information, the Shipping Quotes should automatically be retrieved from the FedEx server. If there is any issue with the communication between your Drupal client and the FedEx server, you'll receive an error message on the checkout screen. You should see a progress bar stating "**Receiving quotes ....**"

If you receive errors, you may also want to check your **Recent Log** entries in Drupal to see a printout of a specific error you may receive. For example, when I tried getting shipping quotes the first time, I received the following error:

> **Error in processing FedEx Shipping Quote transaction.**
>
> **ERROR**
>
> **crs**
>
> **866**
>
> **Origin postal code missing or invalid.**
>
> **Origin postal code missing or invalid.**

This error, most likely, points to an issue with our pickup location zip code because it's telling us that the store origin postal code is missing or invalid. So check to make sure that you have your Ubercart store settings configured correctly. Fix or address any issues that could be causing errors and then try again. Also, confirm that you set a pickup location as the default in your **FedEx shipping quotes** settings.

Once you have successfully got quotes returned from the FedEx server, you should see something like this on your checkout screen:

You can now select the quote you want to use for your transaction, and this quote amount will be automatically applied to the overall cost of the product. I will choose **Home Delivery** here, enter test credit card credentials, and then proceed to **Review my order** and **Complete my transaction**.

When you click on **Review Order,** you should receive a successful FedEx Rate Quote Transaction message (as you've enabled debug to see errors and messages regarding this module).

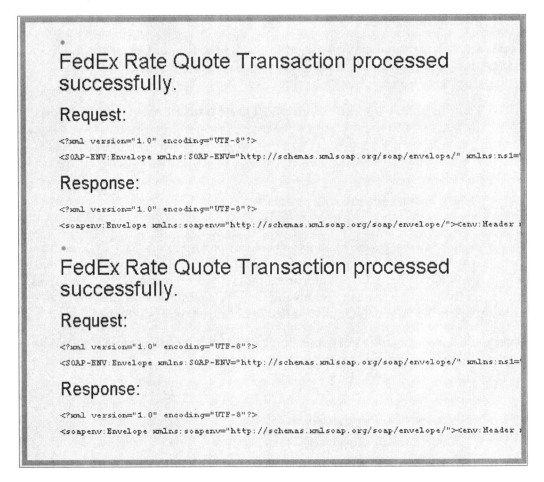

The debug info should give you a successful **Request** showing you the actual XML of the request from the Drupal client to the FedEx server, as well as the successful XML-based response that comes back to your client from the web service. The XML request should look like this:

```
<?xml version="1.0" encoding="UTF-8"?>
<SOAP-ENV:Envelope xmlns:SOAP-ENV="http://schemas.xmlsoap.org/soap/
envelope/" xmlns:ns1="http://fedex.com/ws/rate/v7"><SOAP-ENV:Bod
y><ns1:RateRequest><ns1:WebAuthenticationDetail><ns1:UserCredent
ial><ns1:Key>r0QLxAKaZsA4egau</ns1:Key><ns1:Password>76nUkRUopsU
JxZRoshS0SkeJk</ns1:Password></ns1:UserCredential></ns1:WebAuthe
nticationDetail><ns1:ClientDetail><ns1:AccountNumber>510087941</
ns1:AccountNumber><ns1:MeterNumber>118511868</ns1:MeterNumber></
ns1:ClientDetail><ns1:TransactionDetail><ns1:CustomerTransactionId>***
Rate/Available Services Request v7 from Ubercart ***</
ns1:CustomerTransactionId></ns1:TransactionDetail><ns1:V
ersion><ns1:ServiceId>crs</ns1:ServiceId><ns1:Major>7</
ns1:Major><ns1:Intermediate>0</ns1:Intermediate><ns1:Minor>0</
ns1:Minor></ns1:Version><ns1:RequestedShipment><ns1:ShipTimesta
mp>2010-05-03T09:10:08-06:00</ns1:ShipTimestamp><ns1:DropoffType>RE
GULAR_PICKUP</ns1:DropoffType><ns1:Shipper><ns1:Address><ns1:Postal
Code>21702</ns1:PostalCode><ns1:CountryCode>US</ns1:CountryCode></
ns1:Address></ns1:Shipper><ns1:Recipient><ns1:Address><ns1:PostalCo
de>21769</ns1:PostalCode><ns1:CountryCode>US</ns1:CountryCode><ns1:Re
sidential>true</ns1:Residential></ns1:Address></ns1:Recipient><ns1:R
ateRequestTypes>LIST</ns1:RateRequestTypes><ns1:PackageCount>1</ns1:
PackageCount><ns1:PackageDetail>INDIVIDUAL_PACKAGES</1:PackageDetail
><ns1:RequestedPackageLineItems><ns1:SequenceNumber>1</ns1:SequenceNu
mber><ns1:Weight><ns1:Units>LB</ns1:Units><ns1:Value>4</ns1:Value></
ns1:Weight><ns1:Dimensions><ns1:Length>1</ns1:Length><ns1:Width>1</
ns1:Width><ns1:Height>1</ns1:Height><ns1:Units>IN</
ns1:Units></ns1:Dimensions></ns1:RequestedPackageLineItems></
ns1:RequestedShipment></ns1:RateRequest></SOAP-ENV:Body></SOAP-
ENV:Envelope>
```

Notice that our XML request contains our FedEx account credentials as well as the two distinct postal codes for the requested quote—the origination postal code and the destination postal code. Also, notice that the XML request is wrapped in `<SOAP-ENV:Envelope>` tags that follow the standard SOAP XML request format. The XML request too contains the various functions that the call is making, including the rate request `<ns1:RateRequest>`.

The reply XML code that is returned from the FedEx server is very long, which I'll excerpt here:

```
<?xml version="1.0" encoding="UTF-8"?>
<soapenv:Envelope xmlns:soapenv="http://schemas.xmlsoap.org/
soap/envelope/"><env:Header xmlns:env="http://schemas.xmlsoap.
org/soap/envelope/" xmlns:xsi="http://www.w3.org/2001/XMLSchema-
instance"/><env:Body xmlns:env="http://schemas.xmlsoap.org/
soap/envelope/" xmlns:xsi="http://www.w3.org/2001/XMLSchema-
instance"><v7:RateReply xmlns:v7="http://fedex.com/ws/rate/
v7"><v7:HighestSeverity>NOTE</v7:HighestSeverity><v7:Notifications><v
7:Severity>NOTE</v7:Severity><v7:Source>crs</v7:Source><v7:Code>441</
v7:Code><v7:Message>This shipment met Shipment Weight Minimum
criteria.</v7:Message><v7:LocalizedMessage>This shipment met Shipment
Weight Minimum criteria.</v7:LocalizedMessage></v7:Notifications
><ns1:TransactionDetail xmlns:SOAP-ENV="http://schemas.xmlsoap.
org/soap/envelope/" xmlns:ns1="http://fedex.com/ws/rate/v7"><ns1:
CustomerTransactionId>*** Rate/Available Services Request v7 from
Ubercart ***</ns1:CustomerTransactionId></ns1:TransactionDetail><ns
1:Version xmlns:SOAP-ENV="http://schemas.xmlsoap.org/soap/envelope/"
xmlns:ns1="http://fedex.com/ws/rate/v7"><ns1:ServiceId>crs</
ns1:ServiceId><ns1:Major>7</ns1:Major><ns1:Intermediate>0</
ns1:Intermediate><ns1:Minor>0</ns1:Minor></ns1:Version><v7:RateRe
plyDetails><v7:ServiceType>FIRST_OVERNIGHT</v7:ServiceType><v7:Pac
kagingType>YOUR_PACKAGING</v7:PackagingType> </v7:RatedPackages></
v7:RatedShipmentDetails></v7:RateReplyDetails></v7:RateReply></
env:Body></soapenv:Envelope>
```

Again, this XML reply is wrapped in the `<soapenv:Envelope>` tags.

When you review your order after submitting it, you should see the **FedEx shipping quote** line item in your order summary and the FedEx cost added automatically to your subtotal. On my screen, the line item reads **FedEx Home Delivery**.

So you have learned how to consume web services using your Drupal site from an external server and how a module can be built in Drupal to allow this service to occur. The module developer has integrated the module seamlessly into the Drupal code so that the module performs the SOAP-based client call to the remote server and then integrates the results of the call (the response) into the Drupal-based transaction in Ubercart. The module uses the most current FedEx API WSDLs in the module code in order to make this remote call work.

In this specific scenario, the module is using the `RateService_v7.wsdl`, which is located on your client server in the `/wsdl-testing` folder. This WSDL is also in XML format and contains the XML schema for the actual web service. The WSDL also contains the URL for the FedEx Web Service application and server that the remote call from your client will be routed to. This server is `http://fedex.com/ws/rate/v7`. Here is what the code for this WSDL looks like (in excerpted format because it's a long document):

```xml
<?xml version="1.0" encoding="UTF-8"?>
<definitions xmlns="http://schemas.xmlsoap.org/wsdl/"
xmlns:ns="http://fedex.com/ws/rate/v7" xmlns:s1="http://schemas.
xmlsoap.org/wsdl/soap/" targetNamespace="http://fedex.com/ws/rate/v7"
name="RateServiceDefinitions">
    <types>
        <xs:schema xmlns:xs="http://www.w3.org/2001/XMLSchema" at
tributeFormDefault="qualified" elementFormDefault="qualified"
targetNamespace="http://fedex.com/ws/rate/v7">
            <xs:element name="RateRequest" type="ns:RateRequest"/>
            <xs:element name="RateReply" type="ns:RateReply"/>
            <xs:complexType name="RateRequest">
                <xs:annotation>
                    <xs:documentation>Descriptive data sent to FedEx
by a customer in order to rate a package/shipment.</xs:documentation>
                </xs:annotation>
                <xs:sequence>
                    <xs:element minOccurs="1"
name="WebAuthenticationDetail" type="ns:WebAuthenticationDetail">
                        <xs:annotation>
                            <xs:documentation>Descriptive data to be
used in authentication of the sender's identity (and right to use
FedEx web services).</xs:documentation>
                        </xs:annotation>
                    </xs:element>
                    <xs:element minOccurs="1" name="ClientDetail"
type="ns:ClientDetail">
                        <xs:annotation>
                            <xs:documentation>Descriptive data
identifying the client submitting the transaction.</xs:documentation>
                        </xs:annotation>
                    </xs:element>
                    <xs:element minOccurs="0" name="TransactionDetail"
type="ns:TransactionDetail">
                        <xs:annotation>
                            <xs:documentation>Descriptive data
for this customer transaction. The TransactionDetail from the
request is echoed back to the caller in the corresponding reply.</
xs:documentation>
                        </xs:annotation>
                    </xs:element>
```

SOAP request/call in the FedEx module file

The actual SOAP call that is being initiated is located in the `uc_fedex.module` file. If you open up the `uc_fedex.module` file and look at or around line 331 in the module code, you should see comments noting the beginning of the SOAP `RateAvailabilityService` request code. This code will obtain the rates and services needed to gather the shipping quotes from the FedEx services server. Also, notice that the comments specify that all SOAP call parameters follow the same order in which they appear in the FedEx WSDL file.

Summary

In this chapter, we explored how Drupal can consume web services using the SOAP protocol. This included:

- Defining and introducing the SOAP protocol
- Installing, configuring, and using the **SOAP Client** module
- Installing, configuring, and using the **FedEx Shipping Quotes** module
- Looking in detail at the XML-formatted request call and response that the Shipping Quotes service gives us
- Looking in detail at the SOAP remote call/function that is in the actual module code

In the next chapter, we're going to look at a contributed suite of modules that will allow our Drupal site to communicate with an external web service provided by the web application Flickr. This will allow us to consume Flickr photos into our Drupal website and present photos hosted by our Flickr account within the themed galleries on our Drupal site.

3
Drupal and Flickr

In this chapter, we're going to continue our discussion of how Drupal consumes web services using a specific contributed Drupal module. We're going to practice integrating our Drupal site with the Flickr photo-sharing web application (http://flickr.com) using the contributed Flickr module.

Using Drupal with the Flickr module will give us a hands-on look and demo of how we can use complex web services along with Drupal blocks, CCK, and Views to build intricate and dynamic frontend displays that present photo data from Flickr on our Drupal site. We will also look at the awesome flexibility and rich presentation of photo content that the Flickr module and its web service integration with Drupal can give us.

We will install and configure the Flickr module to communicate with the Flickr Web Services and display dynamic Flickr photo galleries on our Drupal site.

To summarize, in this chapter we will:

- Access the Flickr Web Services using the Flickr module
- Use Flickr contributed modules to manipulate and use our Flickr Web Services with Drupal
- Enable and configure Flickr module blocks and display these blocks on our site

Accessing Flickr

Flickr is a cloud-based application that allows for the easy uploading and sharing of photos. You can search for photos on the Flickr website and sort the results by relevance, that is how recently the photos were posted and how interesting the photos are. You can also search for specific photographers or groups. For example, if I do a search for "firehouse", I get about 49,760 results that have been tagged as firehouse when they were uploaded to Flickr. On the same search result screen, I'll see links to groups related to this topic or tag. For example, there is a group called **Firehouses**. If I click on that Group link, I'll get all the photos that have been posted to this specific group or pool.

The next screenshot shows the Firehouses Group pool on Flickr:

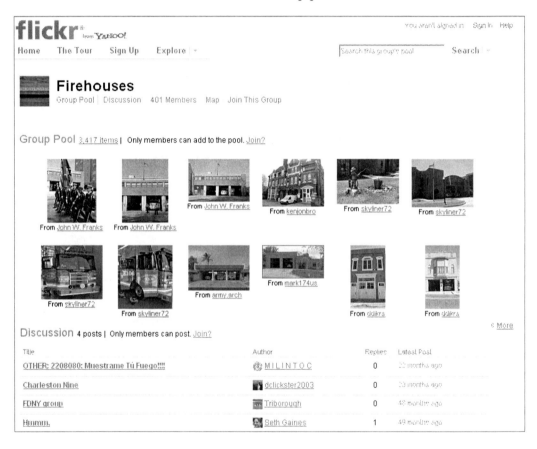

Your Flickr account

If you create an account on Flickr, you can upload photos to galleries within your account, and you can subsequently tag the photos and create sets of photos in your account. These images get posted to your photostream. Your photostream is then available for viewing through the Group pool for a specific topic as long as you have posted photos to that group and tagged your photos appropriately.

I go by the screenname of **backdrifting07** in my Flickr account. You can view my account at `http://www.flickr.com/photos/starlights/`. This URL shows all of my public photos:

If you start posting photos to your Flickr account regularly, you may want an easy method of feeding your Flickr photos into your Drupal site so that you can display and share the photos with your Drupal site's visitors and users. To do this, you will use a variety of modules to connect to the Flickr Web Services.

In this chapter, we're going to learn how to integrate our Flickr photos and photosets with our Drupal site by installing, enabling, and configuring the Drupal Flickr module. We'll use this module on our Drupal site to consume the Flickr Web Services.

For more on the history of Flickr, read the detailed Wikipedia article available at: `http://en.wikipedia.org/wiki/Flickr`.

Flickr module

The Flickr module (http://drupal.org/project/flickr) allows you to connect to the Flickr Web Services through its API and access your Flickr photos. You can filter specific photos or photosets as well as photo sizes using this module. This allows you to share a specific photoset with your Drupal site and render specific sizes, including a small square, thumbnails, small, medium, large, and original. There are currently multiple versions of the Flickr module available for both Drupal 6.x and 5.x. We're going to use the latest 6.x version.

Let's go ahead and download and install the Flickr module on our Drupal site. I'm going to download the 6.x-1.2 version of the module. I'll upload the module to my /sites/all/modules directory. Once you upload, go to your main modules admin page and enable the entire Flickr suite of modules that show up in your Flickr module's fieldset. These include the following:

- Flickr (allows for integration with Flickr Web Services)
- Flickr Block (adds blocks to your Drupal site with Flickr content)
- Flickr Filter (a filter for accessing and inserting specific photos)
- Flickr Sets (support photosets)
- Flickr Tags (add tagging capability to the module and service)

Signing up for a Flickr API key

To use the module, you'll need to sign up for a Flickr API key and credentials. To sign up for a Flickr API key, go to the main Flickr API services site at http://www.flickr.com/services/api/. Click on the **API Keys** link, and if you are logged into your Flickr account when you do this, you should be redirected to a page where you are asked to create your first app. You should see a link to create the app as well as a link to access an **App Garden FAQ**. Click on the **Why not create your first?** app link as shown:

This will launch the **The App Garden** page where you can follow the instructions to get an API key:

- Click on the **Request an API Key** link to get started.

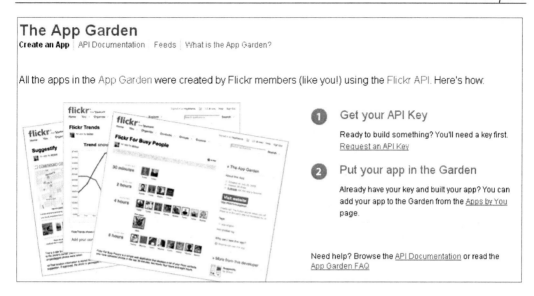

You'll be asked to choose whether your app will be a non-commercial or commercial app. For this example, let's choose to go with **APPLY FOR A NON-COMMERCIAL KEY**:

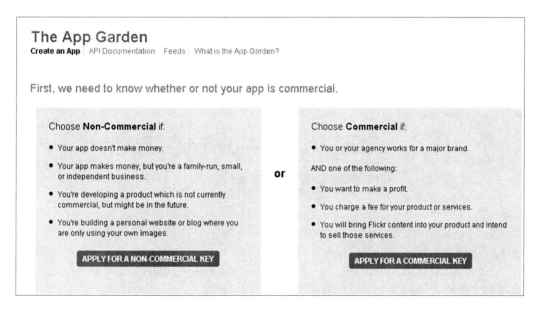

Click on **Non-Commercial** button.

You will need to name your app, so let's name it **Drupal Web Site Integration** for this example. You can also add a detailed description of the app you are planning to build. Agree to the terms of service and click on **Submit**.

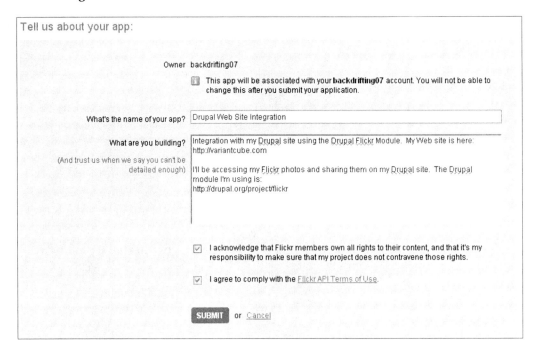

When you click on the **SUBMIT** button, you'll be redirected to a web page that shows your API key and secret code:

Make sure to print this page out, and keep the key and code in a safe place. You'll need both of these to utilize the Flickr module. We're now ready to access Flickr via our Drupal site. Let's configure the Flickr module.

Configuring the Flickr module

Now visit the module's configuration page by going to **Site Configuration | Flickr** or /admin/settings/flickr.

Enter your **API Key** and **API Shared Secret** key details. Select the **Update interval** to indicate how often you want to check that the Flickr API cached service calls are up-to-date. Also, select how many photos you want to show per photoset. So, this would display 30 photos of a photoset in your Drupal node, for example:

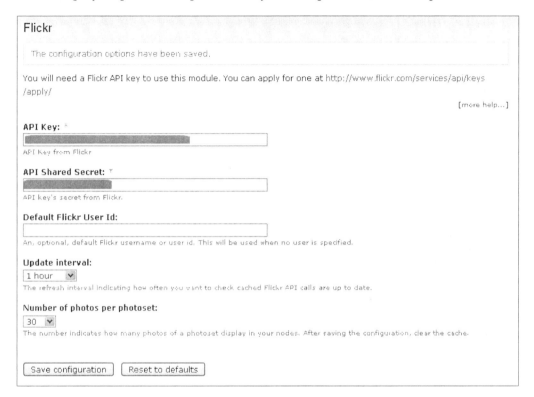

Save your configuration.

Adding the Flickr filter

The next thing you need to do, before adding your Flickr photos, is to add the Flickr filter to your active default input format. On your Drupal site, you will have either a Filtered HTML, Full HTML, or PHP Filter set as your default site input format. The input format configuration is located at **Site configuration | Input formats** or at /admin/settings/filters. I'm using the Filtered HTML input format on our example site, so I'm going to visit the configuration page for this input format by clicking on the **Configure** link in the **Operations** column of the **Input format** table. On your input format configuration form page, make sure to enable the **Flickr linker** filter. This will allow you to embed the Flickr token code into your Drupal nodes to access photos and photosets:

By enabling the **Flickr linker** filter, you will be able to enter specific Flickr-based tokens into your node's content. The format of the token code that you'll be adding looks like this, for inserting individual photos:

```
[flickr-photo:id=230452326,size=s]
```

To insert photosets, you'll be using this code:

```
[flickr-photoset:id=72157594262419167,size=m]
```

So go ahead and check the **Flickr linker** box and then save your Drupal input format configuration.

Setting Flickr module permissions

Finally, make sure that you have given Flickr module permissions to your anonymous and authenticated site users. Go to your **User Permissions** and look for the **flickr module** permissions. Enable the preferred permissions for your site:

flickr module		
administer flickr	☐	☐
view all flickr photos	☑	☑
view own flickr photos	☑	☑

Testing the Flickr module

Let's go ahead and test the module and access our Flickr photos. Here, I'm going to access one of my photosets. To do this, I will need to know the ID of my photoset. So I'll open up the photoset in Flickr first. This is my **Light Experiments** photoset: http://www.flickr.com/photos/starlights/sets/72157594379081863/.

Let's create a new page in Drupal. I'm going to go to **Create content | Create Page** and add a new node to my site. I'll name the node after my photoset **Light Experiments**. I'll then paste the following code into my node's body textbox:

```
[flickr-photoset:id=72157594379081863,size=m].
```

Notice that this photoset code contains the ID of my photoset and the size is set to **m** for medium. The Flickr module supports multiple sizes for the display of the images in your Drupal site. The sizes are the following, including their size code. The size code is what is added to the `flickr-photoset` code as shown above. For example, in our code we've set the `size=m`.

- s — small square, with 75px by 75px dimensions
- t — thumbnail, with 100px on the longest side
- m — small, with 240px on longest side
- -- — Medium, with 500px on longest side
- b — large, with 1024px being the longest side
- o — original image

So I've chosen to display the photos at the small size **m** of 240px for one dimension. You can insert other sizes to experiment here.

I'll also check to make sure the input format is set to use the input format that has the Flickr image input enabled. To do this, expand the Input format field set under your body text editor box and then make sure that the **Filtered HTML** input format radio button is selected. I'll then save my page. Here's a screenshot of what you should see on your **Create Page** form, including the **Title** field, **Body** field, and **INPUT FORMAT** fieldset:

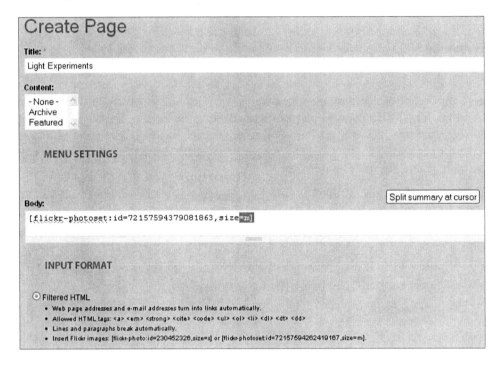

After saving your new page, you should see your images appear in your node. If you click on one of the images in your Drupal node, it will open a specific image in Flickr. We have successfully accessed our Flickr images using the Flickr module.

Depending on how many photos per photoset you have configured to show, the node will show this number based on your Flickr module configuration. If you want to show more photos, you'll need to tweak your configuration. If you change this number after you've posted the node, make sure to clear your Drupal cache so that the new amount of photos will get accessed and will show on your node. Go ahead and try tweaking this.

In addition, if you want more control over the layout and display of your image gallery in Drupal, you can quickly make a tweak to your theme's CSS file and specify your tweaks to the following CSS variable in your site's main theme CSS file. The Flickr module adds the following class variable to all Flickr images. The class is **.flickr-photo-img**. You'll see this variable in your **img src** if you view your image using Firebug. This screen shows you the variable you want to target in your Firebug view:

Now, if you want to tweak this CSS so that your layout of gallery images shows no padding between each image, you can tweak the vertical-align value to be on top instead of text-bottom. Making this tweak in your CSS file will cause the images to display totally flush to each other. With these types of images, this tweak can enhance the overall impact of the gallery display. So the tweak I made here is:

```
.flickr-photo-img {
vertical-align:top;
}
```

When I make this tweak, my corresponding image gallery layout looks like this:

Notice that now all the images are flush in their display.

If you want to add padding between your images so that they sit on their own in the frame of the layout, you can make this addition of padding elements to your CSS:

```
.flickr-photo-img {
padding:10px;
vertical-align:top;
}
```

Adding this padding will make the overall layout in my theme become two columns of images with 10px of padding between the images:

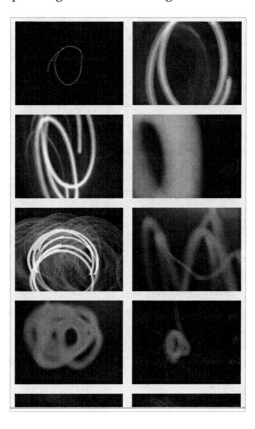

As you can see from these examples, with a tiny amount of CSS tweaking, we can get some really beautiful gallery layouts.

Flickr module blocks

We have successfully displayed our photoset as a Drupal node. Let's go ahead and enable the Flickr blocks that come with the module. Go to your **Site building | Blocks** configuration page, and in your disabled Drupal blocks you'll see a selection of Flickr blocks that you can use. The following blocks are available:

- Flickr group photos
- Flickr random photo from photoset
- Flickr random photos
- Flickr recent photos
- Flickr recent photosets
- Flickr user page photosets
- Flickr user page random photos
- Flickr user page recent photos

Each of the Flickr blocks contains its own configuration settings that we'll take a look at in detail now.

Flickr group photos

This block allows you to show photos from a specific group. Click on the **configure** link next to the block and you'll launch the configuration page for the specific block. Notice that this block allows you to type in a group ID into the **Show photos from this group id** text field. You can tell the block to show a specific number of photos (**from 1-30**). You can also tell the block to size the photos.

Let's use the following settings:

- Add a group ID to the block configuration
- Show four photos
- Choose the square 75x75 pixel size.

I'm going to use the Polyhedra group from Flickr. The group's URL is: `http://www.flickr.com/groups/polyhedra/pool/`.

You may be tempted to just paste the group's URL into the **Show photos from this group id** field. The problem with this is that the URL is not the actual group ID. So, if you copy the URL into the field, you'll generate an error when trying to enable the block in your theme's regions.

If the ID is wrong in your block configuration, you may get the following error (notice that I received the following error when pasting the polyhedra group URL into my group ID field):

Flickr error 1: Group not found

 If you are not sure how to get the actual group ID for a photostream or Group you are viewing in Flickr, you can use this utility to get the numeric Group ID. It's called **idGettr** and is available at http://idgettr.com/. Enter your photostream URL and then click on the **Find** button. Consequently, the Group ID will be shown.

Add the correct ID and then enable your block. The block configuration form should look like this:

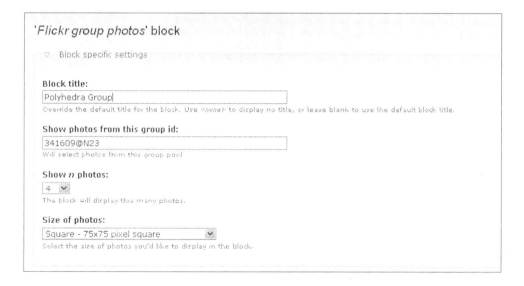

You may also receive an error telling you that you do not have permission to view the group photos in your block—this may be due to a group disallowing permissions to share photos through the web services. The error will be:

Flickr error 2: You don't have permission to view this pool

If this happens, you may need to create your own Flickr group for your own photos and then try using this group ID in your block.

The Polyhedra group is a publicly accessible group, so you should be able to show its photos in your block. After enabling the block, you should see the resulting images showing up in your block on your site. It should look similar to this:

I've named the block **Polyhedra Group,** so that's the title that appears in the block when you enable it. If you set the block title to **<none>**, the block title will be set by Flickr automatically and will read **Flickr Group photos**.

If you enable your block in a different region of your site or tweak the block's CSS, you can also get some interesting column layouts for the included photos. Here's an example:

As you can see, you can start to build some very interesting and fun photo galleries on your Drupal site through your Flickr galleries. By combining a node view of Flickr photos, along with a block view of a specific group's photos, you will start to construct a beautiful series of galleries on your Drupal site that leverage both Drupal for layout purposes, and the Flickr API, for its powerful web service. This can act as a nice supplement to your other image capabilities and the functionality of your Drupal site:

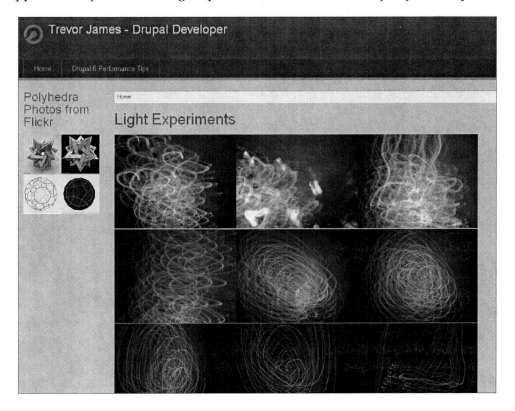

Flickr random photo from photoset

Let's go ahead and configure the next Flickr block called **Flickr random photo from photoset.** This block will feed in random photos from a Flickr photoset. The configuration is similar to setting up the Flickr Group Photos block. You add the following:

- **Block title**
- **Flickr User Id**
- **Show *n* photos**
- **Size of photos**
- **Flickr Photoset Id**

Go ahead and complete these fields. You can leave the **Flickr User Id** field blank because it will use the default user ID set in your Flickr module configuration. Also, you can set up the number of photos to show in this block. So, if you just want to show one random photo, you can set the number of photos to 1. Each time a user refreshes the Drupal page, the block shows on it and feeds in a new random photo from the Flickr photoset. Remember that here you are entering the ID of a photoset and not a group. So I'm going to add the photoset ID for my Light Experiments public gallery and that is **72157594379081863**. Your block configuration form should look like:

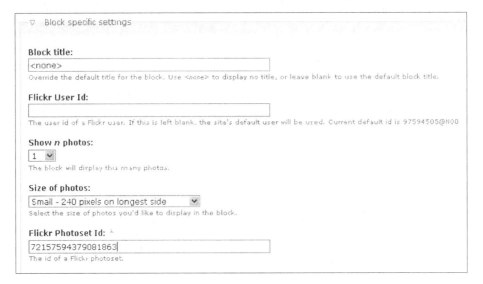

Go ahead and add your settings to this block to try it out. Enable it to see the results you get. I have also changed the size of the photos to display at **Small – 240 pixels on longest side**.

I should now be showing a random photo from my photoset on my Drupal site in one of the regions, if I've enabled this block:

Do a quick refresh of your site's page in the browser, and you should see a new random photo appear. Pretty cool!

Flickr random photos block

The Flickr random photos block allows you to show randomly selected photos from a specific user's photosets. So, for example, you can leave the **Flickr User ID** field blank on this block configuration and the block will pull in random photos from the site's default Flickr API user account. Let's go ahead and try this. Complete the following items on the block's configuration page and then save the block:

- **Block title**
- **Flickr User Id**
- **Show *n* photos**
- **Size of photos**

I'm going to enable this block on my site's home page at the top of the main content region so that these photos appear above my site's posts. I'm going to show four photos at the thumbnail size each of 100px dimension.

Enable the block and you should see something similar to this:

If you do not give the block title field a value, the default that the Flickr module will provide us is **Flickr random photos**.

Flickr recent photos and recent photosets

The recent photos block is similar to the random photos block, but it allows you to filter the photos to just the most recent images you have posted to your Flickr account. So, if you set this to display two photos, it will grab the two most recently posted photos from your Flickr account.

The recent photosets is similar to this, but it allows you to show all of the photos from a specific photoset. You can show your most recently posted photoset.

Go ahead and try out both of these blocks.

Flickr user page photosets, user page random photos, and recent photos

To use the Flickr user page photosets, user page random photos, and recent photos blocks, you will first need to make sure that you have added your Flickr user identifier to the **Flickr settings** field on your user account profile form. This identifier is your Flickr username or the e-mail address associated with your Flickr account.

These blocks allow each user on your site to configure their own Flickr blocks of images and show these images on their own user account profile page.

Let's try this. Edit your user profile and add your **Flickr identifier** to the field:

Save your user profile page and then, as soon as your user page loads, you should see an entire photoset display, depending on how many photosets you chose to show in the block configuration. I enabled the block to display in the bottom content region of my theme and so it shows up at the bottom of my user profile page. The cool thing about this block display is that if you show the photos at 75x76 pixel dimensions, the photoset displays very closely to the Flickr photoset display of thumbnails. You should see a photoset on your user page similar in layout to this:

Try this with the two remaining user-based Flickr blocks: Flickr user page random photos and Flickr user page recent photos. You should get similar results.

Summary

In this chapter, we explored how Drupal can consume photo content from the popular photo-sharing web application Flickr. We installed and enabled the Flickr module and explored in detail on how to:

- Configure Flickr modules with Flickr API key
- Test the Flickr filter functionality by adding Flickr filters to our nodes
- Test the Flickr module using the Flickr filter code
- Enable and test Flickr module blocks

In the next chapter, we're going to integrate our Drupal site with the Amazon Web Services and show how we can easily consume Amazon's content into our site, and display dynamic shopping carts and build a rich e-commerce-based website using the Amazon suite of web service modules.

4
Drupal and Amazon

In this chapter, we're going to continue our discussion of how Drupal consumes web services using specific contributed Drupal-based modules. We'll also look at consuming web services from the popular shopping marketplace site — Amazon. com — using the Amazon module and its integration with the Amazon Web Services (AWS) cloud.

The Amazon and Amazon Store modules will give us a hands-on look and demo of how we can integrate product data from Amazon and display this data on our Drupal site. We will also look at the awesome flexibility and rich presentation of content that these modules and web services can give us on our site.

We'll install and configure both the Amazon and the Amazon Store modules to communicate with our Amazon associate account and we'll practice filtering in specific Amazon products, including books, CDs, DVDs, and other items into our Drupal nodes.

To summarize, in this chapter we will:

- Access Amazon Web Services using the Amazon module
- Use the Amazon Store module to integrate an Amazon Associate Storefront with your Drupal site
- Access Amazon products and product API using the Amazon module
- Sign up for an AWS account and configure our Amazon module
- Test our Amazon module configuration by looking up an Amazon product
- Use Amazon Example content type
- Use Amazon filters

Accessing Amazon

Amazon.com provides a web service and a Product Advertising API that you can leverage and consume with your Drupal site. The AWS provides a huge amount of data and information about its books, DVDs, and music. The web service allows you to filter this product data into your Drupal nodes and to set up actual Amazon-like storefronts within your Drupal site. To do this, you will use the Amazon module and associated contributed Amazon Web Service-based modules, including the Amazon Store module.

The Amazon module is a contributed Drupal module that allows for integration with the Amazon Web Services API (specifically, the Amazon Product Advertising API). It allows Drupal to consume AWS and integrate these services with a CCK (Content Construction Kit) based product type. When we install the Amazon module we'll need to install two required modules, CCK and Features. We'll discuss the installation of both of these in the next section of this chapter. If you are running a Drupal 5.x site, you may have been using the Amazon associate tools module (http://drupal.org/project/amazontools). This module is now only supported for Drupal 5.x, and the Amazon module has replaced it for Drupal 6.x and Drupal 7.x.

The Amazon module allows for integration with the **Views** module. The module supports the AWS to consume Amazon product data, including page counts, MPAA (Motion Picture Association of America) ratings, price, editorial reviews, customer reviews, lowest price, Amazon price, ISBN, and more.

Various input filters are available and the module allows for integration with the Drupal core search functionality. The module also allows for token support for product data.

You will need an Amazon API key to use this module. To sign up for an Amazon API account, you need to visit the Amazon Web Services site at http://aws.amazon.com/. Click on the **Sign Up Now** button for a free AWS account. You will also want to sign up for a Product Advertising API account. You can get that account at https://affiliate-program.amazon.com/gp/advertising/api/detail/main.html.

Related modules include the Amazon store module that integrates an entire Amazon storefront with your Drupal site along with a shopping cart.

 If you are a developer, you can help contribute to the module by volunteering your time to improve documentation, provide patches, help build tests using the Simple Test suite, and Sponsorship module features.

Download the module and install to your /sites/all/modules folder.

To connect to products and data about products on the Amazon cloud, you'll need to know the product **ASIN (Amazon Standard Identification Number)**. This is the unique identifier that the service will use for integration with your Drupal site. On any Amazon product, you can locate the ASIN in the **Product Details** section. The ASIN is also visible in the URL for the actual product. For books in the Amazon catalog, the ISBN-10 number is same as the ASIN, so look for the ISBN-10. Generally, the Amazon product URLs follow this pattern:

```
http://www.amazon.com/Drupal-Performance-Tips-Trevor-James/dp/
ASIN-NUMBER-HERE.
```

Here's an example:

Product Details
    Paperback: 240 pages
    Publisher: Packt Publishing (February 12, 2010)
    Language: English
    ISBN-10: 1847195849

Signing up for an Amazon Web Services account

Go ahead and sign up for an Amazon Web Services account at the AWS website. You'll be able to sign up with your existing Amazon account if you already have an Amazon.com account. Once you sign up, you will receive an e-mail with your login credentials and AWS credentials. The e-mail will also provide you with details on how to access your unique Access identifiers that are required to make your Drupal site client send valid web service requests to the Amazon servers.
There will be a link to your access identifiers in the e-mail you receive.

When you visit the **Security Credentials** section of your AWS account, you'll be provided with three sets of credentials. Access credentials will include your **Access Key ID** and links to creating associated **X.509 Certificates** and **Key Pairs**. You will also have information about your **Sign-in/login** credentials for your account and finally your AWS account ID. You should jot down and remember your AWS account ID and your Access Key ID for using the Amazon module.

Installation and initial configuration of the Amazon module

Let's go ahead and upload and extract the Amazon module to our server, and enable it in our module admin area.

The modules that are included in the main Amazon module are the following:

- **Amazon API** — the main module for integrating with the AWS
- **Amazon Examples** — gives an Amazon CCK type as a demo/example
- **Amazon field** — this gives your Drupal site a CCK field for Amazon products
- **Amazon Filter** — allows your Drupal users to use the [amazon] filter tag to embed Amazon product information directly into your site's nodes
- **Amazon legacy importer** — you can use this if you have legacy data to import into your Drupal 6 site from an older Drupal 5 installation of the Amazon module
- **Amazon media** — allows you to store data for Amazon products, including books, DVD, and music
- **Amazon search** — this integrates the **Amazon search API** for searching Amazon product information with the core Drupal search module

Let's enable all the modules except for the **Amazon legacy importer** because we're not importing Drupal 5.x data.

If you enable the **Amazon Examples** module, make sure you also install and enable the CCK (Content Construction Kit) and Drupal Features modules. These modules are required to use and configure the **Amazon Examples** module and the corresponding **Amazon Examples** content type that this module enables. The CCK module is available at: http://drupal.org/project/cck and you can find the Features module at: http://drupal.org/project/features.

Go ahead and install the CCK and Features modules, and then enable the previously mentioned Amazon modules (all except for the **Amazon legacy importer**).

	Amazon		
Enabled	**Name**	**Version**	**Description**
☑	Amazon API	6.x-1.0	Provides integration with the Amazon Ecommerce APIs. Required by: Amazon legacy importer (disabled), Amazon Examples (disabled), Amazon Filter (disabled), Amazon media (disabled), Amazon search (disabled), Amazon field (disabled)
☑	Amazon Examples	6.x-1.0	Provides Amazon module CCK type and view as a demo Depends on: Amazon API (disabled), Amazon media (disabled), Amazon field (disabled), Features (disabled), Views (enabled), Content (enabled)
☑	Amazon field	6.x-1.0	Provides a CCK field type for Amazon products. Depends on: Amazon API (disabled), Content (enabled) Required by: Amazon legacy importer (disabled), Amazon Examples (disabled)
☑	Amazon Filter	6.x-1.0	Lets writers use the [amazon] tag to embed Amazon product information in text. Depends on: Amazon API (disabled)
☐	Amazon legacy importer	6.x-1.0	This module is used only to import legacy Drupal 5 Amazontools data. After upgrade it should be disabled. Depends on: Amazon API (disabled), Amazon field (disabled), Content (enabled)
☑	Amazon media	6.x-1.0	Stores extended Amazon product information for books, music, DVDs, and software. Depends on: Amazon API (disabled) Required by: Amazon Examples (disabled)
☑	Amazon search	6.x-1.0	Provides an API for searching Amazon product information, and integration with the Drupal search system. Depends on: Amazon API (disabled), Search (enabled)

Once the modules are enabled, go to the main Amazon configuration page at **Site Configuration | Amazon API** (/admin/settings/amazon). Drupal will tell you that you need to configure the module with an **Access Key ID** and an **Amazon AWS Secret Access Key** once you enable the modules. It will also provide you with a link to the **Settings** page. On the **Settings** page, you need to specify the location of the store you are going to use (US, UK, Japan, and so on). You also need to configure the **Amazon Referral Settings**. This allows you to determine who should receive any percentage of the referral transaction and cost. Set this to use your own associate ID if you want to receive a bonus when you sell a product.

If you choose to receive a commission, this is where you'll be required to sign up for an Amazon Product Advertising API. Go to: https:// affiliate-program.amazon. com for the same. Once you sign up, you'll need to click on your **Manage Your Account** link to retrieve your access information and keys for the Drupal module.

Also note that until you add your Amazon API keys to the module configuration page, you will receive a notice on your Drupal **status report** reminding you to configure the module.

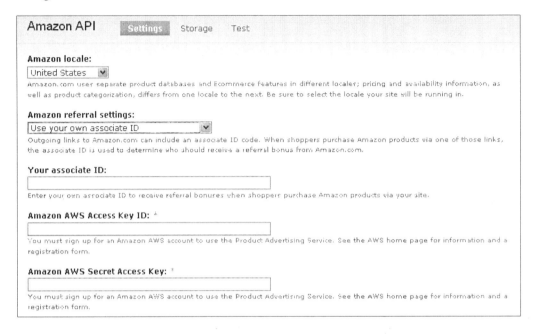

Go ahead and enter your **associate ID, AWS Access Key ID**, and **Amazon AWS Secret Access Key**. Save your module configuration. You're now ready to use the module and web service.

Testing configuration

Once you have saved your key credentials, click on the **Test** link on the module configuration page to send a test request to the AWS server. This will confirm that you have configured the web service configuration correctly. On the **Test** page, you can add a valid Amazon product ASIN. Click on the **Look up Product** button and the Drupal site will request data about the Amazon product and display it if the test is successful.

If the test fails, you may get the following error message that gives a link to your recent log entries: **Test failed for this ASIN**. Please check the **error log** for messages. The error I received was HTTP code 403:

> **HTTP code 403 accessing Amazon's AWS service: SignatureDoesNotMatch, The request signature we calculated does not match the signature you provided. Check your AWS Secret Access Key and signing method. Consult the service documentation for details.**

If this happens, check to make sure you have entered your security credentials correctly. Notice here that in this case I have left one digit off from my secret access code. I re-entered this code and then ran the test again.

If a successful test is run, you should get a result on your Drupal site showing the product data, including the **Title** of the book, **Author**, **Publisher**, and **Binding**. You should also receive an Array response, and finally, all of the product details, including the **In Detail** and associated product information about the book. It will look similar to this:

Also notice here that the product title link will go to the Amazon product page. In this URL, you should see your AWS Account ID. It will follow the `SubscriptionID=&tag` URL format.

Using the Amazon module

The easiest way to start using the Amazon module set once you have enabled and configured it is to use the **Amazon Examples** functionality. If you have installed the CCK and Features modules as explained earlier in this chapter, the **Amazon Examples** module adds a content type with a specific Amazon content type to your Drupal site. You can use this pre-built content type on your site. This provides the easiest method of getting Amazon data to show up linked from your Drupal nodes.

Once you enable the **Amazon Examples** module, you'll have a new content type called Amazon Example. You can access this by going to **Create Content | Amazon Example**. The Amazon Example content type contains one custom content type field labeled **ASIN**. This field allows you to enter the numeric product ASIN item.

Since this ASIN field is a content type field you can leverage the power of the **Amazon Examples** module by adding this ASIN custom content type field to any of your content types via your **Manage Fields** functionality. For example, if you want to add this field to your **Page** type, you can edit your **Page** content type and then add the Amazon item: field_asin (ASIN) field to your Page type via the **Manage Fields** configuration. For now, we'll just add a product using the actual **Amazon Examples** content type.

Testing the Amazon Example content type

To test the Amazon content type, go to **Create content | Amazon Example.** Add a title to your node and then add the **10-digit ASIN** for a product to the **ASIN** field.

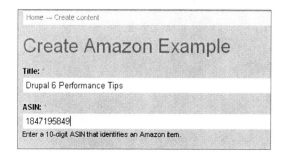

Save your node. If you entered the correct ASIN, you should see a resulting node that contains the node title and a link to the product. A thumbnail image of the product will also show.

When you click on the link, the product page will open a corresponding detail node on your Drupal site showing the product details, including all the specific detail data consumed through the Amazon Web Services. This includes the item description, buying options, and Customer Reviews, if there are any available on Amazon.com for the product in question. You should get a path that is similar to the following and includes the item ASIN number. For example, for this product the path is: `/amazon_store/item/1847195849`.

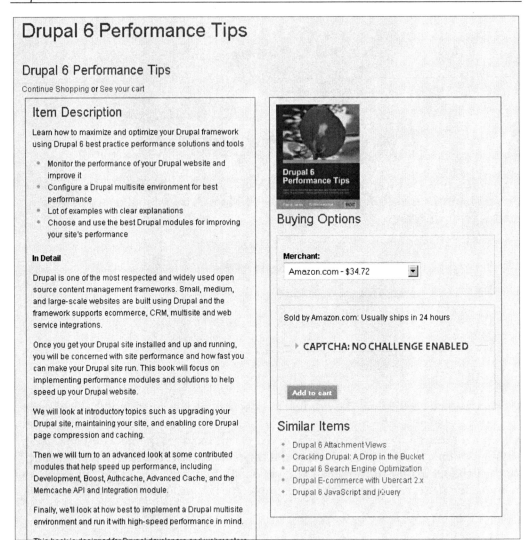

Using the Amazon content type with Views

The Amazon Example content type also includes a default view that you can access if you have the **Views** module enabled. If you do not have the Drupal Views module installed you can download Views from here: `http://drupal.org/project/views`. To access the view, go to your **Site Building | Views** and look for the link to the **amazon_example_view** in your **Views** listing.

Default Node view:
amazon_example_view (examples)   Edit | Export | Clone | Disable

Path: amazon_example_view   Amazon Example View
Page

If you click on this link, you will see the **Amazon Example View**. This view should show any results of nodes you have entered into your site using the Amazon Examples content type. Your view should look something like this:

Notice that the View page displays as a Table style layout and includes the Drupal node ID, the Amazon **ASIN**, **Product Title**, **List Price**, **Publisher**, **Publication date**, and a product image linked to the Amazon product page if available.

Because this is a page View, you can click to Edit your View and make tweaks to the View itself to enhance the function of the display. The View edit display will show you all of the Fields available, any View relationships you have configured, and any View filters.

With this View you can see how much power and flexibility you have, using the Amazon module on your site.

If for some reason you cannot see the Amazon View or are encountering any other issues with the View, make sure you have confirmed that the Drupal **Features** module is enabled on your site and that you have configured the **Features** module to enable the **Amazon Examples** features. You can do that by going to **Site Building | Features** (or /admin/build/features). You should see a tabbed display that looks like the following screenshot:

Once you have checked the box and saved your settings, you should now see your **Amazon Example View** and be able to edit your View. Your **View settings** for the Amazon page View should look like this:

Using the Amazon filters

Make sure you have enabled the Amazon filters module. This module adds a specific Amazon filter input type to your Input Types in your Drupal site. Go to your **Site Configuration | Input Formats** and configure your site's default input format. You will see an Amazon Filter checkbox in the **Filters** section. Check this box to enable the Amazon filter. This filter will allow your content editors to use the **[amazon]** filter tag to embed the Amazon product content directly into a Drupal node through the body textbox.

The **[amazon]** tag filter will allow you to enter any Amazon-specific product data that can be filtered. For example, you can use this formatted input tag— [amazon <ASIN> <action>] — to enter the following types of data:

- [amazon 0596515804 thumbnail] — this will show the product name and thumbnail image
- [amazon 0596515804 full] — this will show the full product data in your node
- [amazon 0399155341 author]
- [amazon 0596515804 asin]
- [amazon 0596515804 isbn]
- [amazon 0596515804 publisher]
- [amazon 0596515804 productgroup]

The Amazon module's documentation provides a full list of all the tokens available to you. You can view that list at http://drupal.org/node/595464.

Testing the Amazon input filter

Let's go ahead and test the filtering component of the Amazon module. First, let's create a new node on our site using the **Create Content | Page.** Give your page a title, and then in the body textbox add the following filter tags:

```
[amazon 1847195849 full]
```

Make sure that you enter your product's correct ASIN. Save your node. You should see the product data embedded within your node. Click on edit and add some more tokens to your node to test their return output from AWS. For example, I added the following to my node:

```
[amazon 1847195849 detailpageurl]
[amazon 1847195849 salesrank]
[amazon 1847195849 publisher]
[amazon 1847195849 manufacturer]
[amazon 1847195849 studio]
[amazon 1847195849 label]
```

Amazon Store module

The Amazon Store module allows you to connect to the Amazon Product Advertising API and display an Amazon marketplace store on your Drupal site as long as you have an Amazon Store account and store marketplace configured. With your Amazon Associates ID credentials (as explained in the previous sections), you can get commissions on sales of any products sold through your web services-connected Amazon store.

To use the Amazon Store module, you'll need to have the Amazon module installed and enabled (as per the instructions given in the previous section) and you will also need to be running PHP 5.2.x or higher on your web server. The Amazon and Amazon Store module require PHP 5.2 due to the **SimpleXML** library. **SimpleXML** gets bundled with PHP 5.2. The other requirement is the hash function used for preparing keys for the Amazon API. So for the keys to integrate correctly, you need to have PHP 5.2.

If I check my PHP info through a Drupal status report, I see that with PHP 5.2, I get the **Simple XML** libraries:

SimpleXML	
Simplexml support	enabled
Revision	$Revision: 293036 $
Schema support	enabled

In addition, Drupal-contributed modules such as Panels and Thickbox extend the functionality and layout of the Amazon store when it's embedded in your Drupal site, so it's good to have these modules installed and enabled.

You can download and install the module through its project page at: http://drupal.org/project/amazon_store. There is also a detailed documentation about the Amazon Store module at http://drupal.org/node/494402.

Let's go ahead and install the Amazon Store module and also make sure that we have the Drupal Panels module installed (http://drupal.org/project/panels). I'll be installing the current versions of both modules. The Amazon Store module is at version 6.x-2.1-rc2 and the Panels module is at 6.x-3.7. To use the Panels module, you will also need to install the required CTools (Chaos Tools) module. That project page is available at http://drupal.org/project/ctools.

Once you have uploaded the two modules, go ahead and refresh your modules admin page, and enable both **Panels** and the **Amazon Store** module.

From the previous sections on the Amazon module, you should already have your main Amazon module settings configured, including your Amazon credentials in your Drupal site, so you can continue to use these for the **Amazon Store** module and the examples that follow.

Using the Amazon Store module

Once you enable the **Amazon Store** module, you should now see a new module settings page available to you through the **Site Configuration | Amazon Store Settings** or by going to `http://variantcube.com/admin/settings/amazon_store`.

By default, the module ships with a store already configured and displayed in your Panels. The default panel page for the store is at the `/amazon_store` URL. If you go to `/amazon_store`, you will see an **Amazon Store** embedded in your Drupal site along with search functionality that allows your site visitors to search for products by category, key word (book title, for example), sort (that is, relevance, bestselling, and so on), and narrow the search (narrow by subject, and so on). So by going to your **Amazon Store** page, you would see something similar to this:

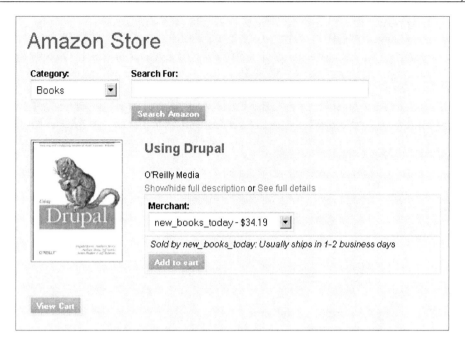

If you click on the **Add to Cart** button, you can add the Amazon product to your shopping cart on the Drupal site. Clicking the **View Cart** button allows you to go to your cart and then checkout via Amazon.com. To purchase the item, you'll be redirected to Amazon.com and you'll notice that the Amazon.com path contains the associate ID corresponding to your Amazon module settings.

Configuring your Amazon Store

You can configure your **Amazon Store Settings** to display a more specific set of product data. Go to your **Amazon Store** module settings at **Site configuration | Amazon Store Settings**. Here you can configure how the actual store display will be set up on your site. You can choose to display the **search form** and the specific search criteria such as **narrow by**, **sort form**, and **category selection** dropdown. You can allow for the searching of all the Amazon sellers or merchant products or just Amazon-specific products.

You can also specify the default products that will show up on the search layout page by category and whether the default Amazon search index should show (and show a random product), or you can specify specific **browsenodes** by **browsenode ID** and also a default item list by ASIN. For this example, I'm going to set the **Default Merchant ID** for search to **All** and the **Default search index selection** to **Books**. I'm also going to select the radio button for the **A list of Amazon ASINs** specified next and then note the specific ASINs that I would like to add to my store. Again, this shows you how flexible the web service is. You can show search functionality for all Amazon products, or you can go as granular as you like and only search for a specific sets of ASINs.

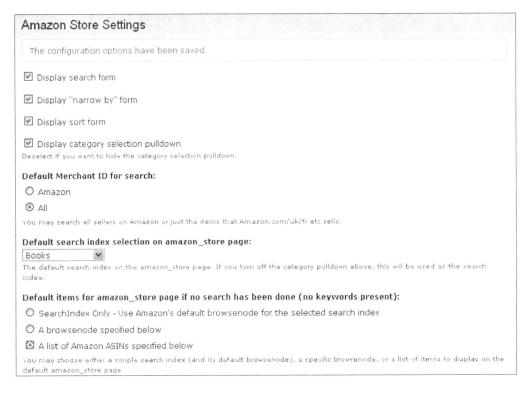

Add the product ASINs to your **Default Item,** list making sure to separate them with commas. You can add up to 10 products to display on your default store home page.

Select the refresh schedule for caching purposes and also select the categories to include in the search functionality. For the refresh schedule, it's suggested to set this to to refresh less than every 24 hours so that you keep product data and prices current. As per the Amazon license agreement, you cannot cache items for more than 24 hours. I have set this refresh schedule to **12 hours**.

I'm also going to remove some of the category checkboxes because I'm going to focus on selling media through the Variantcube.com store. So I'm going to uncheck all categories except for **Books**, **Digital Music**, and **DVD**. I'll also leave MP3 Downloads and Music checked. Save your **Amazon Store** module settings.

Testing your Amazon Store

Now that you have tweaked your **Amazon Store Settings** to customize it to specific products, let's go ahead and test out the store layout and display. You should now be able to navigate to the `/amazon_store` URL and you should see your specific ASIN products displaying on your storefront. You should also see two hyperlinks under the title of the product allowing you to **Show/hide full description** of the item and a link to **See full details**. Clicking on these links will then refresh the display of the product with complete product details on your site. The **Show/hide full description** link uses jQuery to show the data directly on your **Amazon Store** page and the **See full details** link will load a node on your site containing the product details.

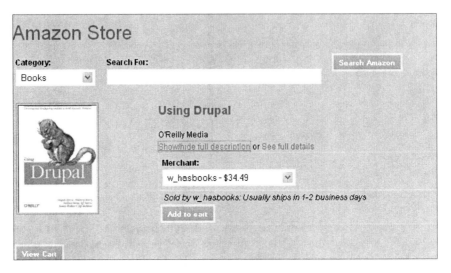

I can also do a search for the keyword "drupal" in the **Search For** box and then click on the **Search Amazon** button. It will return a list of all of the Drupal book items and display this list in our Drupal site using the following URL: `http://variantcube.com/admin/settings/amazon_store?Keywords=drupal&SearchIndex=Books`.

Also, if you add a product to your shopping cart and then proceed to click on the **Checkout** at **Amazon** button, you'll notice that the Amazon checkout URL will load and it will contain your associate ID in the URL. For example:

```
https://www.amazon.com/gp/cart/aws-merge.html?cart-id=178-5653400-
1389741%26associate-id=9068-5531-9855%26hmac=dQKWzdaGEaxOJ/Tv2/9VEgit
8xM=%26SubscriptionId=AKIAI7P3QWWSCXEOUHWQ%26MergeCart=True.
```

Summary

In this chapter, we explored how Drupal can consume web services using the Amazon and Amazon Store modules. We installed and enabled each module and learned how to:

- Access Amazon products and product API using the Amazon module
- Sign up for an AWS account and configure our Amazon module
- Test our Amazon module configuration by looking up an Amazon product
- Use Amazon Example content type
- Use Amazon filters
- Use Amazon Store module.

In the next chapter, we're going to continue our detailed exploration of Drupal-contributed modules that interact and connect with multimedia-based web service APIs including the Kaltura and CDN2 video service platforms.

5
Drupal and Multimedia Web Services

In this chapter, we're going to continue to look into the Drupal modules that allow for integration with popular web services. We started an exploration of the Flickr module and Flickr Web Services in *Chapter 3*, *Drupal and Flickr*. We'll return to look at how we can take our photosets and embed them as full-throttle Flash-powered slideshows directly on our Drupal site. So, we'll be exploring how Drupal works with the Flickr Web Services in more detail, using the Media: Flickr module.

We're also going to turn our attention to other types of multimedia, including videos, and look at how we can integrate our Drupal site with two popular video hosting services, CDN2 and Kaltura. Both of these services offer a freely available API to use in our Drupal site, and both offer Drupal-based modules to create the interface and UI. Both have benefits and drawbacks and we'll explore all of this in detail.

To summarize, in this chapter we will:

- Upload video files to the CDN2 web server and use the CDN2 web service
- Use the Kaltura module and web service to upload and distribute the video content on your site
- Post photosets to our Drupal site using the Media: Flickr module and embed these photosets in a dynamic Flash slideshow player through the Embedded Video Field module

CDN2 video

Video is a popular media uploaded to Drupal websites. Site developers want methods of uploading large video files, in multiple video formats including Flash Video (FLV), QuickTime, Windows Media, and HD. With Drupal, you an easily upload video files to your nodes and allow them to be downloaded and viewed locally by your site visitors on their client machine. This is not always the preferred solution for uploading video content due to file sizes, quality, time spent in uploading and managing the files on your server, and complexities of module configurations, using the Flash Node or SWFTools module. Some of these modules may require more configuration time from your site content editors than they want to spend. You will want to store your video files on external servers, so these files do not bog down your own server resources.

The CDN2 Video module has been developed by a firm called WorkHabit (http://www.workhabit.com). This module allows you to upload multiple video file formats to the WorkHabit transcoding server and stream the resulting uploaded video through the WorkHabit web service on your Drupal site. The benefit here is that the WorkHabit web service takes care of the transcoding and embedding of the video file, using best practice streaming solutions on their servers and using their application software. You can then feed this video into your Drupal site using the web service API. The service uses a SOAP-based web service framework similar to the Amazon service. So, if you know how to program using SOAP, you can integrate the CDN2 service into many web-based applications, including Drupal.

CDN2 supports Flash Video (FLV), QuickTime, DVD, Windows Media, and JPEG (for thumbnail images) formats. Videos are stored on the WorkHabit network, and use sophisticated caching mechanisms that allow for your video to be viewed and downloaded quickly. When the video is delivered to your Drupal site, you can still control all aspects of its playback using module mechanisms such as the Flowplayer (http://flowplayer.org/) module through SWF Tools. The CDN2 module seamlessly integrates your videos with Flowplayer. The large benefit to you, as a Drupal developer, is that you can host your large video files on external servers via the WorkHabit web service, and this relieves stress from your own server running your Drupal site.

There is a wealth of information about the WorkHabit API and service on their website at http://www.workhabit.com/products/cdn2. If you visit the WorkHabit website, you'll notice that they advertise CDN2 as **the world's first video platform built specifically for Drupal**. This service helps you to make the video upload process easy and fast for your clients and your content editors.

The CDN2 web service is free to install and sign up for—you can easily sign up for the API credentials for your Drupal site for free on the CDN2 website. WorkHabit does bill you for your video uploads, based on the file size. So, if you have a 1GB file, it will cost you $2.50 to upload it to the CDN2 web service. They then charge based on the usage of the video by your site visitors. You can get all the pricing information on the CDN2 site at `http://www.workhabit.com/products/cdn2/pricing`. In addition, the CDN2 FAQ page is a good resource and they explain in detail how the service is integrated with Drupal. For example, when we install the CDN2 module on our Drupal site, it integrates the API directly into our content types by making the video a CCK field. This is a benefit because the service allows you to take the video file, upload it to their server, and then integrate it into your content type through a CCK field. The video will then be embedded into your node. This will then allow you to theme your video nodes and use the same Drupal-based functionalities (comments, attachments) on these CDN2-powered nodes.

Let's go ahead and sign up for a CDN2 web service account and try embedding some videos into our Drupal site using the service and module.

Accessing the CDN2 web service

To use CDN2, we'll need to do two things to get started. First, we need to download the module from the CDN2 project page: `http://drupal.org/project/cdn2`.

The current version is **6.x-1.10**. Upload and extract the module to your `/sites/all/modules` directory as per normal module extraction and installation methods. Refresh your modules admin page and you'll see a new section called Media and the CDN2 modules will be listed.

Let's go ahead and enable the **CDN2 FlowPlayer** and the **CDN2 Video** modules. Save your module configuration. The **CDN2 Dash Media Player** module allows you to embed your CDN2-based videos in a Dash player utility. This **CDN2 Dash Media Player** is another version of a Flash-based video player similar to **CDN2 FlowPlayer**. In this chapter and in the examples, we're going to focus on Flow Player instead of the Dash Media Player.

Enabled	Name	Version	Description
☐	CDN2 Dash Media Player	6.x-1.10	Integrates the Dash Media player module into CDN2 Depends on: CDN2 Video (disabled), Dashplayer (missing), Flashvideo (missing), Content (enabled)
☑	CDN2 FlowPlayer	6.x-1.10	Integrates the popular FlowPlayer FLV player into CDN2 Depends on: CDN2 Video (disabled), Content (enabled)
☑	CDN2 Video	6.x-1.10	Video uploading and transcoding service Depends on: Content (enabled) Required by: CDN2 Dash Media Player (disabled), CDN2 FlowPlayer (disabled)

Signing up for the CDN2 web service

Before we configure the CDN2 module and test it out, let's go ahead and sign up for the CDN2 web service. To sign up, you can visit this page on the WorkHabit website: `https://signup.workhabit.com/`.

Complete the sign-up form. During the sign-up process, you will need to specify the full URL path to your site's domain of the Drupal site where you want the videos to appear. You will also need to agree to their beta-hosted services agreement. While you wait for the confirmation and credential e-mails to show up in your inbox, you can review the CDN2 documentation in their guide. There are some requirements you'll need to implement before using the service. The following are required to make the module run correctly:

- Drupal 5 or 6
- Drupal CCK module
- PHP 5.2 or greater
- PHP SOAP extension enabled
- `jquery_update` module installed and working in your Drupal site
- PEAR library enabled on your server
- PEAR `Crypt_HMAC` library
- MCrypt library

Most likely your server based on the first three chapters in the book, will have these items installed and enabled, but if you need to enable any specific libraries or extensions including SOAP or PEAR, there are instructions on how to do so in the CDN2 guide.

You can also check your PHP info page through the Drupal status report to confirm that you have the **mcrypt** and **soap** extensions enabled. You should see the **mycrypt** extension as follows:

mcrypt

mcrypt support	enabled
Version	2.5.8
Api No	20021217
Supported ciphers	cast-128 gost rijndael-128 twofish arcfour cast-256 loki97 rijndael-192 saferplus wake blowfish-compat des rijndael-256 serpent xtea blowfish enigma rc2 tripledes
Supported modes	cbc cfb ctr ecb ncfb nofb ofb stream

Directive	Local Value	Master Value
mcrypt.algorithms_dir	*no value*	*no value*
mcrypt.modes_dir	*no value*	*no value*

The **soap** extention details would look something like this:

soap

Soap Client	enabled
Soap Server	enabled

Directive	Local Value	Master Value
soap.wsdl_cache	1	1
soap.wsdl_cache_dir	/tmp	/tmp
soap.wsdl_cache_enabled	1	1
soap.wsdl_cache_limit	5	5
soap.wsdl_cache_ttl	86400	86400

If you refresh your status report in Drupal, you should see green confirmation rows stating that the CDN2 module is installed correctly:

✓ CDN2: PHP SOAP Extension	Installed
✓ CDN2: PHP Version	5.2.13 (Compatible)

Configuring the CDN2 module

To configure the CDN2 module, go to your module settings page at **Site configuration | CDN2 Settings**. The settings page is split into four tabbed sections:

- **CDN2 Formats** — this section launches a page that allows you to choose which video formats you want the service to support
- **CDN2 Settings** — this section gives you the web service API fields
- **CDN2 Video Tracking Settings** — this section allows you to insert Google tracking code to enable Google to track your video content
- **CDN2 Workflow settings** — this section allows to you set auto publishing and set cron configuration

Under the **CDN2 Workflow** settings, let's set our nodes to "**Do not automatically publish**". We will want to upload the video file and then preview our node before publishing. You can also decide to enable cron or not. You may want to enable cron to run if you are serving a large amount of video content through the CDN2 web service because this will help you to get the most recent cached content from the CDN2 server. The **CDN2 Settings** are as follows:

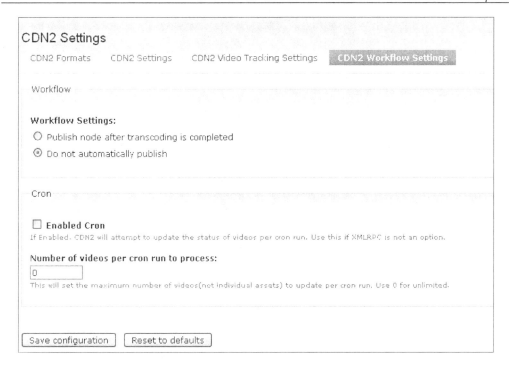

The **CDN2 Video Tracking Settings** allow you to enter your Google Analytics account number so that Google can track statistics on how many people are viewing your videos. You can also add a tracking path that Google will use when running its statistics. This path will show up in your Google account when you run reports, as shown in the following screenshot:

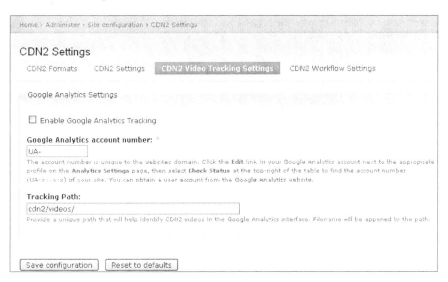

The **CDN2 Settings** tab will launch a form where you can enter your CDN2 web service Client ID and Secret Key. You should receive both of these API credentials from WorkHabit through an e-mail. The CDN2 web service's **SOAP endpoint** will also be noted as a server URL automatically and a URL where you'll be uploading your video content.

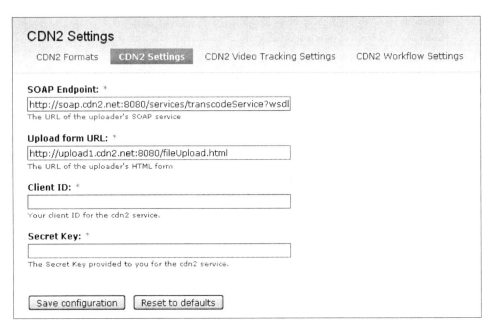

Finally, click on the **CDN2 Formats** settings link and the **Formats** form will load. This page will list all the **Allowed Presets** that the CDN2 web service allows for transcoding your video files as shown in the following screenshot. These include iPod, Flash, MPEG, Windows Media, QuickTime, and Flash Video:

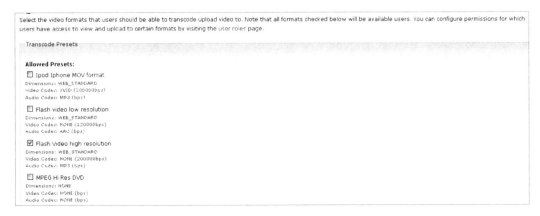

Let's go ahead and choose the **Flash Video high resolution** as our format (as shown in the previous screenshot) because we'll be uploading Flash FLV files in the next screenshot. The module will use the **Flow Player** as the preferred Flash player to embed the Flash video. Save your configuration as shown:

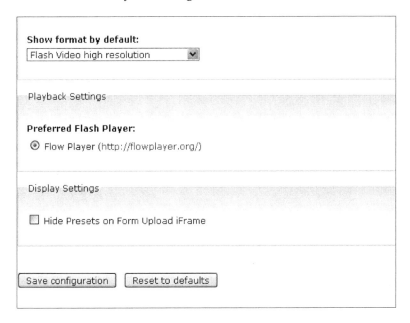

Adding videos using CDN2

To add video files to our Drupal site, the first thing we'll need to do—once we have configured the CDN2—is to create a content type for our video content. If you are already posting videos to your site using another content type or the Flash node, this is fine. You can create a brand new content type to support your CDN2 videos. Let's walk through this process step-by-step.

First, let's create the content type. We'll call this type **Video**. Go to **Content management | Content types | Add content type**. Type **Video** as the **human-readable name** and **video** as the **Type**. Then add a description. Save your content type as follows:

Content types   List   Add content type   Fields   Export   Import   Templates

To create a new content type, enter the human-readable name, the machine-readable name, and all other relevant fields that are on this page. Once created, users of your site will be able to create posts that are instances of this content type.

Identification

Name:
```
Video
```
The human-readable name of this content type. This text will be displayed as part of the list on the *create content* page. It is recommended that this name begin with a capital letter and contain only letters, numbers, and **spaces**. This name must be unique.

Type:
```
video
```
The machine-readable name of this content type. This text will be used for constructing the URL of the *create content* page for this content type. This name must contain only lowercase letters, numbers, and underscores. Underscores will be converted into hyphens when constructing the URL of the *create content* page. This name must be unique.

Description:
```
This is the content type to handle CDN2 video uploads.
```
A brief description of this content type. This text will be displayed as part of the list on the *create content* page.

Now, click on **edit** next to your content type. Click on the **Manage fields** link. Add a new field with the following info:

- **Label**: **CDN2 Video**
- **Field name**: **field_cdn2**
- Select the **CDN2 field** type from the **Field Type** select box
- Make sure your field **Form element** is set to **CDN2 Field**

Click on the **SAVE** button. The details are as shown in the following screenshot:

When you configure your CDN2 video field, the module is going to test the connection to the web service. If you have not added the API credentials to your Drupal site yet, you'll receive an error stating: **Unable to contact CDN2 service. Video uploads are currently disabled**. Make sure you enter your CDN2 service credentials before continuing.

Also, make sure to check that you have configured the permissions correctly so that your content editors can upload and view videos on your site. Go to your main Drupal user permissions page and make sure you set appropriate permissions for both transcoding and uploading videos, and also for viewing your CDN2 videos, as shown in the following screenshot:

Permission	anonymous user	authenticated user
cdn2 module		
administer cdn2	☐	☐
delete cdn2 video	☐	☐
delete own cdn2 video	☐	☐
transcode cdn2 video to 320x240_thumb	☐	☑
transcode cdn2 video to flash_flv_high_res	☐	☑
view cdn2 video transcoded with 320x240_thumb	☑	☑
view cdn2 video transcoded with flash_flv_high_res	☑	☑
view upload status	☐	☑

Uploading videos with CDN2 content type

Let's go ahead and test the CDN2 video upload field with our new Video content type.

Go to **Create Content | Video**, and this will open the Video content type form. Give your video node a **title**. Add a description for your video to the **Body** field. This is optional. But again, it shows you how you have the same flexibility to add metadata and other content to your CDN2 Video content type just as you do with other Drupal content types.

On your CDN2 Video form, you'll see your custom content type field directly under the **File Attachments** section of your form. It should provide an **Upload a video** label followed by a **Browse...** button. You'll also see checkboxes for the various formats you chose in your CDN2 module settings. In our case, we will see a checkbox for **Flash Video high resolution** and **Default web standard video thumbnail** as follows:

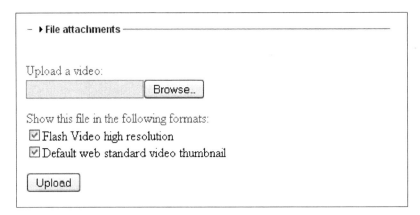

Browse for a Flash video you want to upload. Click the **Upload** button. You will see an Upload Progress bar as the video uploads to the CDN2 web server. Once uploaded, you may get a message from CDN2 stating:

Your video has been uploaded. It can take some time to process, so be patient.

Please make sure you submit this page before continuing, otherwise your video will be lost.

Go ahead and **Save** your video page so that you do not lose any node data. Bear in mind that because we are using a web service to process and post our video file, it may take a while to see the results on your Drupal site. The CDN2 web service needs to transcode and process the file as well as the CDN2 notes in their guide because this process can take quite a bit of time. So check back often on your site to see the status; you can also contact WorkHabit with your account to check on the status of your upload. This is the only drawback of using a web service to host your video file. You are ultimately on the web service's timetable and schedule as far as when the video will be posted. You may also run into more issues posting video to a web service if they do not receive the video file correctly at their end or if there's another issue or error in the transcoding or uploading of the file. Just be aware that these issues can crop up since you are relying on another web server and service to provide this functionality.

This is the resulting node I see, once I post my video file to the CDN2 server:

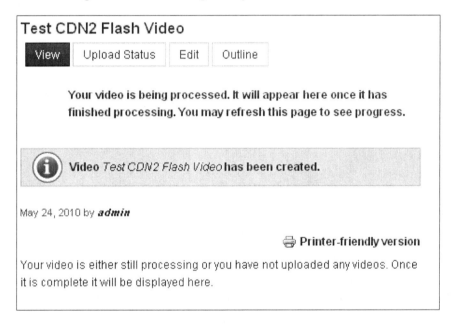

Using the Kaltura module and web service

Like the CDN2 module and web service, Kaltura Open Source Video is a project that offers a web service that you can integrate with your Drupal site. The module offers hosting on Kaltura servers for streaming versions of video at a cost. You can get the first 10GB of uploaded video and streaming as part of a free trial. You can also connect to the web service via the community-supported self-hosting version for free.

The module allows you to upload video in any format, same as CDN2. Videos are transcoded in the the Flash FLV format. You can also import videos from your other video application sites such as Flickr. The video content is uploaded and hosted by Kaltura's servers and the module allows you to connect to its web service. Like CDN2, you can also add a video upload field to your content types and the module allows for integration with other Drupal functionalities and modules such as Views, Comments, Statistics, and Taxonomy. There are both Drupal 5 and Drupal 6 versions currently available.

Signing up for the hosted solution will give you 10GB of free hosting and streaming. You can get more information on this once you sign up on the Kaltura website at: `http://corp.kaltura.com/`

The biggest difference between this service and CDN2 is that Kaltura also allows you to host videos using their application on your own servers so that you can set up your own version of the Kaltura web service on your servers.

In this example, we're going to walk through setting up a trial version of Kaltura hosted on the web services' servers.

The documentation of the module, including a downloadable PDF of the Kaltura Drupal manual, is at `http://drupal.kaltura.org/documentation`. This document contains the entire Kaltura Drupal specification and technical architecture outlined and explained for the Drupal developer. There is also a basic usage tutorial available at `http://drupal.kaltura.org/node/147`.

Accessing the Kaltura service

Let's first go ahead and install the Kaltura module on our site. Follow the same process you have used in the earlier chapters to install the module. Once you install the module (currently the latest version is **6.x-1.4**), refresh your modules admin page and enable the associated Kaltura modules that will be showing under the **Kaltura Media Management** section. The modules include the main **Kaltura**, the **Kaltura as CCK field**, **Kaltura Media Comments**, **Kaltura Media node**, **Kaltura remix node**, and **Kaltura Media Views**. Kaltura allows you to integrate with CCK and Views through these modules as shown:

Enabled	Name	Version	Description
∇ Kaltura Media Management			
✓	Kaltura	6.x-1.4	Infrastructure for managing video, audio and photos - allows to upload and import media files, manage them, and even allow users to collaboratively add and remix media Required by: kaltura as CCK field (disabled), Kaltura Media Comments (disabled), Kaltura Playlist (disabled), Kaltura Media Views (disabled), Kaltura Media Node (disabled), Kaltura Media Remix Node (disabled)
✓	kaltura as CCK field	6.x-1.4	provides 2 new CCK fields based on the kaltura nodes Depends on: Kaltura (disabled), Content (enabled)
✓	Kaltura Media Comments	6.x-1.4	enable users to post video comments in the drupal comments system Depends on: Kaltura (disabled)
✓	Kaltura Media Node	6.x-1.4	Upload and view video audio and images, storing each media item as a node. Depends on: Kaltura (disabled) Required by: Kaltura Media Remix Node (disabled)
✓	Kaltura Media Remix Node	6.x-1.4	Edit videos, music and photos on a web based editor. Create collaborative video mixes Depends on: Kaltura (disabled), Kaltura Media Node (disabled)
✓	Kaltura Media Views	6.x-1.4	View your top videos, most viewed, users videos, etc'. Depends on: Kaltura (disabled), Views (enabled)

Once you enable the Kaltura modules, you will see a message telling you that you need to **sign up for a Kaltura Partner ID to complete the installation**. To do that, click on the link that the module provides: **Get a Partner ID**. Kaltura has built a registration form right into your Drupal site that you can use to sign up. Complete the form and then click on the **Complete Installation** button.

Once you click to complete the installation, the **Server Integration Settings** page will launch and it will give you a report on whether the Drupal to Kaltura web service integration was successful. A test request will be sent to Kaltura and the status of that request will be submitted back. Cron will also run and a test will be performed to see if you have the required **CrossDomain.xml** file in your site's root directory.

Your Partner information will also be shown including your Partner ID and your e-mail address. The details are as shown in the following screenshot:

If you see the error message about the `crossdomain.xml` file being missing, you can locate this file in your module's directory. Copy the XML file to your site's root directory and this should fix the error message. Refresh your **Server Integration Settings** page and the cross domain status should be resolved.

You should also receive an e-mail from Kaltura that contains your **Partner ID, Sub-Partner ID, Admin password, Web service admin secret**, and **Web service secret keys**. You do not need to add the keys to your Drupal Kaltura configuration because the module does all this for you through the automatic partner sign-up process that we just walked through.

One of the benefits of using Kaltura over CDN2 is that Kaltura builds its API registration process directly into the module configuration so that you do not need to leave your Drupal site to complete the registration process. In addition, there are no user permissions to define for the Kaltura module's functionality.

Importing and uploading Kaltura video content

The Kaltura module gives your site two new content types automatically. Go to **Create Content | Kaltura Media Node** to create a new node that contains your uploaded video file. This content type form will open up in a pop-up style modal LightBox window. You can browse to select the video file you want to upload. I'm going to browse for and select a Flash (FLV) file. Once you browse for the video file and add it to the **Upload Videos** modal screen, click on the **Upload!** button.

An upload progress screen will show as follows:

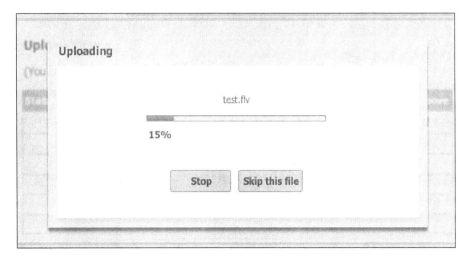

Once the upload is completed, you can click on the **Next** button. Once you do that, it will launch a detail page where you can add **Tags** for your videos and the **Title** of your video, as shown in the following screenshot. Click on the **Finish** button when done.

As soon as this is done, a dialog box will appear asking you to confirm that you are not violating any terms of use per Kaltura's agreements. You also need to state that the media is user submitted media license under the Creative Commons licensing specifications. For more information on Creative Commons licensing, see: `http://creativecommons.org/`. Click on **OK**. Another progress menu will show. Kaltura will then show you a confirmation screen telling you that the files are being converted and that the process is complete. Click on the **Finish** button.

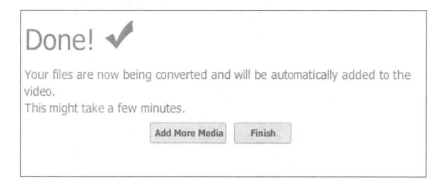

You will be redirected to a View page that shows you thumbnail images of your uploaded video(s). You can click on the Video title link to open up the node that contains the embedded video file.

Using the Media: Flickr module

In *Chapter 3, Drupal and Flickr*, we used the Flickr module and its set of associated Flickr web server-based modules. This allowed us to embed photos from our Flickr photosets, photostreams, and groups into our Drupal website through the Flickr web service API. In this chapter, we're going to return to our discussion of Flickr's web service by trying out another Drupal module called **Media: Flickr**. This module will allow us to map our Flickr photosets into an embedded media field in our custom content type. The module works in tandem with the **Embedded Media Field** module. Once you have both modules installed, you can add your photoset URL into the embedded media field and your photoset will then be displayed as a navigable slideshow on your Drupal site.

So we're going to install and configure two modules here — the **Embedded Media Field** and the **Media: Flickr modules**.

Currently, the **Media: Flickr** module is released for Drupal 6 (version **6.x-1.11** is the most current version). Download the module from its project page here at: `http://drupal.org/project/media_flickr`.

Note here that in order to use the **Media: Flickr** module, you'll need to sign up for a Flickr API key which you may have done already in *Chapter 3, Drupal and Flickr*. So you should be good to go.

The **Embedded Media Field** module is available at: `http://drupal.org/project/emfield`. Go ahead and install that module as well. Once you have installed the modules, navigate to your modules admin page and enable the **Embedded Media Field** and **Embedded Video Field** modules in your **CCK** section as well as the **Media: Flickr** module in your **Media** section as shown in the following screenshot. Save your module configuration.

	Media: Flickr	6.X-1.11	Embedded Video Field provider file for Flickr.com photosets. Depends on: Embedded Video Field (disabled), Embedded Media Field (disabled), Content (enabled) Required by: Media: Flickr - XSPF Playlist (disabled)

You should see a status message stating: **Media: Flickr's tables have been installed successfully**.

Now, you need to configure the **Embedded Video Field**. To do this, go to **Content Management | Embedded media field configuration**. Scroll down on the configuration form page until you see the **Embedded Video Field** section. Expand it and then look for the **Flickr Photosets configuration**. Expand that. Here, you will see a default checkbox checked for allowing content from the Flickr photosets. Leave that checked. You can also choose to store images locally on your server. For now, let's leave this unchecked, so we'll store our images over on Flickr's server.

Finally, you can set the maximum local saves per page load. This allows you to control how many files can be stored locally from your Flickr set on your local server. So, for example, you can load the first 10 images (the default) locally on your site and server location, and then the remaining photos in the set will be stored on Flickr's server.

Below this, you will need to add your API credentials again for your Flickr Developer's account. You need to add them again here so that you can use the **Media: Flickr** web service. Go ahead and enter your credentials and then click on the **Save Configuration** button.

▽ Flickr Photosets configuration

These settings specifically affect slideshows displayed from Flickr.com.

☑ Allow content from *Flickr Photosets*
If checked, then content types may be created that allow content to be provided by *Flickr Photosets*.

☐ Store images locally
If checked, then images from Flickr will be stored locally.

Maximum local saves per page load:

```
10
```

This will limit the number of remote files that will be stored locally from Flickr per page load when storing a photoset locally, causing the rest in that specific view to be displayed from the remote location. If you set this to 0, then all such files will be stored on the initial slideshow view. Note that setting this to 0 or to an arbitrarily large number can cause the initial view to take a very long time, or even cause the browser to time out. Also note that this setting has no effect if the images are not to be stored locally.

▽ Flickr API

You will first need to apply for an API Developer Key from the Flickr Developer Profile page.

Flickr API Key:

```
ced3d4c1f7a44b149cb6dfcb8e2b69a9
```

Please enter your Flickr Developer Key here.

Flickr API Secret:

```
b721a674f81f4916
```

If you have a secret for the Flickr API, enter it here.

If, for some reason, you do not see the Flickr API credential fields available in the **Flickr Photosets configuration** fieldset, scroll up on the configuration page until you see the **Embedded Image Field** fieldset. Depending on the version of the **Embedded Media Field** module and the **Media: Flickr** modules you are using, the API fields may be in this **Image** fieldset. Go ahead and check the **Allow content from Flickr** box inside the **Flickr Configuration** fieldset and then add your credentials. You should see a fieldset screen like this:

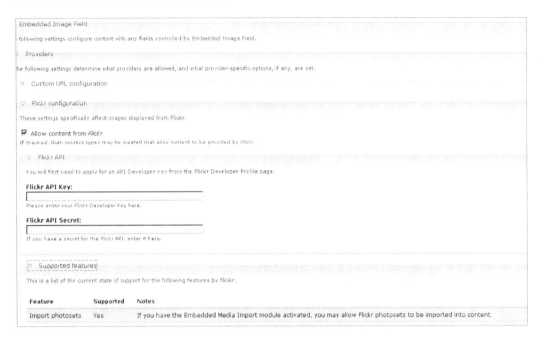

Now, you can go about editing the content type that you want to add the embedded video field to. I'm going to use the same Video content type I've already created on my development site for the CDN2 Videos and I'll add the embedded video field to it. Click on your **Manage fields** button and add a new field named **Flickr Photoset**. Give the field a `field_name`, and then select the **Embedded Video** field type and the **3rd Party Video** operation as shown in the following screenshot:

Click on **Save**. You will be redirected to a new form page titled **Flickr Photoset**. This is the form that allows you to select which provider you want to use. Check the **Flickr Photosets** box for the Flickr provider as follows:

Select which third party providers you wish to allow for this content type from the list below. If no checkboxes are checked, then all providers will be supported. When a use the URL they enter will be matched to the provider, assuming that provider is allowed here.

Providers:
☐ archive.org
☐ Blip.tv
☐ Dailymotion
☑ Flickr Photosets
☐ Google
☐ GUBA

Next, you can expand the **Media: Flickr settings** section. This contains the configuration for the web service. You can simply leave the configuration set to the defaults for our examples as shown:

▽ Media: Flickr settings

These settings only affect Flickr slideshows.

▽ Media: Flickr settings for video size

These settings only affect Flickr slideshows when displayed in the video size.

Media player (video size):

| Default Flickr slideshow (flash) ▼ |

Please select the player to display Flickr photoset slideshows in the video size.

▷ Media: Flickr settings for JW Image Rotator in video size

▷ Media: Flickr settings for JW Flash Player in video size

▽ Media: Flickr settings for preview size

These settings only affect Flickr slideshows when displayed in the preview size.

Media player (preview size):

| Default Flickr slideshow (flash) ▼ |

Please select the player to display Flickr photoset slideshows in the preview size.

▷ Media: Flickr settings for JW Image Rotator in preview size

▷ Media: Flickr settings for JW Flash Player in preview size

Save your field settings.

Now, let's go ahead and post a new node with an embedded Flickr photoset. Go to **Create Content | Video** and give your node a title. You'll see a new video upload field labelled Flickr Photoset. This is the field you will paste your Flickr photoset URL into. Go ahead and grab a Flickr Photoset URL path, and then paste it into your field. Here's the photoset URL I'll be using: `http://www.flickr.com/photos/starlights/sets/72157594379081863/`

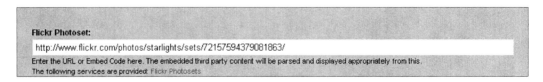

Click on your **Save** button and then you'll see your refreshed node. Your node will load with the embedded photoset slideshow. I used the default module player settings for a Flash-based player. Click on the **Play** button icon that's overlaid on the first image to start the slideshow as shown in the following screenshot:

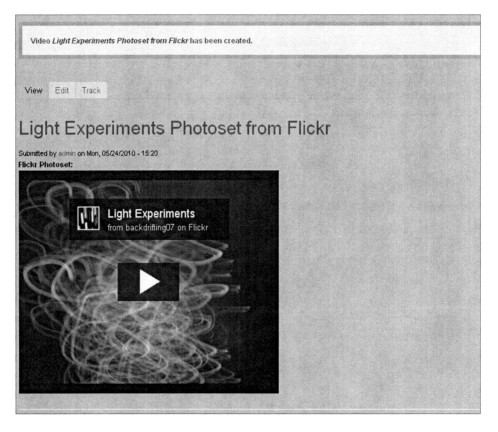

Also, since you are using the **Embedded Video field** here, make sure that your anonymous users and authenticated users have the correct field permissions to view the **Embedded Video field**. So, check the permissions boxes to allow your users to view **field_flickphotoset** as shown:

You should now be able to view the slideshow and navigate through it using the embedded player controls as follows:

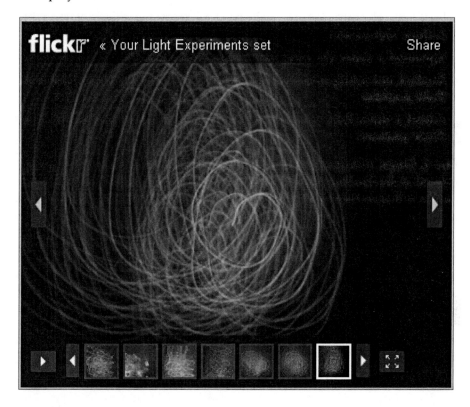

So, we have completed our example of embedding a Flickr photoset directly into our Drupal node using a custom content type that contains the **Embed Video field**. We pasted our photoset URL and now we have a beautiful Flickr-based Flash player of our images embedded in our site. The embedded Flash player allows you to navigate through each slide and also toggle to full-screen view mode.

Summary

In this chapter, we explored how Drupal can consume multimedia-based web services using contributed modules including CDN2, Kaltura, and Media: Flickr. We installed and enabled each module and explored in detail the following functionality:

- Enabled and configured the CDN2 module and integrated with the CDN2 web service

- Added video content to our Drupal site using a custom content type and CDN2 video field

- Enabled and configured the Kaltura Video module and integrated with the Kaltura web service

- Uploaded a video file using the Kaltura video module

- Enabled and configured both the Media: Flickr and the Embedded Media Field modules

- Added a video field to our custom content type and posted a URL to our Flickr photoset

In *Chapter 6, Drupal Web Services the Easy Way: The Services Module*, we're going to look in detail at the Services module and test some simple service callbacks using this module. We will also show a simple example of building a custom callback module.

6
Drupal Web Services the Easy Way: The Services Module

In this chapter, we're going to turn our attention to the Drupal Services module. The Services module is a contributed module that gives you a variety of built-in custom service modules to test and use. This will allow you to enable both servers and services on your Drupal site from one main module backend configuration and administration area. The included services allow you to call content and output data from Drupal's default and contributed comment, file, menu, node, search, system, taxonomy, user, and views modules. Calling these services will allow you to get content from your Drupal site and display it on another Drupal site, both on your server and externally. In our examples, we'll be focusing on consuming and feeding content from one Drupal site to another, however you could also use the Services module to integrate with external web service applications that are not Drupal based.

The Services module also contains flexibility so that you can program your own custom service module and integrate it with the method calls that already come packaged with the main Services module. In this chapter, I'll show you how to program your own custom module and integrate this with the Services module, and subsequently, to return a list of nodes from one of your content types.

To summarize, in this chapter we will:

- Install and enable the Services module and explore what the Services module offers our Drupal site(s)
- Test simple default Services module callbacks
- Program our own custom callback module that will return a simple text string such as `hello world`
- Expand our custom module to return a list of nodes of a specific content type

The Services module—what is it?

The **Services** module is currently at version **6.x-2.2** and is available through its module project page at: `http://drupal.org/project/services`. Note that if you are using a version of the Services module that is pre-**6.x-2.2** (2.0.x or below), there have been significant changes in the 2.1+ release. You can fix your previous installation by going to: `http://drupal.org/node/800590` and reading the documentation. This offers fixes to address security issues with the earlier releases of the module.

The module provides a standardized API method of integrating external web services (to consume web services) and internal web server modules (that provide services) with your Drupal site. In our previous explorations, we've looked at specific Drupal modules such as the Amazon and the Flickr modules that allow for integration with those specific web applications through the Drupal interface. The Services module expands the web services and Drupal integration frontier by presenting one module to use that can integrate the web service callbacks with external server applications such as XMLRPC, JSON, JSON-RPC, REST, SOAP, AMF, and more. Each of these servers provides specific modules at drupal.org that you can install and enable to work with the Services module. Some examples of these pluggable server modules are:

- JSON server: `http://drupal.org/project/json_server`
- JSONRPC server: `http://drupal.org/project/jsonrpc_server`
- REST server: `http://drupal.org/project/rest_server`
- SOAP server: `http://drupal.org/project/soap_server`
- AMFPHP: `http://drupal.org/project/amfphp`

All of these server modules require the Services module to be installed and enabled in order to work. We will look at the use of three of these servers in this section: AMFPHP, SOAP, and REST. The module also provides authentication mechanisms that allow for integration with your Drupal user base and permissions.

The benefit to using the Services module is that it allows for web service integration with multiple applications, while using the same standard module code and programming. The other large benefit is that the module is supported and developed widely throughout the Drupal community. The module provides the following features:

- Service API that allows other Drupal modules to consume Drupal content and integrate with external applications
- Server API that allows your Drupal site and server to act as a web service to provide services using the REST and SOAP protocols

- Provides a user friendly administrative interface

- Provides a testing environment and allows for easy management of API keys

- Integrates with core Drupal including Drupal files, nodes, taxonomy, users, and the Views and system modules

The module provides a detailed handbook at drupal.org: `http://drupal.org/handbook/modules/services`. There is also a Services user group available through the Groups.Drupal.org website: `http://groups.drupal.org/services`.

For a list of servers that work with the Services module, go to: `http://drupal.org/node/750032`.

Here is a list of web services—many of which have Drupal modules developed—that integrate with the Services module: `http://drupal.org/node/750036`.

The Services module—why use it and what does it buy you?

The Services module helps to reduce the amount of time you need to spend writing your own web service modules because this module provides a standard interface for a number of the common web service application environments. This module works well for developers who are using Flash and Flex, and who want to integrate their Drupal site with their Flash applications. JavaScript developers will also benefit from using this module by using the JSON backend server module integration.

Mobile developers who want to write applications to use with their Android or iPhone devices will find that the Services module helps to speed up this type of development. Overall, the module is a great benefit to any developer who is looking to integrate his/her Drupal site with external web applications and services.

Deployment module

One project that will interest Drupal users and developers is the Deployment module (`http://drupal.org/project/deploy`). Drupal developers are often faced with the challenge of moving Drupal content and structure from a staging or development site to the client's production version of the site.

Currently, the best method for this has been to just duplicate the nodes and structure on your production site as closely as possible. You can export Views and CCK types and fields, but it's difficult to move over content. The Deployment module is a framework of modules that allows developers to move and stage content automatically over to their production site version. This module uses the Services module to allow for communication with remote Drupal sites. An example of how this happens is when the Deployment module tracks all changes to your node content and then uses web services to transfer the edits and changes over to your production or staging website. The module was developed by teams of developers from Palantir.net and the Foreign Affairs magazine that needed to move large amounts of data from one Drupal site to another.

We'll look at using Deployment in detail in this chapter, and try moving Drupal data from one site to another. This is one of the most promising modules that utilizes the Services module. It's currently in a development version so we'll need to test it out and tread lightly, but it can be used in a development environment.

Content distribution

This is another new module that works intensively with the Services module. The Content distribution module (`http://drupal.org/project/content_distribution`) allows for automatic content migration from one Drupal site to another when that content has been updated. So you can use this module in a way similar to RSS or aggregation—if you have content on one Drupal site that you want to push out to one or many other Drupal sites. This uses a one-to-many content model. You can also queue the updated content to push at specific subscription instances—based on when the accepting site has subscribed to the content updates. This module relies extensively on using the Services module.

Installing and enabling the Services module

Let's go ahead and install the module. Grab the latest version from the project home page and download it. Install the module to your `/sites/all/modules` folder.

When you upload the `module` folder—if you look inside the folder—you'll see two sub-folders: `servers` and `services`. The `servers` folder contains the web services module code you are going to use. The core module contains support for the xmlrpc server. The `services` folder contains modules for providing web services of Drupal-based content including comments, files, menus, nodes, search, system, taxonomy, users, and views. Each of these folders is a sub-module of the Services module.

Once installed, go to your main modules administration list in your Drupal site and look for the **Services** sections. The module page will contain sections for the main core **Services** module, authentication, the server modules, and the services modules. Go ahead and enable the main core **Services** module, the **Key Authentication** module, the **XMLRPC Server,** and the **Services** modules. Save your module configuration.

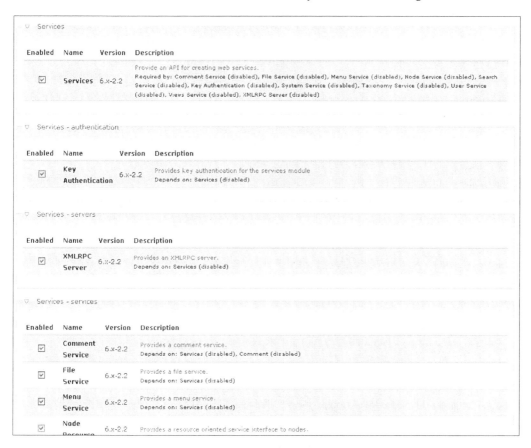

Once you enable the modules, you will have access to an administration page in Drupal to view your installed and enabled Servers and Services, and to check on your main core Services settings. Go to /admin/build/services or visit **Site building | Services**. This page allows you to easily browse your installed Servers and Services modules. You can also view any API keys you have added to your site to use with your servers and services by clicking on the **Keys** button, and overall Services settings by clicking on the **Settings** button.

Currently, we only have core Servers and Services modules installed and enabled, so you'll see a **Browse** page that looks like this:

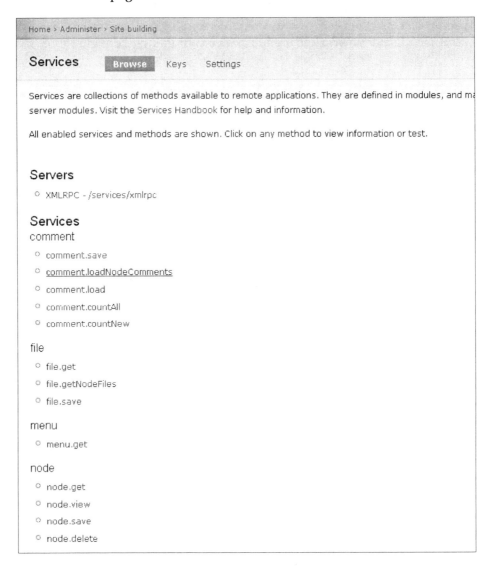

The **Keys** screen lists all of your installed API keys as well as a button to create a new key:

The **Create key** screen allows you to title your application or web service, add an allowed external domain that you will be communicating with (the external web service domain), and then an optional method access if you want to add a specific Drupal-based functionality, such as searching all of your users or searching content—the web service you're communicating with can then access your site to consume these services and access this data.

Currently, the **Settings** screen will show you any authentication methods and settings you have enabled, and whether you want to apply additional content permissions to your content when it's being consumed. The field permissions on your content types will not be automatically applied during a web service call. By default, all the fields will be returned for your content. So, if you want to apply specific content field level permissions, make sure to check the **Apply content permissions** box as shown in the following screenshot:

Testing a simple service callback

We can go ahead and run a basic test by using our Node Service module to get a node from our Drupal site. To test this, go to your **Services | Browse** screen, and under the node service click on the **node.get** link as follows:

The **node.get** service screen will load. This screen explains what this method call does. It returns node data, so if you have a node on your site you can call that node using this screen to test that the call and request works. The **node.get** function explains that it uses two arguments in its call. You are required to enter a node ID, and then the field list to return is optional. So, you can call the node and then request specific fields from your content (via the content type). Let's test both of these.

I have a node on my site at /node/92. This is a node with one image of a butterfly uploaded through the content type filefield. Let's call this node through our **node. get** screen. In the required **nid** Value field, I will type in **92** (or the specific **nid** you are calling on your site) as shown in the following screenshot:

Click on the **Call method** button and your method call will run. You should get a result returned to you for display on the screen with the following code or something similar, depending on how many fields and values you have in your node that you are calling. Notice that the return shows you all of your node type field values (nid, type, language, promote, moderate, sticky, title, body, and so on). It will also return any field arrays for specific content type fields such as, in this case, the image field (field_photo):

```
Result
stdClass Object
(
     [nid] => 92
     [type] => photo
     [language] =>
     [uid] => 1
```

```
[status] => 1
[created] => 1276191970
[changed] => 1276191970
[comment] => 0
[promote] => 0
[moderate] => 0
[sticky] => 0
[tnid] => 0
[translate] => 0
[vid] => 92
[revision_uid] => 1
[title] => Butterfly 7
[body] =>
[teaser] =>
[log] =>
[revision_timestamp] => 1276191970
[format] => 1
[name] => admin
[picture] =>
[data] => a:1:{s:13:"form_build_id";s:37:"form-007e566c85152583f81
e77157874f494";}
[field_photo] => Array
    (
        [0] => Array
            (
                [fid] => 30
                [list] => 1
                [data] => Array
                    (
                        [description] =>
                        [alt] =>
                        [title] =>
                    )

                [uid] => 1
                [filename] => P1100340.JPG
                [filepath] => sites/default/files/P1100340.JPG
                [filemime] => image/jpeg
                [filesize] => 9860
                [status] => 1
                [timestamp] => 1276191968
            )

    )

[og_groups_both] => Array
    (
    )

[og_groups] => Array
    (
    )
```

```
    [last_comment_timestamp] => 1276191970
    [last_comment_name] =>
    [comment_count] => 0
    [taxonomy] => Array
        (
        )

    [files] => Array
        (
        )

    [locations] => Array
        (
        )

    [location] => Array
        (
        )

)
```

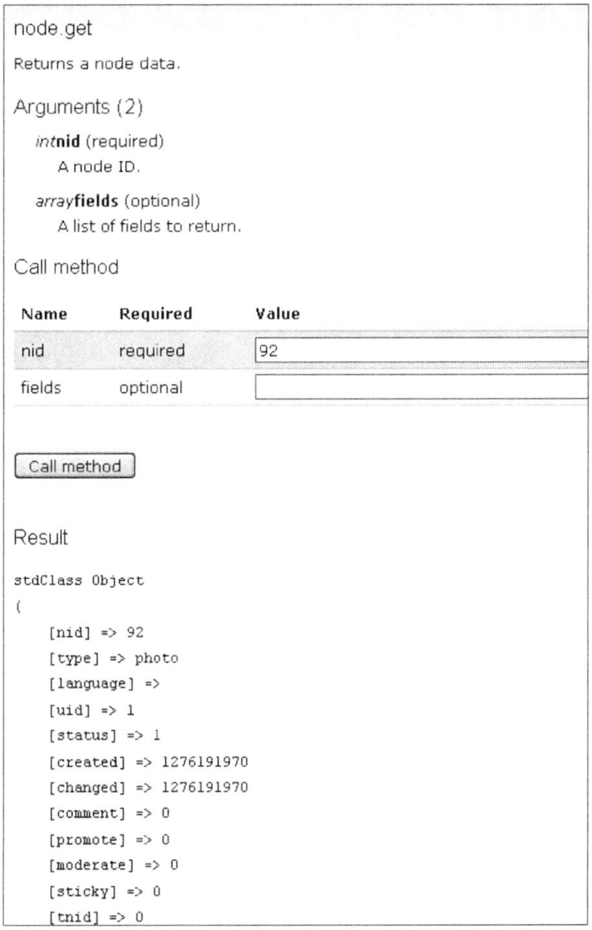

---

node.get

Returns a node data.

Arguments (2)

  *int***nid** (required)
    A node ID.

  *array***fields** (optional)
    A list of fields to return.

Call method

Name	Required	Value
nid	required	92
fields	optional	

[Call method]

Result

```
stdClass Object
(
    [nid] => 92
    [type] => photo
    [language] =>
    [uid] => 1
    [status] => 1
    [created] => 1276191970
    [changed] => 1276191970
    [comment] => 0
    [promote] => 0
    [moderate] => 0
    [sticky] => 0
    [tnid] => 0
```

So, our initial test of the node ID call worked and returned a successful result. Now, let's try limiting our method call to a specific field. This time we'll just return the data for the **field_photo**, our image array for the photo field. In the **fields Value** field, type in the name of the field, in this case **field_photo**. Click on the **Call method** button and you should get a return of just the image field data:

```
Result
stdClass Object
(
    [field_photo] => Array
        (
            [0] => Array
                (
                    [fid] => 30
                    [list] => 1
                    [data] => Array
                        (
                            [description] =>
                            [alt] =>
                            [title] =>
                        )

                    [uid] => 1
                    [filename] => P1100340.JPG
                    [filepath] => sites/default/files/P1100340.JPG
                    [filemime] => image/jpeg
                    [filesize] => 9860
                    [status] => 1
                    [timestamp] => 1276191968
                )

        )

)
```

So, this shows you the immediate flexibility of the Node Services module. You can request a node by its node ID and also request the specific field(s) from that node. If you want to request multiple fields on the call, just type in your field names separated by a comma. For example, the value field would contain **title,field_photo** to call both the `title` and the `photo` fields as shown in the following screenshot. Make sure to not avoid spaces and to separate values with commas, as shown:

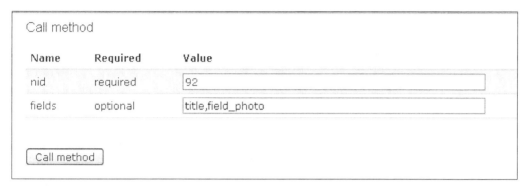

Go ahead and test some more of the Services modules. You may want to try `file.get` to retrieve attached file data, `menu.get` to retrieve menu item data, and `user.get` to retrieve user data. Test a few of these to see what types of results you get.

Creating a Services module and running a custom callback

In the last example, we used the Node Service module that comes packaged with the Services module to query our database and return specific node IDs (and respective node arrays). We also queried returning specific content type fields using the **Call method** of the Node Service module that uses the `node.get` function to return the respective node data and specific fields.

We can also write our own custom module and group this module with the other Services modules to return a set of data of a specific content type's nodes. So, for example, we may want to return all of the nodes of a specific content type—in our case, it will be the Photo gallery type that we queried in our previous examples. But, this query will return all nodes from this content type. This example will also show us how to write a custom module for services, how to integrate it with the Services module, and how to test it to return a simple output such as `hello world`. This will be an example of a simple callback that returns a set of nodes eventually. Just like our previous examples, this custom module will also use the `node.get` function. Let's get started writing our custom Services module.

Creating custom Services module

The first thing we need to do is create our custom Services module files. In our `/sites/all/modules/services/services` folder, let's add a new folder for our module and name it `photo_service`. You'll notice the other service modules in the `services/services` folder such as `comment_service`, `file_service`, and more. We're going to place our custom module in this folder.

Once you create the `photo_service` folder, open up your preferred text editor or IDE, and create a new file named `photo_service.info`. Every module in Drupal needs to have a `.info` file. This file contains the metadata and the information needed by Drupal to list the module in the main modules administration page.

Enter the following lines of code into your `.info` file:

```
; $Id: photo_service.info,v 1.1 2010/06/28 $
name = Photo Service
description = Services for our Photo content type.
package = Services - services
dependencies[] = services
core = 6.x


; Information added by drupal.org packaging script
version = "6.x-1.0"
core = "6.x"
project = "services"
datestamp = "06282010"
```

This code tells Drupal the name of the photo service, a description of what it does, the overall module package the custom module is part of (`Services - services`), and any dependencies. In our case, in order for our custom module to work, we'll need to have the Services module enabled as well.

Upload the `photo_service.info` file to the `/services/services/photo_service` folder.

Now, let's go ahead and create our module file. With a text editor or Dreamweaver, let's create a new file and save the file as `photo_service.module`.

Let's add some basic function code to our photo service's module file. In this file, we're going to write our PHP function to return our data array and output our Photo nodes. The following function implements `hook_services()`, and if you need more information on the documentation for this from the Drupal API, visit: `http://drupal.org/node/438416`. A basic understanding of Drupal module development is not required here but certainly will be helpful if you follow along with this example. Go ahead and add the following code to the `.module` file:

```php
<?php

function photo_service_service() {
    return array(
    array(
        '#method' => 'photo.all',
        '#callback' =>'photo_service_all'


    )
);
}

function photo_service_all() {
 return 'hello world';
}
```

As this is a PHP function, make sure to contain the function in an opening `<?php` tag in your module file code (as shown in the previous code). We'll start by naming our function after the specific service we're creating here, which is `photo_service_service`. We want to return an array, and the method we'll use is to return all of the Photo content type nodes. The function name we're going to give this module is a callback function called `photo_service_all`. We'll define that function in the above code as well, and return for testing purposes a simple text string of `hello world`.

Once we have the .info and the .module files in place in our new custom module folder, we can try to enable the module in our Drupal modules administration page. Go to your /admin/build/modules page and look for your custom **Photo Service** module. Check the box next to the module to enable it and then save your module configuration. Our module will not do anything specific yet because we do not have any functions in the module file, but at least we can see it enabled in our main Services module section.

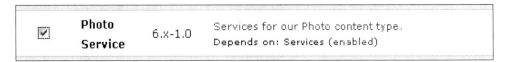

Now that you've added the function to your **Photo Service** module file, try loading your main Services configuration page at **Site Building | Services**. You should see a new service for photos with one method defined as **photo.all**. This method will be hyperlinked on your Services configuration page and will look like this:

Click on the method hyperlink and this will load the **Call method** page for **photo.all**. You'll notice that we have not added any arguments to our function yet. This is just a simple method call that will return text string output. Go ahead and click on the **Call method** button to test this as follows:

When you click on **Call method**, you should get the **hello world** text string as the **Result** displayed on the **photo.all** method page. Our method call works and so far our custom module is working as expected.

Adding to our function to allow for returning Photo nodes data

Let's go ahead and add some more code to our module file so that we can start to return more data besides the simple text string **hello world**. We want to return our Photo nodes and just the nodes of the Photo content type.

```php
<?php
function photo_service_service() {
    return array(
    array(
        '#method' => 'photo.all',
        '#callback' =>'photo_service_all',
        '#return' => 'array',
        '#help' => t('Returns a list of the photo content type
nodes.')

    )
);
}
function photo_service_all() {
 return 'hello world';
}
```

Notice here that we're adding two lines of code after hash tags. We add a `'#return' => 'array'` because we want to return an array of data and we also add a help hash that will show some help text on our method call page. Currently, we have no help text visible, so this will help administrators know what this method call does. Go ahead and upload your module file again and then refresh your method page. You should see the help text appear as follows:

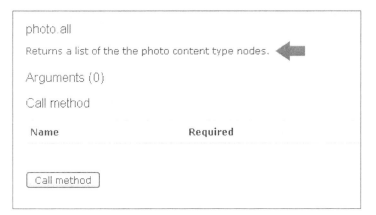

Adding a database query to our custom Services module

Now, we'll replace our function photo_service_all with a database query to return our Photo content type nodes as opposed to the hello world text.

Add the following to your function photo_service_all and remove the previous return hello world. You should now have this in place of that function:

```
function photo_service_all() {
 $result = db_query("SELECT nid FROM {node} WHERE type ='photo'");

 $nodes = array();
 while ($node = db_fetch_object($result)) {
  $output .= node_view(node_load($node->nid), 1);
   $has_posts = TRUE;

 }

 return $output;
}
```

This function is now querying our database and selecting the node ID from nodes, where the type is equal to the Photo content type. This will return an array of nodes and load them for display.

 Here's a helpful hint for dealing with the node_load function. In our code, we want to output our node view and show all the nodes of the Photo content type. To do this, we use the node_load function. You can learn more about this function in the Drupal API documentation available at: http://api.drupal.org/api/function/node_load. If you click on the 45 functions call node_load link, you'll get a list of the examples you can look at for sample code. I chose to use the blog_page_user, which displays a Drupal page containing recent blog entries of a given user. This shows a usage of node_load within a while db_fetch_object call. The code looks like this in this example: $output .=node_view(node_load($node->nid), 1);. I can reuse this code in my function photo_service_all. It's a good practice and habit to use the Drupal API documentation as much as possible when writing your functions because it provides the most up-to-date code for Drupal 6.

Our entire code should now resemble this:

```php
<?php
function photo_service_service() {
    return array(
    array(
        '#method' => 'photo.all',
        '#callback' =>'photo_service_all',
        '#return' => 'array',
        '#help' => t('Returns a list of the photo content type
nodes.')
    )

);
}
function photo_service_all() {
 $result = db_query("SELECT nid FROM {node} WHERE type ='photo'");

  $nodes = array();
 while ($node = db_fetch_object($result)) {
   $output .= node_view(node_load($node->nid), 1);
    $has_posts = TRUE;

   }

 return $output;
}
```

Go ahead and refresh your **photo.all** method call and then click on the **Call Method** button. You should get an array output showing the Photo content type nodes that you currently have on your site. All of the nodes data should be displayed because you're returning nodes with the "photo" type. Your output should look something like this:

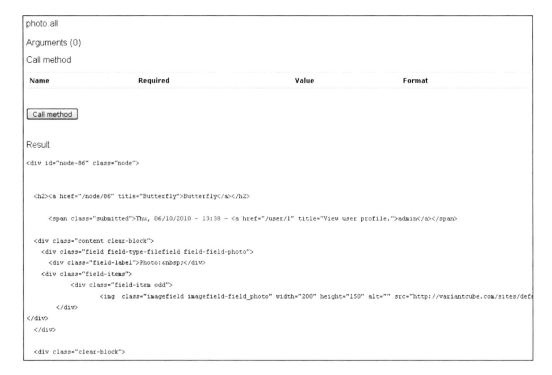

Adding arguments

Let's go ahead and add an argument to our `photo_service` function so that we can specify which fields to return in our output when we run the method call. Currently, we're returning all of the node data, but we may only want to return specific fields. To do this, add the following code to your function `photo_service_service`:

```
'#args'=> array('array'),
```

Then, add the `fields` parameter to our `photo_service` function. So, the function will become:

```
function photo_service_all($fields) {
 $result = db_query("SELECT nid FROM {node} WHERE type ='photo'");
  $nodes = array();
 while ($node = db_fetch_object($result)) {
```

```
    $nodes[] = services_node_load(node_load($node), $fields);

  }

 return $output;
}
```

Summary

In this chapter, we explored how to use the Drupal Services module. We installed and enabled the contributed Services module and looked at the functionality of its servers and services functionality. We learned that we can add server modules to integrate with our Drupal site and content and also serve our Drupal content out to external websites using the pre-packaged Services sub-modules that can be enabled. We did the following:

- Installed and enabled Services module
- Enabled and tested the Node Service sub-module and used the `node.get` function to return method calls of specific node ID data and arrays
- Looked at the authentication methods that are included with the Services module
- Created a custom module that can integrate with our Services module and extend the default functionality of services
- Did a simple method call to return a callback that outputs `hello world` text data
- Returned a more advanced method call by listing all of the nodes and data for a specific content type; in this case, all of the Photo content types' photo nodes

In *Chapter 7, Drupal, Spam, and Web Services*, we're going to look at multiple contributed modules that help your Drupal site integrate with spam prevention Web services and applications including Mollom, CAPTCHA and reCAPTCHA.

7
Drupal, Spam, and Web Services

In this chapter, we're going to practice using contributed modules and web services that will help us to prevent spam submissions on your Drupal site. Currently, one of the easiest methods of preventing unauthorized access to your site by spambots and spam scripts is to install the CAPTCHA module. We're going to install and enable CAPTCHA and also use a web service called reCAPTCHA to enhance the default CAPTCHA functionality.

We'll also look at the web service modules including AntiSpam (a successor to the Akismet module) and the Mollom module. We introduced the Mollom module in *Chapter 1, About Drupal Web Services*, but we'll take a closer look at the Mollom functionality in this chapter.

To summarize, in this chapter we will:

- Install and enable the CAPTCHA and reCAPTCHA modules
- Explore and practice using the Antispam module
- Enable and practice using the Mollom module

CAPTCHA and reCAPTCHA

The Drupal CAPTCHA contributed module allows us to protect our site from machine-based spambots by forcing the site visitor and user to enter a text or image-based code into a form field, before logging into the Drupal site or posting new content to the site. The form field offers a test to the user to confirm that the user of the site is a human being and not a machine. You will see CAPTCHA forms in use on many website forms that are public accessible forms, including, for example, comment post forms and help-desk ticket support requests, to name a few, and you will also see CAPTCHA fields in use on login pages on websites. The CAPTCHA module will prevent form submissions by bots and thus prevent your website from getting filled up with unwanted spam posts.

The CAPTCHA module is currently in its 6.x-2.2 version and you can download it from its project page at `http://drupal.org/project/captcha`. In order to use the reCAPTCHA web service module, you'll need to first install the CAPTCHA module.

The reCAPTCHA module is an extension module of CAPTCHA that allows you to integrate with the reCAPTCHA web service (`http://www.google.com/recaptcha`), which is a web service project sponsored by Google. Google actually uses reCAPTCHA to digitize books for the Web. You can learn more about the reCAPTCHA project at its Google project page. Google also allows you to tie into the reCAPTCHA API by embedding the reCAPTCHA plug-in into your site, and this will show a widget that will ask your site visitors to type two words into a form field. By typing in the words, you can get access to that portion of the website because the site recognizes—through the reCAPTCHA module—that you are a human being typing in the words as opposed to a spambot or script.

The Drupal reCAPTCHA module is available at its project page for download: `http://drupal.org/project/recaptcha`.

Installing and configuring CAPTCHA and reCAPTCHA

Let's go ahead and install, enable, and configure the CAPTCHA and reCAPTCHA modules so that we can then get the reCAPTCHA web service installed and try it out.

Download the latest 6.x versions of CAPTCHA and reCAPTCHA from their respective project pages and install them to your /sites/all/modules directory. Once uploaded, go to your main modules admin page and enable the modules. For these examples, I'm using the 6.x-2.2 version of CAPTCHA and the 6.x-1.4 version of reCAPTCHA. The modules will show up under a Spam control heading in your modules admin list. Enable the **CAPTCHA, Image CAPTCHA, reCAPTCHA,** and **reCAPTCHA Mailhide** modules as shown in the following screenshot.

As the module admin page notes, the reCAPTCHA module uses the reCAPTCHA web service to enhance the default CAPTCHA module. The reCAPTCHA Mailhide uses the web service to protect e-mail addresses from spammers' scripts. Notice that reCAPTCHA is dependent on the CAPTCHA module being enabled.

Enabled	Name	Version	Description
☑	CAPTCHA	6.x-2.2	Base CAPTCHA module for adding challenges to arbitrary forms. Required by: Image CAPTCHA (disabled), reCAPTCHA (disabled)
☑	Image CAPTCHA	6.x-2.2	Provides an image based CAPTCHA. Depends on: CAPTCHA (disabled)
☑	reCAPTCHA	6.x-1.4	Uses the reCAPTCHA web service to improve the CAPTCHA system. Depends on: CAPTCHA (disabled)
☑	reCAPTCHA Mailhide	6.x-1.4	Uses the reCAPTCHA web service to protect email addresses.

▽ Spam control

Save your module configuration. Once you save your module configuration, you will see a message notifying that you can configure the CAPTCHA module on your site. Click on that link to go to the CAPTCHA configuration settings page or go to **User management | CAPTCHA**.

For our examples, I will be adding a CAPTCHA field to the main contact form on the site. So, make sure you have enabled your core contact module and form, and set the appropriate level of user permissions so that both anonymous and authenticated users can submit the contact form. Once you have enabled your site-wide contact form, the form will be available at /contact.

On your CAPTCHA module's **General Settings** admin page, go ahead and set the default challenge type for the site. We'll set this first to **Image (from module image_captcha)** type, though you can also choose the Math type that uses the core CAPTCHA module functionality. This type uses the CAPTCHA image module's functionality.

Next, you'll see that you can set specific challenge types for specific forms on your site by their **form_id**. By default, the module allows you to set the challenge types for the following forms:

- **comment_form**
- **contact_mail_page**
- **forum_node_form**
- **user_login**
- **user_login_block**
- **user_pass**
- **user_register**

Let's set the challenge type to Image for the **contact_mail_page** (this is the default site-wide contact form) and for the user login and register pages.

We'll circle back and change these types to reCAPTCHA once we test out the main CAPTCHA functionality.

You can also choose to add a CAPTCHA administration link to forms (other content type forms) on your site if you want administrator roles and users to have a choice to add CAPTCHA to their specific content type form. Let's go ahead and check that box for now. Finally, you can add your own **Challenge description** text and choose the type of CAPTCHA validation and persistence. I'm going to leave these set to their defaults for now, as you can see in the following screenshot:

Form protection

Select the challenge type you want for each of the listed forms (identified by their so called *form_id's*). You can easily add arbitrary forms with textfield at the bottom of the table or with the help of the *'Add CAPTCHA administration links to forms'* option below.

Default challenge type:

Image (from module image_captcha) ▼

Select the default challenge type for CAPTCHAs. This can be overriden for each form if desired.

form_id	Challenge type	Operations
comment_form	[none] ▼	delete
contact_mail_page	Image (from module image_captcha) ▼	delete
contact_mail_user	[none] ▼	delete
forum_node_form	[none] ▼	delete
user_login	Image (from module image_captcha) ▼	delete
user_login_block	[none] ▼	delete
user_pass	[none] ▼	delete
user_register	Image (from module image_captcha) ▼	delete
	[none] ▼	

☑ Add CAPTCHA administration links to forms

This option makes it easy to manage CAPTCHA settings on forms. When enabled, users with the *"administer CAPTCHA settings"* permission will see a fieldset with CAPTCHA administration links on all forms, except on administrative pages.

☐ Allow CAPTCHAs and CAPTCHA administration links on administrative pages

This option makes it possible to add CAPTCHAs to forms on administrative pages. CAPTCHAs are disabled by default on administrative pages (which shouldn't be accessible to untrusted users normally) to avoid the related overhead. In some situations, e.g. in the case of demo sites, it can be usefull to allow CAPTCHAs on administrative pages.

☑ Add a description to the CAPTCHA

Add a configurable description to explain the purpose of the CAPTCHA to the visitor.

Challenge description:

This question is for testing whether you are a human visito

Configurable description of the CAPTCHA. An empty entry will reset the description.

You can also choose to log wrong responses, which will give you a detailed log of all potential spam submissions. Save your CAPTCHA configuration.

Image CAPTCHA

To tweak your Image CAPTCHA settings, click on the **Image CAPTCHA** button. This will launch the specific Image CAPTCHA settings page. Here, you have control over which characters to show in the code, the code length, fonts, font size, and character spacing. The entire sub-module is very flexible and customizable. Go ahead and tweak these settings to your preference. You can also tweak the color settings that get displayed (background and text colors), the file format for the displayed image, and the distortion level of the image. Try adding salt and pepper noise and line noise to your image to see how this renders. When you are happy with your settings, click on **Save configuration**.

When you save your configuration, you'll notice that the Image CAPTCHA example will change to reflect your new settings, giving you an almost real-time example of your configuration. This allows you to easily refine your CAPTCHA by tweaking it according to your preferences. For example, if it's too noisy you can lessen the amount of line noise.

Log out of your site and go to your /contact form and try out the contact submission along with the CAPTCHA field. You need to log out of the site to test the CAPTCHA field because otherwise the field will only show you to the anonymous users of your site. Anyone with a site admin account and admin credentials will be able to bypass the field. So, it's best to test it when you're logged out. You should have something that looks similar to this:

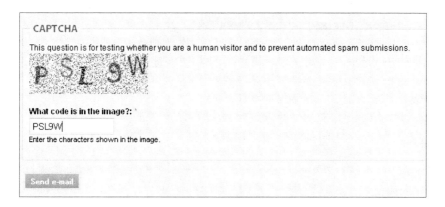

reCAPTCHA

Let's go ahead and enable reCAPTCHA on the site and integrate the web service with our CAPTCHA module. To do this, we'll go to your CAPTCHA settings page again, and this time we'll specify that we want to use reCAPTCHA as the **Default challenge type** for our specific forms. I'll make this tweak for the **contact_mail_page** first, to try it out. Save your CAPTCHA configuration.

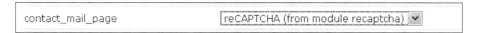

To tweak the specific reCAPTCHA configuration, click on your **reCAPTCHA** button at the top of the CAPTCHA configuration page. In order to use the reCAPTCHA web service, you need to enter a public and private key on this page. To sign up for keys, go to the reCAPTCHA website and register for the API keys and for an account. On the reCAPTCHA site, you'll launch a **Create a reCAPTCHA key** form. Enter your website domain into the **Domain** field and then click on the **Create Key** button. You can choose to enable the key on all domains of your server if you select the **Enable this key on all domains (global key)** checkbox. If you are logged into your Gmail account, you'll automatically log in to your reCAPTCHA account as it's a Google-powered web service:

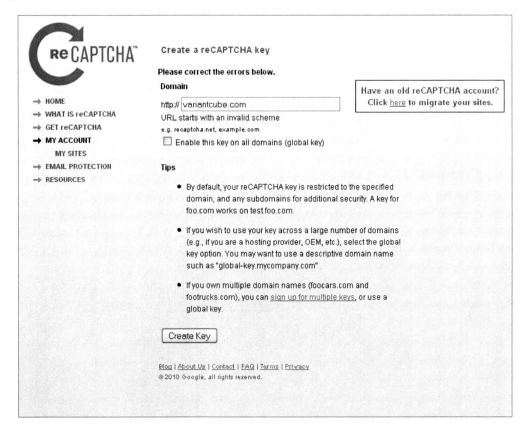

Click on the **Create Key** button. You will get a page that shows you the submitted domain and your new public and private keys and links to reCAPTCHA resources. Make sure to print this page out for your records.

Enter the **Public Key** and **Private Key** details on the reCAPTCHA configuration form in your Drupal site.

You can also choose theme/design settings to use for the reCAPTCHA widget. I'm leaving it set to the default **Red** theme, for this example. Click **Save configuration**.

Now, launch your contact form to test out the reCAPTCHA form. You should see something similar to this:

If you want to look at the reCAPTCHA module code, you can access this in the `/sites/all/modules/recaptcha` folder. Inside this folder are your Drupal module files, and another folder named `recaptcha`. The actual API is wrapped inside the `recaptchalib.php` file that resides in the `recaptcha` folder. This PHP file contains the code defining the reCAPTCHA web service server URLs; a query string that encodes the request out to the servers; the function that posts the request via HTTP; the function that gets and returns the HTML for the actual reCAPTCHA widget and form fields; the function that checks the answer people type into the form fields (`function recaptch_check_answer`); and the part of that function that discards any spam submissions.

I've attached the code for the `recaptchalib.php` file as an appendix in this book, so you can view the code in the code appendices.

AntiSpam

Drupal has a number of contributed modules that control and prevent spam submissions and posts on your site. The Antispam module is the enhanced version of the former Akismet web service module. Akismet utilizes the Akismet web service (`http://akismet.com/`) but the module is no longer supported. The module maintainer recommends downloading and installing the AntiSpam module if you want to patch into the Akismet web service.

The AntiSpam module is available from its Drupal project page at: `http://drupal.org/project/antispam`. The current version of AntiSpam is 6.x-1.2. AntiSpam also supports using web service spam applications such as TypePad AntiSpam (`http://antispam.typepad.com/`) and Defensio (`http://defensio.com/`). Similar to Mollom, if you use the AntiSpam module with a Defensio account, you can leverage the spam ratings that Defensio uses to learn as it defends and actually improves your AntiSpam results.

The AntiSpam module also gives you a new API function named `antispam_api_cmd_spam_check()` that allows your site to check all textual node content for potential spam posts, as long as you have configured the AntiSpam module to work with an external web service application.

Let's go ahead and install and enable the AntiSpam module.

Installing and configuring AntiSpam

Upload the module to your `/sites/all/modules` folder and then enable the module on your main modules admin screen. The module will show up in your **Spam control** section along with the previous section's CAPTCHA and reCAPTCHA modules. Go ahead and enable the AntiSpam module.

Once enabled, you can then enable your AntiSpam module configuration by going to **Site configuration | AntiSpam.** If you have specific questions about the comparison between the functionalities of each integrated spam web service, you can check out the module developer's documentation for a detailed comparison table. Go to: http://www.pixture.com/drupal/node/76 to view the comparison table. There is a charge for the Akismet service for commercial sites but the TypePad AntiSpam service is supported free of charge. There are some fees involved with using the module with Defensio or Mollom as your service. Akismet was built for the Wordpress CMS but the module developer has programmed the AntiSpam module to work with Akismet. TypePad was developed to work with the TypePad CMS, but again, the module developer programmed it to work with this Drupal module.

We're going to try setting up the module to run with the TypePad AntiSpam web service. You'll notice on the AntiSpam configuration page that when you select a service provider radio button, it conditionally opens the specific service API key field. Select the **TypePad AntiSpam** radio button. The TypePad AntiSpam API key field will appear. In order to get an API key for TypePad AntiSpam, you'll need to sign up for a free account at the TypePad AntiSpam API Key sign up web page available at: http://antispam.typepad.com/info/get-api-key.html.

Go ahead and sign up for a TypePad account first. Once you create an account, you'll be asked to sign in first at the TypePad website. Sign in and you'll be redirected to the Get an API Key page. Click on the link to **Get Your API Key.** Your API key will launch in a pop-up window as shown in the following screenshot. Print this out for your records.

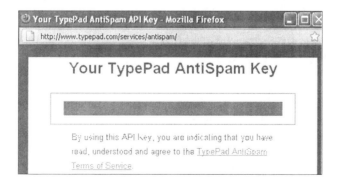

Copy the API key and paste it into your TypePad field on the AntiSpam configuration page. You can leave the service provider connections radio button set to **Enabled**. Also, leave the **Connection timeout** set to its default **10** seconds. Your screen should look like this:

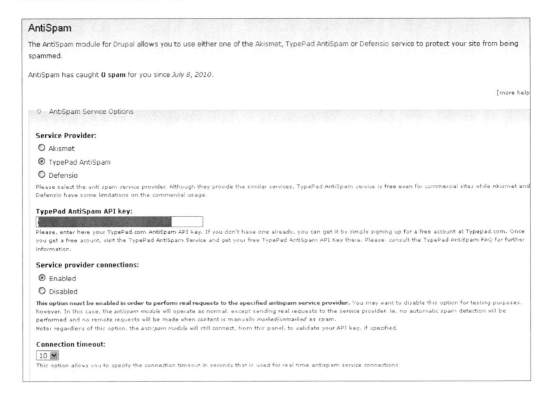

Additional TypePad/AntiSpam module settings

Scrolling down on the main AntiSpam configuration page will give you more options to configure, including how the AntiSpam module handles spam generally, and specifically for your nodes and comments. You can also set your spam counter, statistics, and anti-spambot options here.

For **General Options**, I'm going to leave the defaults set for removing spam older than three days, showing 50 records per page, one spam notification block, and e-mail notifications will be left enabled.

Under the **Node Options**, you can select the specific content types you want to run the AntiSpam functionality on. I'm going to select a few of these, including Blog, Page, and Story. You can select the types for which you want to check spam submissions on your site.

Scroll down to the **Comment Options** settings and leave these set to their "enabled" defaults because we do want to check for comment spam on our site. You can also set your spam counter options and your Statistics chart width. I'm leaving these set to the defaults.

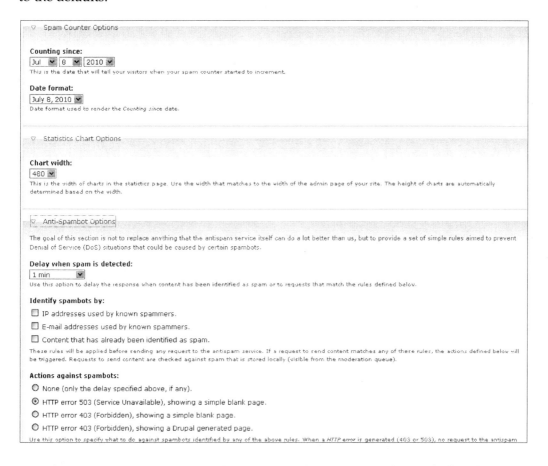

You also have various **Anti-Spambot Options** that you can select including how to use the web service to identify spambots, and what actions to take against spambots. We'll leave these set to the defaults. Save your AntiSpam module configuration.

AntiSpam moderation queue

Node and comment posts will start being monitored now by the AntiSpam module. To view your spam reports and statistics, you can go to the **Content management | AntiSpam moderation queue** report page. The initial **Overview** screen will show you a summary of your nodes and comments content and how much spam has been caught.

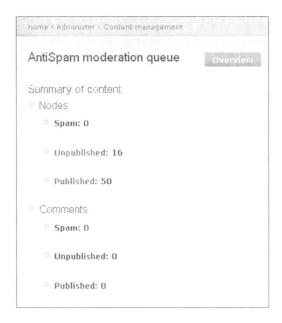

Because you're using the TypePad service, any spam will be caught in real time and your summary will be updated here based on the AntiSpam module cron run that gets fired.

You can also get reports on your Node spam and comment spam specifically by clicking on the Nodes and Comments links. This will give you a list of your unpublished and published Drupal nodes. Finally, if you click on the **Statistics** link, you'll launch a page that shows you a statistics graphic that the AntiSpam module will configure for you showing you Ham, Spam, False Negatives, and False Positives. There's a pie chart graphic and a tabled graphic.

Current Service Provider

○ TypePad AntiSpam

Statistics since July 8, 2010 (1 day)

○ Total Checked: 1 (avg: 1/day)

    ○ Total Spams: 0 (avg: 0/day)

    ○ Total Hams: 1 (avg: 1/day)

○ Total False Negatives: 0 (avg: 0/day)

○ Total False Positives: 0 (avg: 0/day)

○ **Accuracy: 100 %**

Total Statistics

Ham ——— ———False Negative
——False Positive
——Spam

Daily Statistics

■ Spam ▨ Ham

2
1.8
1.6
1.4
1.2

Mollom module

We've explored using the AntiSpam module. We're going to turn our attention to another module that works specifically with the Mollom spam prevention web service application. We introduced the Mollom module in *Chapter 1, About Drupal Web Services* of this book but we'll take a closer look at the module now and use its functionality to see how it catches spam on your site. You can learn more about the Mollom module on its project page and download it from: `http://drupal.org/project/mollom`. In *Chapter 1, About Drupal Web Services*, we already installed and enabled the module as well as the Mollom Test module. Mollom Test allows you to test your Mollom web service functionality without having to worry about getting your own IP or site reported as a valid spammer or spambot. You do not need to enable this module, as long as it's installed when you install and enable the main Mollom module. Both of the modules will show up in your main modules admin listing.

Mollom will also block your comment and contact form spam, and also protect the user registration form on your site and block spam from node content type submissions. It also includes CAPTCHA so you can enable just Mollom for both your spam and CAPTCHA functionality if you choose. There is a detailed handbook and documentation on how to use the module at drupal.org: `http://drupal.org/handbook/modules/mollom` and also on the Mollom website: `http://mollom.com/tutorials/drupal`.

Configuring the Mollom web service

First, we need to make sure we have installed and enabled the module. Upload the Mollom module to your `/sites/all/modules` directory and enable it in your main modules admin list. Then, go to **Site configuration** | **Mollom** to load the main Mollom configuration screen.

Once you load the main Mollom screen, click on the **Settings** tab/link. Similar to the AntiSpam module, you will need to sign up for an account with the Mollom web service. You need an account in order to get the public and private API keys. To do this, go to the Mollom.com website and sign up for a subscription account. You can do this at: `http://mollom.com/user/register`. You'll notice that the Mollom website has been designed and developed using Drupal.

Once you create your account, follow the instructions in the e-mail you receive to log in for the first time. Now, once you log in to the Mollom site, you'll need to add a subscription for your website. Click on the **Manage sites** button and this will launch the Mollom Site manager. Here, you can click on the **Add new site** button to link Mollom to your Drupal site.

The Mollom subscription specification page will load, explaining the multiple subscription levels. For this example, we're going to select the Mollom Free version. This will give you the default level of Mollom spam filtering, CAPTCHA functionality, and cover an unlimited amount of spam posts. For a larger enterprise level website, you may want to select a paid subscription level.

Click on the **Get Mollom Free** button and you'll then be asked to enter your website's URL, type, site language, and site software. Go ahead and complete the form and then click on the **Next** button.

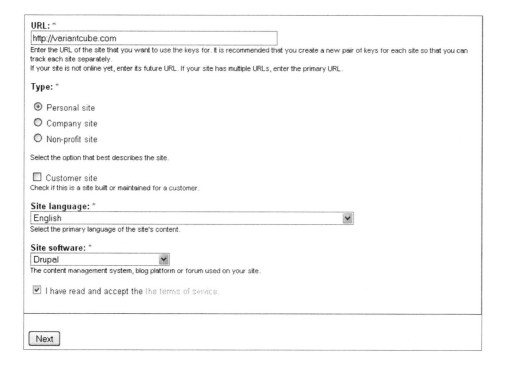

Click the **Complete subscription** button when it appears on the next screen. Once you add the site to your account, you will be presented with a **view keys** link. Click on this link to get your public and private keys. Go ahead and add your public and private keys to your Drupal site Mollom configuration page.

On your **Mollom** settings page in your Drupal site, you can also choose to use a Mollom Fallback strategy. This gives you an option in the event that the Mollom web service application servers are down or offline. You can choose to block all submissions on the site until the Mollom servers come back online, or you can leave all of your forms in an unprotected state and allow all submissions to be posted.

Leave the default to block them all for the moment. Your screen should look like this:

Save your Mollom configuration. You should receive a message stating that:

> We contacted the Mollom servers to verify your keys: the Mollom services are operating correctly. We are now blocking spam.

Choosing the content that Mollom will protect

Now, you need to select the content type forms on your site that will use the Mollom spam and CAPTCHA protection. First, I'm going to make sure to disable my AntiSpam and CAPTCHA modules because in this example I'm only going to use the Mollom web service.

I'm going to add the `Comment: Comment form` to my Mollom configuration. I'll analyze the subject and comment fields of the comment form.

Save your comment form configuration. I'm also going to add the **User: User registration form**. Save your User registration form configuration. You are now protecting both the comment forms and the user registration form process. User registration form protection will use CAPTCHA while the comment form will analyze the form fields for textual spam data.

At any time, you can remove or configure these operations by clicking on the **Configure** and **Unprotect** links. You can go ahead and test the Mollom CAPTCHA functionality by enabling your user registration settings and form. Log out of your site and then go to `/user/register` and you'll see the Mollom Word verification CAPTCHA field.

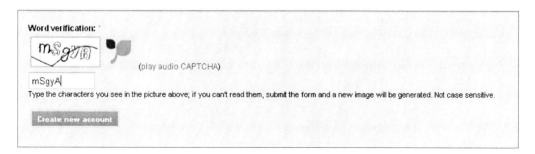

Mollom reports and statistics

You can get a graph statistics report of your Mollom spam activity by going to **Reports | Mollom statistics**. The graph will show all Ham (not spam) operations accepted and any spam posts that have been blocked. Try entering a user and adding the wrong CAPTCHA. When you enter the wrong CAPTCHA (for example, if you type the word in with the wrong spelling), Mollom will record this in its statistics. First, you will receive this error message on the user frontend:

> **The CAPTCHA was not completed correctly. Please complete this new CAPTCHA and try again.**

Now log in to the site as the admin user and go to your **Reports | Recent log entries**. You'll see that the Mollom web service records all incorrect CAPTCHAs in your recent logs. You'll also see an incorrect CAPTCHA array warning submitted by an anonymous user. The type should be designated as Mollom:

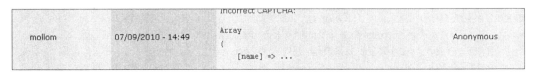

Click on the Array code and the entire Array message will load. It should look similar to this:

```
Incorrect CAPTCHA:
Array
(
    [name] => trevor4admin
    [mail] => drupalbuilders@gmail.com
    [pass] => test
    [og_register] => Array
        (
            [72] => 0
        )

    [timezone] => -14400
    [op] => Create new account
    [submit] => Create new account
    [form_build_id] => form-bf28474138716b1ac49f0c40baa8c0b5
    [form_id] => user_register
    [mollom] => Array
        (
            [session_id] => 1278701353-1007093762bf6aa773
            [captcha] => dddssdf
        )

)
```

The Mollom application service reports on the username, e-mail, and password that the user or potential spammer was trying to enter into the user registration form. So, this gives you a large amount of data about the CAPTCHA attempt. It actually gives you the CAPTCHA text that the user has entered.

Before you begin testing your content type or comment form submissions, you'll want to read the following paragraph on how to safely test Mollom without affecting your site's reputation negatively. You don't want to get blacklisted by Mollom as a spammer by running some tests on your site.

Mollom allows you to bypass the production version of the web service by putting the web service into a plugin developer mode so you can run some spam submission tests. To do this, go to your Mollom site manager within your Mollom account and click on **Edit your Mollom site subscription**. You'll return to the site details screen. On this screen you'll see a checkbox to Activate Mollom plugin developer mode. Check this box and you will then be able to use Mollom in test mode. When you enable this developer functionality any request that goes to the Mollom web service from your Drupal site will be treated as a test call by Mollom. Bear in mind that if you have just enabled your Mollom account, it can take up to 60 minutes for Mollom to change your site subscription to developer mode. So you'll need to wait up to one hour before testing.

Click on the **Update** button and then return in about an hour to submit a test spam post.

Once you submit some test spam posts, and later when Mollom begins catching and reporting on real spam posts and submissions, you can get a full graphical report from your Drupal Mollom Statistics. Load the **Mollom statistics** page and you'll see a table graphic that shows you all of your spam posts in a graphic visual report. If you do not have a lot of spam posted to your site the graphic will appear empty and look like this:

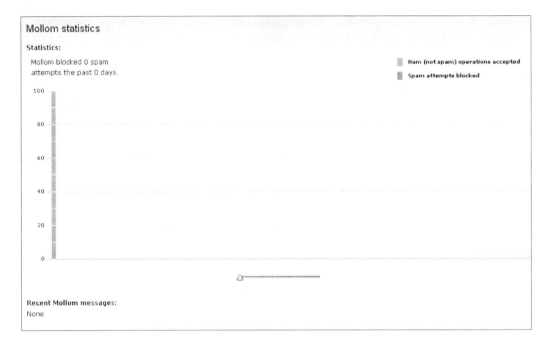

Eventually, your visual will look something like this:

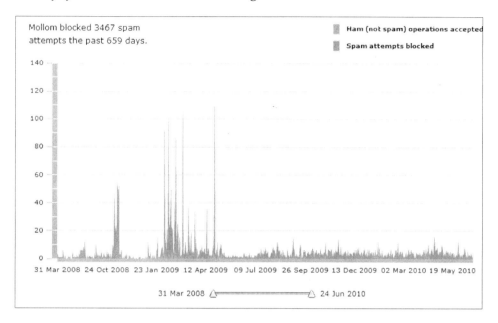

Summary

In this chapter we looked in detail at a variety of contributed Drupal modules that interface with spam prevention web services including the AntiSpam module and the Mollom module. The AntiSpam allows us to use the Akismet, TypePad, or Defensio web services, and the Mollom module allows us to interface our site with the Mollom web service API. Here's a brief summary of what we did in this chapter:

- Installed and enabled the AntiSpam module
- Interfaced the AntiSpam module with the TypePad spam web service
- Installed and configured the CAPTCHA and reCAPTCHA modules
- Added the reCAPTCHA web service API to our reCAPTCHA module configuration
- Installed, enabled, and configured the Mollom module and integrated the module with the Mollom web service API
- Tested all the above modules by posting spam and trying to bypass the CAPTCHA mechanisms on login and user registration

In *Chapter 8 , Using XML-RPC*, we'll return to a discussion of Drupal content and how to connect our Drupal site with web applications, including Google documents, using the XML-RPC protocol.

8
Using XML-RPC

In this chapter, we're going to look in more detail at how Drupal uses the XML-RPC protocol and how this protocol can help integrate your Drupal site with external web service-based applications and servers. We'll set up a Google Documents account and learn how to leverage the XML-RPC protocol to post our Google text documents automatically over to our Drupal site and show how these documents will turn into Drupal-based nodes automatically. This will allow us great flexibility in how we can publish rich content to our Drupal sites.

While setting up our Google Documents to Drupal integration, we'll explore the BlogAPI core Drupal module and its configuration.

Then, we'll look in detail at how to sync Drupal node content from one Drupal site to another using the XML-RPC protocol. We'll return to a discussion about using the Services module to help set up this sync.

To summarize, in this chapter we will:

- Enable the BlogAPI module and configure it
- Define how the XML-RPC protocol works in your Drupal site
- Take existing Google Documents and populate those documents over to a Drupal site so that they become nodes and web content on your site
- Sync Drupal content between two Drupal sites using XML-RPC, the Services and Deployment modules

XML-RPC and Drupal

Drupal 6 supports the XML-RPC web service specification by default. In the root level of your Drupal site, you can locate the XML-RPC PHP file, named `xmlrpc.php`. This file contains the code that allows Drupal to respond to remote procedure calls that are posting data to your site; and also to send GET requests to other servers and applications using the XML-RPC specification.

By way of review, the XML-RPC specification allows for remote procedure calls to use XML as their format and HTTP as the transport mechanism. XML-RPC sends requests (POST and GET) over the HTTP protocol via your web browser to get and send content. The actual remote procedure call is encoded in XML to make for a consistent specification and protocol that multiple websites and applications can use and respond to. The Drupal core includes the file you need to send and receive XML-RPC. In this chapter, we're going to look at a few cases for using XML-RPC on your Drupal site. One of them will show you how to take a Google Document from your Google Docs account and post that document to your Drupal site as a node. So, you can easily take a document on the Google server and post it over to your client Drupal site. The benefit of this is that you can construct your web content using Google's free docs utility and interface and then post that content to your site as a web page. All this happens via the BlogAPI web service using XML-RPC and via the XML-RPC file in your root install.

Incoming XML-RPC post requests are handled by the `xmlrpc.php` file that lies in the root of your Drupal site install. If you browse to this file via your web browser (`http://yoursitename/xmlrpc.php`), you should see a message that states: XML-RPC server accepts POST requests only. Notice here that the server your site is on will handle any post requests that come into it, but for security purposes, the server/site may not allow you to send out POST or GET requests to another application without some tweaking. If your site only handles POST requests, you may need to talk with your server/site administrator to tweak the XML-RPC settings so that you can also send out requests.

First, we're going to try an example using Drupal, BlogAPI, and Google Docs to POST Google Docs content to your Drupal site. We'll then look at a functionality that allows us to sync content between two Drupal sites. Both of these methods use the `xmlrpc.php` file and framework for providing web services.

Drupal Blog API and Google Docs

Drupal's Blog API module comes shipped with Drupal core and it supports using multiple XML-RPC-based BlogAPIs including the Blogger API, MetaWeblog API, and Movable Type API. Google Documents also supports this framework of blog APIs and allows for integration with your Drupal site.

Blog API is a core module that works in association with the blog content type but also with other content types on your Drupal site. By using one of the APIs that Google Docs supports in tandem with the Drupal Blog API, you can publish content from your Google Docs account to your Drupal site at the click of a button. So, the pieces that we'll need to make this work are the following:

- Blog API module enabled in your Drupal site
- `xmlrpc.php` file at the root level of your Drupal site
- A Google Docs account set up and configured
- A Google Document that you want to post to your Drupal site

A note about the Blog API module: this core Drupal module supports various XML-RPC-based blog APIs including the methods we listed above. We're going to interface the Blog API module with the MetaWeblog API. You can learn more about the Blog API module on drupal.org at `http://drupal.org/node/295`. For more information on the MetaWeblog API, you can visit its specification page available on the XML-RPC website at `http://www.xmlrpc.com/metaWeblogApi`.

Another detail to keep in mind here is that the XML-RPC file, `xmlrpc.php`, in your Drupal root is the API URL of your site's blog(s). So, this is the API URL that you're going to use to communicate with Google Docs.

Enabling and configuring Blog API

The first thing we need to do on our Drupal site is enable and configure the Blog API module. This is a core module but it comes disabled by default. Go to your **Site building | Modules** and enable the Blog API module:

Once the module is enabled, you can configure it at **Site configuration | Blog API**. Go here and you'll be asked to enable the module for external blogging clients. This is basically allowing you to enable various content types on your site (both custom content types and the core Drupal types) to allow for external blogging clients to post to these types. We'll select the **Blog entry** as the default type we want to allow external sites to post to:

Next, you can configure specific file settings for the type of content you want to allow posts for. We're going to leave this set to the defaults and allow image files and document files to be posted. Your field should contain the following: **jpg jpeg gif png txt doc xls pdf ppt pps odt ods odp**. This will allow Google Docs formats to post as well.

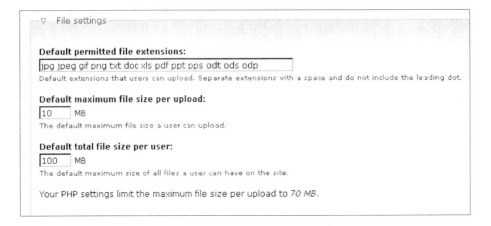

You can also set the **Default maximum file size per upload** and the **Default total file size per user**. I'll set these to **10 MB** and **100 MB** respectively. On a production site, you'll want to use discretion here and be careful as to how much data you're allowing your users to upload.

Click on the **Save configuration** button.

Setting up a Google Documents account

The next thing you'll want to do is set up a Google Docs account if you do not already have one. Go to: `https://docs.google.com` and sign up for an account.

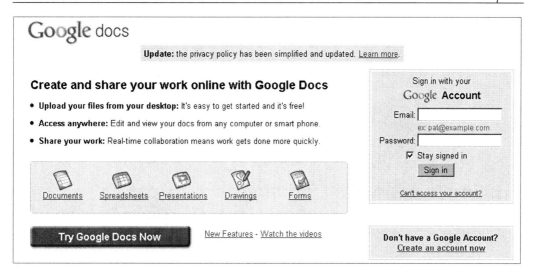

If you already have a Google account for Gmail, for instance, you can access Google Docs via your Gmail account. I'm going to assume here that you have some experience using the Google applications including Gmail and Google Docs.

Once you have an account, go ahead and create a document by using the **Create new | Document** functionality.

We're now all set up to start posting content from Google Docs. The way this will work is that we're going to configure our document in Google Docs to post to our Drupal site through the xmlrpc.php file. Because we have set up our Drupal site to allow posts to the Blog type (as per the above Blog API settings), this is currently the only type on our site that we can post to. We're also going to authenticate the Google Document to post to a specific user account on our Drupal site via the username and password of that account. We'll create a specific role and user account on our site to use just for posting Google Documents. This will help to keep the site secure and prevent the content from being posted by anonymous users or by authenticated users who do not have permissions to post on the site, using the Blog API module.

Go ahead and create a role called **Google Docs** and also a user account on your site to utilize this role. Make sure this role has permissions to **access content** and **create blog entries**.

In order for the Google Docs role to post content to your site from Google Docs, you will need to give them a blog API-specific module permission. The permission is **administer content with blog api**. Make sure the role you want to allow to post has this permission checked in the /admin/user/permissions. That permission row looks like this:

Posting the Google Document to Drupal

Before posting a document from Google to Drupal, you will need to make one configuration setting tweak in your Google Docs account. The latest version of the Google Document editor does not support publishing a Google Document to Blog software automatically yet, so you need to re-enable the older version of the document editor. To do this, click on the arrow icon next to your **Settings** link in the Google Docs header area and then select **Documents settings**:

Once the **Settings** screen launches, select the **Editing** tab. On the **Editing** screen, un-check the box next to **Create new text documents using the latest version of the document editor**.

Now, create or open up a document that you want to post on your Drupal site. With the document open in Google Docs, click on the arrow next to the **Share** button in the top right corner of the document. Select the **Publish as web page...** choice:

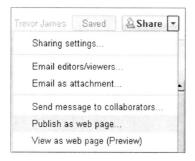

This will launch the **Publish this document** screen. Google will show you some bold text stating: **This document has not been published to your blog**. There will be a button titled **Post to blog**, and a link that allows you to change your blog site settings at any time. You should see this screen at this point:

Click on the **change your blog site settings** link and a pop up modal window will appear. The window is titled **Blog Site Settings**. On this form, we'll enter our Drupal web service information.

Select the radio button for **My own server / custom** because we'll be posting to our own Drupal site. The API we'll want to select is the **MetaWeblog API**. For the URL field, we want to add the absolute path to our xmlrpc.php file. So, type in: http://yoursitename/xmlrpc.php.

In order to authenticate properly and run via a secured connection, we want to add our Drupal user account information in the **Existing Blog Settings** section. Here, enter the Drupal username of the specific user you've created, your user's password, and then, optionally, you can enter the title of your blog. If you leave the **Blog ID/ Title** field blank, Google Docs will automatically fill it in with the name of the user's blog. So, in this example, I'm authenticating to the **trevor2** user account and I'll leave the blog field blank.

Under **Options** make sure to check the **Include the document title when posting** if you want your Document title to appear in the Drupal blog post title field (as shown in the following screenshot):

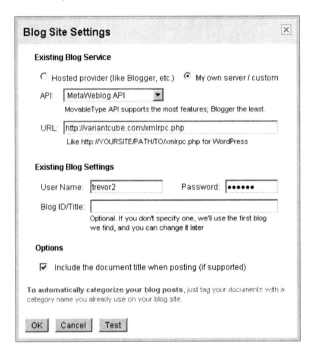

We're now set up to run a test. Click on the **Test** button. If everything is configured correctly, you'll see a message that states: **Test completed: your settings appear to be correct**.

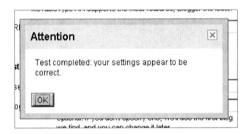

Click on the **OK** button on the **Attention** pop-up box.

Now, click on the **OK** button of the **Blog Site Settings** box. This will return you to your Google Docs **Publish this document** screen. Now that you have configured the settings, you're ready to post to your blog. Click on the **Post to blog** button.

Click on the pop up warning that will appear telling Google it's **OK to post to your blog now**:

Google will go into **Working ...** mode and then post the document. Once it posts, Google will report that **This document has been published to your blog**. There will be two new buttons that will appear. **Republish post** allows you to tweak your document and settings in Google Docs and then republish the blog post. The new post will overwrite the existing one on your Drupal site.

You can also click on the **Remove from blog** button to automatically remove the post from your Drupal site. The nice thing here is that you can control all of this directly from Google Docs without having to republish or delete anything on your Drupal site:

Testing and viewing the document on your Drupal site

Log in to your Drupal site and check your Content listing. You should see your new Google Docs blog post at the top of your content queue listed as a **new** post:

Now, click on the Title of your post and you'll launch the full node of the Google Docs post:

If there were hyperlinks or images in the Google Document, these will also now appear in your Drupal node. Formatting may change slightly from the original document since we're essentially making a web page of the document. Your theme's HTML code may tweak the formatting of the original document.

Now, go to your blog on your Drupal site and you should see the corresponding Google Document as a new blog post on your blog. On your blog home page, the post will come in using the post settings that are configured on your Drupal site. This will show the teaser in the form of the blog title field linked to the node and a teaser of the content. You should see something similar to this:

The cool thing about this is that your Drupal RSS feed for your blog posts will inherit and show this new blog post. Click on your RSS icon to view your feed and see your post's teaser in your RSS feed.

If you view your site's recent log entries, you'll see the entries for the additions of the blog content from Google Docs. You should see a message in your logs that states **blog: added Title of your Doc using blog API**. If you click on that link, you'll get the details of the log message. On this **Details** page, you'll see the actual Location URL showing you how the `xmlrpc.php` file parses out the request to post. You'll see that the `xmlrpc.php` file generates a unique URL path for each post request.

Details	
Type	content
Date	Tuesday, September 21, 2010 - 15:00
User	trevor2
Location	http://variantcube.com/xmlrpc.php?rnd1440437502=347481825
Referrer	
Message	blog: added *Fire station* using blog API.
Severity	notice
Hostname	72.14.194.17
Operations	view

Removing posts

If you want to remove the document from your Drupal site, there are two methods of doing this. You can simply click on the **Remove from blog** button on your Google Docs **Publish this document** screen. You can also navigate to your main Drupal content listing and delete the post from there, or via the node edit form. Since the post is now a node on your site, you can use all Drupal functionality to edit and manipulate the content of the post. Note here that if you make changes to the node on Drupal, it will not make the corresponding tweaks or edits to the document on your Google Docs account. This is a one-way communication service only from Google Docs to Drupal.

You'll also notice that the post does get a node ID.

To try removing the post from Drupal via Google Docs, click on the **Remove from blog** button. Google will confirm you want to remove the post from your blog. Click on **OK**. At this point, the post is removed and if you refresh your post page on your Drupal site, you will get a "Page not Found" error.

You have successfully posted a Google Document to your Drupal site and can manage that node on your site. This is a very powerful feature of using xmlrpc on your Drupal site.

Syncing content between Drupal sites

As a Drupal developer and site manager, you will most likely be running a development or staging server and a production site and server in tandem. You'll install your contributed modules and add content on your staging site first to test it out. You will then want to move this content over to the production site. You can choose to rebuild the content on the production site based on the configuration, content, and workflow that you used on the staging site. However, with a huge amount of content you're going to want an easier method of staging your content over to the live production site. There are methods of transferring this content from your staging to your production site at the click of a button, completely dynamically and automatically. These methods rely on using the XML-RPC protocol and the Services module. We'll look at this functionality in this section.

Using the Deployment module with Services

We're already familiar with using the Services module from *Chapter 5, Drupal and Multimedia Web Services*. We're now going to use the Services module again, but also introduce a new module into our workflow. This module is known as the Deployment module and its project page is available on drupal.org at: `http://drupal.org/project/deploy/`. This module is currently in a development version, so we're going to use it on a localhost environment. It's a very powerful module in that it integrates seamlessly with the Services module functionality and also gives us a method of moving content from a parent staging website to a child production site. In these examples, I'm going to refer to the staging site as our parent site and our child site as our production site.

To follow along with the examples in this section, you will want to install Drupal on your localhost. You'll then want to install a second site so you have two sites to work from and you can then easily migrate content from one staging site to a production site example. A good method of getting two sites installed quickly is to use the Acquia Drupal Stack installer that is available from the Acquia website at: `http://acquia.com/products-services/acquia-drupal`. The stack installer is available as a free download and it easily allows you to set up multiple sites that share the same common Drupal core. For more on how to install Acquia Drupal, see the Appendix in this book.

The Deployment module

Deployment is under active development and only has a development release for Drupal 6.x, so make sure to use only this module on a test server and site platform until it has a stable release. The module allows you to move Drupal data, including nodes, taxonomy, files, users, and more, from one site to another. You can also move all core and some contributed configuration items including content types, views, system settings, and more. This means you can move your custom content types and views from one site to another.

You can also push out updates to content. So, you can deploy a node to a second site and then go back to the staging site and edit that node. You can then deploy the updated node and the update will override the original deployed node. The Deployment module offers a wealth of documentation via its project page at: `http://drupal.org/node/408762`. The module relies heavily on the use of the Services module so you'll need to make sure you have Services installed first in order to use Deployment. The module only works with the current development or latest versions of the Services 2.x release.

Deployment works by using XML-RPC and the Services module. This functionality allows you to push content from a staging site to a second site by means of an API key, or session ID key if you're just using site admin user #1 logins on both sites. We'll be looking at this in more detail when we try the example.

Installing, enabling, and configuring Deployment

First, you need a content type and some content to push from staging to production. Make sure you have CCK enabled and that you have a custom content type and some nodes you want to push.

> There is a known issue with the Deployment module in the event that you have the core Drupal upload module enabled on your site. The service event will still occur when you migrate the content but the node will not show up on the production site. For this example we're going to make sure we have disabled the Upload module on our sites so that our examples will work. This is one of the reasons that this module is still in active development, because it does contain this bug or issue.

We're going to be installing the Deployment module on a brand new staging and production site. These are both new installs, so their databases and site structure at this point match entirely. For these examples, we'll be using this methodology. If you are using Deployment and Services on a staging and production site that has been in use for a while, you'll need to follow the instructions for using the modules on existing sites provided at the module handbook pages. There are slight differences and the most important issue is that you need to make sure both sites match in terms of database structure and content type/node structure.

In both cases, we need to make sure that the sites' time zones match because if the date/time zone settings on both sites do not match this can cause sync issues. To check this, go to your time zone settings at **Site configuration | Date and time**. Make sure the default time zone settings here match the time zone settings on your production site. As long as they match, you should not experience any issues with this.

You also need to make sure that the Services module is installed and enabled on your production site so that this site can receive post requests to XML-RPC from your staging site calls. Make sure you are using the 2.2.x version of Services for Drupal 6. Go ahead and enable the main Services module and its associated modules including Key Authentication, XML-RPC server, System Service, Node Service, UUID service, and User service. To be safe, you can simply enable all of the Services modules on production.

If the Services module prompts you to enable any required dependent modules go ahead and do this. You now have enabled XML-RPC on your production site and you should be able to browse to this URL and get an XML-RPC message: `http://production.localhost:8082/services/xmlrpc`. The message should tell you that the XML-RPC server accepts POST requests only.

Now, we're going to install the Deployment module on both of our sites, staging and production. Download the latest development version of the Deployment module from its project page and install this module to your `/sites/all/modules` directory. If you are using Acquia's multisite capabilities here, you can simply install the module once to your main site's `/root/sites/all/modules` and then enable the module to use on your staging and production sites.

We want to enable the Deployment module, Node Deployment, User Deployment, and UUID. You can also enable the other associated Deployment modules such as **Deploy Comments** and **Deploy Content Type** depending on what specific content you plan to push from your staging site. Make sure to enable **Taxonomy Deployment** as well because we want to move any tags and vocabs that are associated with our nodes. **Deploy Dates** requires the Date and CCK (Content) modules to be enabled on your site. **Deploy Files** requires the Filefield and CCK modules to be enabled. If you receive errors that you cannot enable these specific Deployment modules, then make sure you have installed and enabled the required modules (Date, Filefield and CCK).

Enabled	Name	Version	Description
☑	**Deploy Comments**	6.x-1.x-dev	Deploy comments using the Deployment framework Depends on: Deployment (enabled), Comment (enabled)
☑	**Deploy Content Type**	6.x-1.x-dev	Deploy content types using the Deployment framework Depends on: Deployment (enabled), Content Copy (enabled), Content (enabled)
☑	**Deploy Dates**	6.x-1.x-dev	Deploy CCK date fields using the Deployment framework Depends on: Deployment (enabled), Date (enabled), Content (enabled), Date API (enabled), Date Timezone (enabled)
☑	**Deploy Files**	6.x-1.x-dev	Deploy filefield files using the Deployment framework Depends on: Deployment (enabled), FileField (enabled), Content (enabled)
☑	**Deploy Nodereferences**	6.x-1.x-dev	Deploy CCK nodereference fields using the Deployment framework Depends on: Deployment (enabled), Node Reference (enabled), Content (enabled), Text (enabled), Option Widget (enabled)
☑	**Deploy System Settings**	6.x-1.x-dev	Deploy system settings using the Deployment framework Depends on: Deployment (enabled)
☑	**Deploy Userreferences**	6.x-1.x-dev	Deploy CCK userreference fields using the Deployment framework Depends on: Deployment (enabled), User Reference (enabled), User Deployment (enabled), Content (enabled), Text (enabled), Option Widgets (enabled)
☑	**Deployment**	6.x-1.x-dev	Framework to deploy Drupal data between servers Required by: Deploy Comments (enabled), Deploy Content Type (enabled), Deploy Dates (enabled), Deploy Files (enabled), Node Deployment (enabled), Deploy Nodereferences (enabled), Deploy System Settings (enabled), Taxonomy Deployment (enabled), User Deployment (enabled), Deploy Userreferences (enabled)
☑	**Node Deployment**	6.x-1.x-dev	Deployment for nodes Depends on: Deployment (enabled)
☑	**Taxonomy**	6.x-1.x-dev	Deployment for taxonomy terms and vocabularies

If you enable the **Deploy Dates** module, you may need to tweak the time zone settings again so that they match between both of your sites. Check your status report for any errors regarding your **Date and time** zone settings. I needed to go into the **Date and time** zone requirements and set the time zone name on my staging site. Just make sure to do this on production as well so you can maintain your sites' sync.

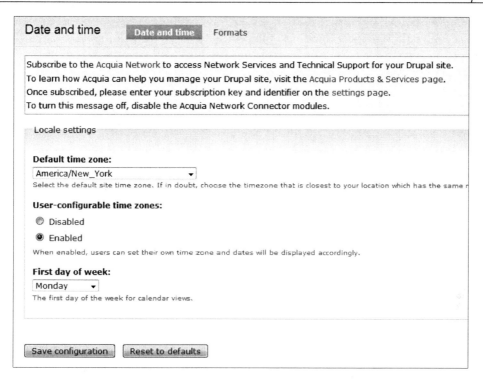

Save your staging module configuration. Now, on our staging site, we have the Deployment module enabled. To configure the Deployment server on your sites, go to your staging sites' **Site building | Deployment**. Click on the **Servers** button and this will launch the deployment servers page:

Click on the **Add a new server** button. For the name of your server, type in **Production** because we want to deploy content to the production version of our site. For the URL, you need to type in the URL path to your production's xmlrpc server. So that should be similar to this: `http://production.localhost:8082/services/xmlrpc`.

Click on the **Save Deployment Server** link.

You have now successfully configured your staging site to work with Deployment.

Now, go to your production site and confirm that you have enabled Services; and that you have installed and enabled the Deployment module on your production site. Now, on your production site, you need to enable key authentication within your Services settings so that we can enable authentication for our XML-RPC and our staging site can successfully communicate with our production. The way we'll do this here in this example is to enable key authentication for session IDs. Then, if we're logged into both sites during deployment as the main user or one admin user, the deployment should work because both user accounts will authenticate across sites through the session IDs.

To do this, go to your **Site building | Services** page and then click on the **Settings** button link. Under the **Authentication module** settings, select **Key authentication**. Then, uncheck the **Use keys** checkbox but make sure to leave the **Use sessid** checkbox enabled. Save your settings.

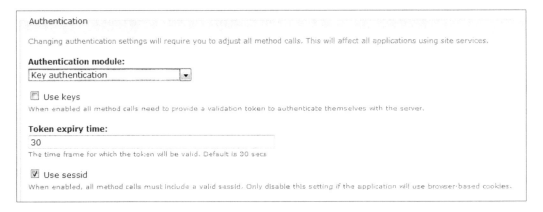

We're ready to deploy content. First, let's add a vocab and some tags to our site. Go ahead and set up a basic taxonomy that you can associate with your Page content type. Add some tags:

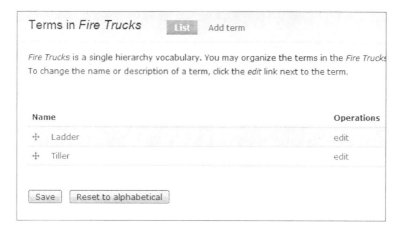

Go ahead and add some content to your site using the Page type. Make sure to tag the content when you add. Add a few nodes to use for this example.

Once you have content published to your staging site, go to your main Content listing page. In the update options for this page, you'll see a new **Deploy** option in your drop-down menu. Select the content nodes you want to deploy and then select the update option **Deploy**. Click on **Update** and the Deploy page will load:

Make sure the server location you want to deploy to is set to **Production,** and then type in your user Drupal user #1 username and password. This should be the username and password of the /user/1 account on your Drupal site. Click on the **Submit** button.

At this point, you should see various processing screens load—you'll see messages including **Processing deployment plan dependencies** (as shown in the following screenshot) and **Pushing deployment plans**.

Let these processes run. At the end of the processing, you'll be redirected to a **Deployment Log Details** page that shows you the exact deployments that ran. In our case, you should see a deployment for your taxonomy vocab, the number of tags you added, and the number of nodes you pushed. You should see a detailed description of each deployment as well as the status result. In our case, it should say "Success" as the result.

Deployment Log Details

Module	Description	Result	Message
taxonomy_vocabulary	taxonomy vocabulary: Fire Trucks	Success	
taxonomy_term	taxonomy term: Tiller	Success	
node	page: New Pierce Tiller Truck for Raleigh, NC	Success	

To see if the nodes successfully transferred, open up your production site and go to your content list. You should see the nodes in your production content listing. The node should be flagged with New. If you open the Node, you should see the linked tags on the node page. If you go to your Taxonomy listing, you should see that the vocab transferred and the specific tags for your vocab also transferred over.

Congratulations! You have successfully deployed node content and Taxonomy terms from your staging site to your production site. You can see how powerful this module is and how much you can do using the XML-RPC server. This is a great method of deploying content and keeping sites synced.

The other thing you can do here is make edits to your recently transferred node on your staging site. Go ahead and update the node with new content. Then, deploy the node again and you'll replace and override the production node with your updated version. It will keep the same node ID but will add the new content. So, you can use the Deployment module to move new content and update existing content on production. For example, if you remove a tag from the node content and then push that node again, the node on the production site will update accordingly. The cool thing is that the tags will all still be on production but your node will only show the tag as per your most recent update.

At any time after you run a deployment task, you can view the **Deployment Log** on your staging site. The log will show you a table with each of your deployment runs logged as a row item. It also tells you the server you deployed the nodes to. When you deploy node content, the deployment plan is titled **Nodes Now**:

Deployment	Plans	Servers	Deployment Log	Settings	
Plan		**Pushed By**		**When**	**To Server**
Nodes Now		admin		2010-07-23 16:09	Production
Nodes Now		admin		2010-07-23 10:25	Production
Nodes Now		admin		2010-07-23 10:14	Production
Nodes Now		admin		2010-07-23 10:05	Production

If you click on the **Nodes Now** link, it will launch the detailed log of that specific deployment.

You can try deploying other types of Drupal content including custom content types and Views. There are more instructions for this advanced deployment on the module's handbook pages. In the future, the module will have functionality for deploying user accounts as well.

Summary

In this chapter, we took content from a Google Documents account and deployed this content over to our Drupal site using the XML-RPC protocol and the Blog API core module. We also used the Deployment module to enable migration of content from a staging to a production Drupal site. In summary, we did the following:

- Enabled the Blog API module and set up a Google Documents account
- Synced content from Google Documents to our Drupal site publishing a Google text document as a Drupal node
- Installed and enabled the Deployment module on a staging site
- Configured Services module on our production site
- Deployed node content and taxonomy vocabs and terms from our staging site to our production site

In *Chapter 9, Twitter and Drupal*, we'll return to a discussion of Drupal content and how to connect our Drupal site and its nodes and user process to the popular Twitter social networking application.

9
Twitter and Drupal

In this chapter, we're going to integrate Twitter with Drupal. If you have a Twitter account, you can post your tweets to your Drupal site automatically at the same time you post them to your Twitter home page. You can also post node content from your Drupal site to your Twitter home page as tweets. We'll look at configuring this integration in detail and also look at setting up automatic actions and triggers to occur when you save a new node content on your Drupal site.

In this chapter, we will install and enable a few Twitter-based modules to allow for integration with the Twitter web service API, including the Twitter module, Daily Twitter, and Tweet modules.

To summarize, in this chapter we will:

- Enable the Twitter module and configure it
- Post tweets from our Twitter account to blocks on our Drupal website
- Post links to nodes and node content from our Drupal site to our Twitter home page
- Enable and configure the Tweet module

Twitter and Drupal

Twitter is a popular and widely used micro-blogging application and website. You can sign up for a Twitter account and post tiny snippet-based blog entries, 140 characters or less, to your Twitter home page. You can log in to your Twitter account and post your 140 character entry into the **What's happening?** text area box and then click on the **Tweet** button to publish it. The tweet will appear on your account's home page—your default Twitter home page—and it will be shared on the main Twitter home pages of your followers.

To send a tweet to another user, you can use the hash tag in front of their username in your post. So, for example, if I was going to send myself a tweet, I would add this in my text area box before adding my post: `#jamesweblabs`. For more on the history and functionality of Twitter, check out the Wikipedia entry at: `http://en.wikipedia.org/wiki/Twitter`. Twitter also has a detailed Help and support documentation section on its main site at `http://support.twitter.com/`.

You may want to integrate Twitter with your Drupal site, to do things such as posting all of your most recent tweets into a Drupal block that will appear on your home page. You also may want to run this block automatically via a web service integration so that the block updates automatically whenever you post a new tweet to your Twitter account. Drupal and Twitter can easily integrate through these web services by using contributed modules.

In this chapter, we're going to install, configure, and use the Twitter module so that we can integrate our Twitter account with our Drupal user account; we can also post tweets to the sidebar block on our site. With the Twitter module, we'll also expose some of its fields to the Views module and be able to create more powerful and dynamic listings of Twitter-based content.

We'll also look at other contributed modules including Tweet.

The Twitter API

The Twitter API and service integration with Drupal uses the REST (Representational State Transfer) API protocol and a Streaming API protocol. Twitter does state in its API documentation that the service does not offer unlimited usage. Twitter does impose limits on the number of requests and updates made to its service API. The REST service is `HTTP`-based and uses `GET` and `POST` requests. `GET` is used to retrieve data so, in our case, this will be used when our Drupal site tries to receive the latest Tweet posted to your Twitter account. `POST` requests are used when you submit, update, or delete node data that you have sent over to Twitter and posted as a Tweet using the Twitter module.

Using REST as the protocol, the API does support various formats for data transfer including `XML`, `JSON`, `RSS`, and `Atom`. For more details on the Twitter API and how to use it, see the Twitter API documentation for developers at: `http://dev.twitter.com/pages/every_developer`.

The Twitter module

The Twitter module is available via its Drupal project page at `http://drupal.org/project/twitter`. The module allows for integration with Twitter's API web service. It allows you to integrate your Twitter account with your Drupal user account; post Tweets to a block in Drupal; and allows your Drupal users to post to their Twitter account using Drupal node content. Drupal Views also integrates with the module and you can create your own customized Views-based listings of Twitter content.

The module gives you a default block called **User Tweets** and also a user profile page titled **user's tweets**. We'll set both of these up in the examples that follow.

Integrating the Twitter module with Drupal

Download the **6.x-3.0-beta2** version of the Twitter module. This is the **Other release** version, not the **recommended release**. The reason we're going to install the **Other release** version is that recently Twitter changed their web service API to use authentication provided by the OAuth protocol. This change happened recently, in September 2010, when Twitter redesigned their website and made other security improvements and enhancements to their API.

In order to support OAuth in the integration, you need to make sure to use the **3.0-beta2** version of the Twitter module. You can download it from:

`http://drupal.org/project/twitter.`

It's listed under the **Other releases** heading:

Other releases			
Version	**Downloads**	**Date**	**Links**
6.x-3.0-beta2	Download (35.19 KB)	2010-Feb-19	Notes

Once downloaded, upload this Twitter module folder to your /sites/all/modules location on your web server. You also need to download the OAuth module and add that to your /sites/all/modules. OAuth is required by the Twitter module, so you must install it. We'll be discussing OAuth in more detail in *Chapter 12, Authentication Services*, but for now, just install it so you can use the Twitter functionality. The OAuth module is available at: http://drupal.org/project/oauth. Again, with this module, you need to make sure to use the **other release** (earlier version) of **6.x-2.02**. This **2.x** version is the version that works with the Twitter **3.0-beta2** module. Make sure you have the correct versions of both of these modules before uploading to your site. This is very important. If the module versions are not the ones mentioned here, you may run into errors or other issues with functionality. So, make sure to install these exact versions.

Other releases			
Version	**Downloads**	**Date**	**Links**
6.x-2.02	Download (26.15 KB)	2009-May-29	Notes

Go ahead and upload both of these modules to your /sites/all/modules. Once uploaded, browse to your modules admin page and look for the **OAuth** and **Twitter** module suites under the **Other** modules fieldset. For OAuth, you're looking for the **Oauth** and the **OAuth Client Test** modules.

Enable the OAuth module as shown in the following screenshot:

| ☑ | OAuth | 6.x-2.02 | Enable the world wide standard OAuth for authentication. Required by: Twitter Signin (disabled) |
| ☐ | OAuth Client Test | 6.x-2.02 | A generic client that might be used by developers that want |

Then, scroll down and look for the **Twitter, Twitter actions, Twitter Post**, and **Twitter Signin** modules. Enable all four of these modules:

witter	6.x-3.0-beta2	Adds integration with the Twitter microblogging service. Required by: Twitter Messaging (disabled), Twitter actions (disabled), (disabled)
witter actions	6.x-3.0-beta2	Exposes Drupal actions to send Twitter messages. Depends on: Twitter (disabled)
witter Post	6.x-3.0-beta2	Enables posting to twitter Depends on: Twitter (disabled)
witter Signin	6.x-3.0-beta2	Adds support for "Sign in with Twitter" Depends on: Twitter (disabled), OAuth (disabled)

Save your module configuration.

Registering your website with Twitter

Now that we've installed the necessary modules on our Drupal site, we need to set up the Twitter side of our functionality. In order to integrate the Twitter module with the Twitter web service, you need to create two Twitter-related items. The first is a Twitter account. If you do not already have a Twitter account, you can go to `twitter.com` and sign up for a brand new Twitter account. Go to:

`https://twitter.com/.`

Click on the **Sign Up** button and then proceed through the account sign-up steps.

Setting up a Twitter application

Now, we need to configure a new Twitter developer application. Once you have a Twitter account, log in to your Twitter account and then go to the `twitter.com/apps` URL to sign up for a new developer's application on Twitter. Make sure you are signed into your Twitter account already when you go to the apps URL. Launch the apps URL from:

`https://twitter.com/apps.`

This page will show you any applications you have configured in Twitter. For our site, we're going to set up a brand new application, so, click on the **Register a new application** hyperlink:

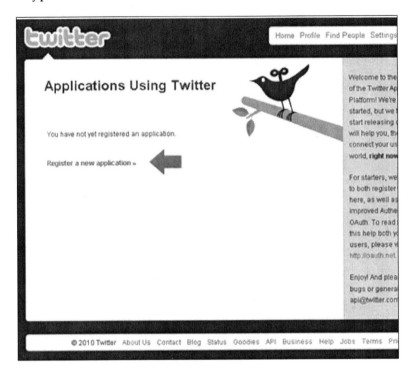

Clicking on that link will load a **Register an Application** form as shown in the following screenshot. Let's fill that out with the following info:

- Application Name
- Description of application
- Application Website (this is the URL of your website)
- Organization Name
- Website address (again this is the URL/home domain of your website)

Scroll down on the form and then complete the form by adding and completing the following fields:

- Application Type—make sure to select **Browser** here
- Callback URL—this is the callback URL that the Drupal Twitter module provides

The Callback URL is information that is provided by your Twitter module settings inside your Drupal site. To locate the correct **Callback URL** to add to the application sign-up form, go to your Twitter setup configuration settings in your Drupal site by browsing to: **Site configuration** | **Twitter setup** (admin/settings/twitter). On this page, you will see the Callback URL noted at the top of the **OAuth Settings** fieldset. You should see something similar to this:

Go back to your Twitter application sign-up form and add this **Callback URL**.

Now, make sure the **Default Access type** is set to **Read & Write**. Finally, make sure to check the **Yes, Use Twitter for login**. This will allow you to authenticate your posts to your Twitter account username and password when you try to post Drupal content to your Twitter account. So, make sure that box is checked. Your app form should now look like this:

Complete the **reCAPTCHA** field at the bottom of the form and then click on the **Save** button.

Twitter will load a page confirming your application is successfully configured and show you your application details. This includes your **Consumer key**, **Consumer secret**, **Request token URL**, **Access Token URL**, and **Authorize URL**. For integration with our Drupal site, we're going to need the **Consumer key** and **secret**.

Leave this app details confirmation page open and then open up your Drupal site in another browser tab.

Configuring the Twitter module once you have your app setup

With your Drupal site open, go back to your Twitter module configuration form in your Drupal site at the following path: `admin/settings/twitter`.

Here, you want to copy and paste your Twitter Consumer key and secret code into the respective fields for **OAuth Consumer key** and **OAuth Consumer secret**. Also, make sure to check the box next to **Import Twitter Statuses**. This will allow for your Drupal site to request posts from your Twitter account and add links to these tweets on your user account page, and also in a **User Tweets** block in one of your site's regions. This is what allows for the total cross-pollination and integration of your Drupal site with your Twitter account. It's very powerful and flexible for running the Twitter import functionality on your site.

Finally, set the **Delete old statuses** drop down to **1 week**. This will keep your Tweets block up to date on your Drupal site and show only updated and recent tweets.

Let's go ahead and do that. You should have a screen that looks like this:

Go ahead and **Save configuration**.

Now, let's check and tweak some of the other Twitter module settings before we test our posts. Click on the **Post** link at the top of your Twitter setup page.

On this page, you can specify what content types and respective Drupal content you want to announce and post to your Twitter account. Let's make sure we check the boxes next to the **Blog entry**, **Page**, and **Story** types. Of course, you can enable all of your content types if you need to, but for this example, we'll just post our new blog entries over to our Twitter account.

The **Default format string** field shows you the format of the link that will be posted over to your Twitter account announcing your new Drupal content. So, when you post a node to your Drupal site using the blog type, the post will appear on your Twitter account in the following format as a hyperlink back to your post on Drupal:

New post: !title !tinyurl

This will show the Drupal node title, `!title`, value along with a `tinyurl` formatted hyperlink back to your Drupal post. So, for example, the resulting post on Twitter will look like this:

·New post: Testing post to Twitter http://tinyurl.com/33jnclx — 1 hour 53 min ago

Your **Post** screen should now look like this:

Save your Post page configuration.

Setting up OAuth configuration

Now, we need to check our **OAuth** settings. Go to **Site configuration | OAuth** or here:

`/admin/settings/oauth`.

Make sure you check the box for **HMAC-SHA1 OAuth cryptography** because this is the security method that Twitter and OAuth use for this type of integration:

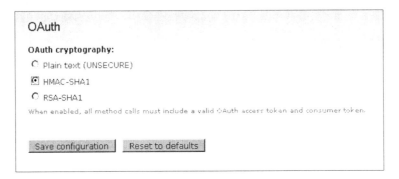

Setting up your user account to integrate with Twitter

Now, we need to tweak our user account settings so that our logged-in user account can communicate with its respective Twitter account and utilize all of the settings and configuration we set in the above instructions.

In our example, we're going to authenticate our main /user/1 admin account with the Twitter account we are using for our site. In many cases, you may want to allow each user on your site to post to their own Twitter accounts. This is possible but these instructions focus on using one account globally for your Drupal site. On a production level website, you also probably will not want to authenticate the main super /user/1 admin account over to your Twitter account due to security reasons (since this is the main admin account on the site). Again, here this will serve as a good example for our demo.

First, go to your user account page for the account you are currently logged in as. I'm logged in as the admin account, so I'll go to: /user/1.

Now, on the main user account page for /user/1, click on the **Edit** tab. When you do this, you'll se e a new secondary menu of options on the Edit form. You should see a **twitter accounts** link. Click on that link:

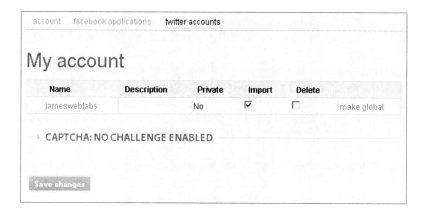

Now, click on the **Add account** button.

The site will redirect to a Twitter authorization web page asking you to allow your site's access to your Twitter account. Click on the **Allow** button:

Twitter should authorize and redirect you back to your Drupal site's `/user/1/edit/twitter` page. It knows to do this because you set up your **Callback URL** to work with your Twitter account. Now, you will see that your new Twitter account is listed in a table on your main Drupal account page. You should see a screen that looks like this:

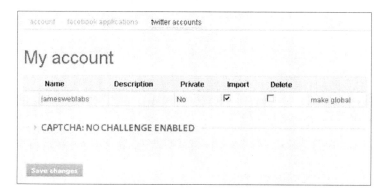

This shows us the name of the Twitter account, and the Import status of the account for whether you want your Twitter tweets imported to your Drupal site automatically. There will also be a link to make this account global, to be used across your entire website and by any user logged into your site if you allow the user permissions. For now, we will not make the account global. We only want to use this Twitter account with our /user/1 account in these examples.

We have configured our Twitter application, the Twitter module, and our authentication methods and permissions. We're now ready to test posting our Drupal nodes announcements over to our Twitter account.

Posting your Drupal nodes as tweets to your Twitter account

Let's go ahead and post a new piece of content to our Drupal site and post it as a tweet to our Twitter account. Go ahead and locate a blog post or create a new blog post on your site. On the edit form of your post, you should now see a fieldset titled **Post to Twitter.com**. There is a checkbox in this fieldset titled **Announce this post on Twitter**. Check this box if it is not checked by default.

When you check the box, the format of the Tweet URL will appear in the URL field. If you do not want the **New post** part of the formatted URL to appear, you can safely delete that, but make sure to leave the remaining part of the formatted URL: **!title !tinyurl**.

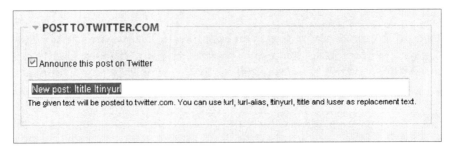

Now, **Save** your node.

Once you click on **Save**, you should get a notification box that tells you that the node has been **Successfully posted to Twitter**:

Go ahead and launch your Twitter profile home page, and you should see the new post at the top of your Twitter timeline:

Click on the `tinyurl` link and you should be directed back to the node on your Drupal site. So now, your Twitter readership can easily see that you have tweeted a new Drupal post and they can click on the link to launch the post on your Drupal site and read it.

Congratulations! You have successfully taken a Drupal node and announced it on your Twitter site.

Showing tweets in blocks on your Drupal site

The Twitter module ships with a default block called User Tweets that will show Twitter tweets and statuses on your site's user profile pages. This means that each user account that has configured a corresponding linked Twitter account can show their User Tweets block on their user profile page.

To activate the block, go to your **Site building | Blocks** admin page and look for the User Tweets block in your disabled blocks section. Enable that block to show in a specific region on your site. You can configure this block like any Drupal block to show for specific roles and on specific pages of the site.

Now that we have the `user/1` account configured to use the Twitter web service, we can browse to our `user/1` account page and once we have enabled the User Tweets block, we should see this block of tweets appearing in our right sidebar area. You should see a block of content that resembles this:

admin's tweets

- New post: Drupal 6 Panels Cookbook announced http://tinyurl.com/2ffbskm — *4 days 17 hours* ago
- New post: Drupal 6 Panels Cookbook announced www.variantcube.com/liu — *5 days 22 hours* ago

The user's tweets block is configured from a View that the Twitter module installs on your site in your Views administration area. You get two default Views when the Twitter module is installed. On your user account profile page, if you click on the Twitter link or tab in your account, you will get the resulting View page of your user's tweets. This View display should correspond to the block display of your user's tweets block. If you launch the path `/user/%/tweets` for a specific user ID, you'll get the following page display (or something similar to this):

admin's tweets

New post: Drupal 6 Panels Cookbook announced http://tinyurl.com/2ffbskm — *4 days 18 hours* ago

New post: Drupal 6 Panels Cookbook announced www.variantcube.com/liu — *5 days 22 hours* ago

Depending on how you have the View configured, the user's tweets block will show a certain number of tweets and potentially use a pager.

Let's go ahead and take a look at the Views configuration for our tweet content and make some adjustments to both the page and block view so you see how the block and page displays of your tweets can be enhanced and tweaked.

Twitter module page and block Views

The Twitter module ships with a default View called **tweets**. This provides a huge amount of flexibility and power when it comes to methods of displaying your user's tweets on the website. Since you can use Views in block and page formats, here you can publish and display your tweets in multiple layout options and configurations. The other great thing about the tweets views is that they use arguments in order to show tweets for a specific user account. So, you can easily learn how to use arguments with Views by studying the setup and configuration of the tweets View. Let's do that now.

 If you need introductory material and tutorials on using the Drupal Views module, the module is covered in detail in two Packt titles: *Chapter 3, Getting Started* of *Drupal for Education and E-Learning* (https://www.packtpub.com/drupal-for-education-and-e-learning/book); and *Chapter 3, Adding Products and Services* of *Drupal 6 Site Builder Solutions* (https://www.packtpub.com/drupal-6-website-builder-solutions/book).

The tweets View is configured for both a page and a block view. The View will look like this in your Views list:

Default Twitter message view: **tweets**	Edit | Export | Clone | Disable
Path: user/%/tweets	Displays Twitter.com status messages for users who have associated
Block, Page	Twitter accounts.

Click on **Edit** and let's look at the View configuration. Notice that the View is split up into a default **Tweets** View, a **User page**, **User block**, and a **Global block** view:

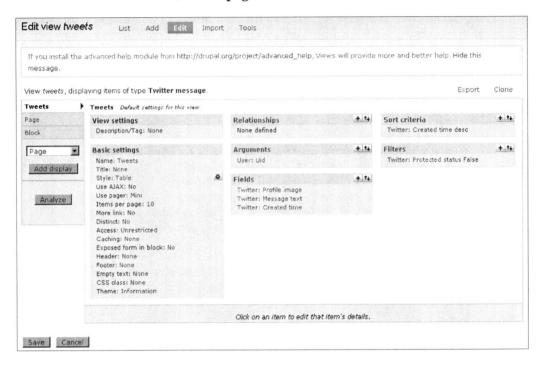

The default view **Tweets** sets some default configuration for all of the Views to share. It styles the view as a Table, uses a mini pager, and displays ten tweets per page. It uses a View argument for **User: Uid**. This sets an argument that the View should only return tweets for a specific user account when the path typed into a browser address field is of the following: `/user/%/tweets`. The title of the resulting page will be `%1's` tweets; and the argument type is User ID from URL. If you look at the argument configuration, you should see this:

The default view also filters in the following fields: **Twitter: Profile image**, **Twitter: Message Text**, and **Twitter: Created Time**. These are the fields that get displayed out in the block content. So, for example, if you wanted to remove the **Created Time** text, you could do that by deleting the field from the View output.

The page and block Views show the same content and use the same argument. The page version displays 10 items per page, while the block only shows the top 5 tweets. The page View also displays the Twitter account profile image if there is one in the Twitter account in question. If you view the user tweets page, you'll see that the profile image appears in the first column of the table next to each tweet. If you view the source code for the View table using Firebug, for example, you'll see that the profile image URL is something similar to this: `http://a3.twimg.com/profile_images/448761483/P1060536_normal.JPG`

So, all of the profile images are populating via the Twitter service domain (a3. twimg.com). You can test that this is the correct profile image by going to your Twitter account and viewing your profile image (as a View image in the browser). You should get a matching profile image name, with a potentially different scale version of the image. I get this when I review the URL of the image via Twitter:

```
https://s3.amazonaws.com/twitter_production/profile_images/448761483/
P1060536_bigger.JPG
```

You have successfully added a View block and View page of your admin user account's tweets to your Drupal site. You can now get real time tweet updates on your Drupal site as they are posted to your Drupal account. You also know how to configure and tweak your displays of these tweets using the core Twitter module tweets View as a model. Since you can display your tweets as Views, if you are a themer you now also have the power to theme these displays. Theming the Views is a bit beyond the discussion and topics of this book, but for more information on theming, see the module documentation at: http://drupal.org/node/412748.

Finally, if you want to set up specific rules using the core triggers and actions modules that post nodes automatically to your Twitter home page without having to check the box on each node, you can do this. The Trigger module includes a hook to the Twitter module that allows you to configure a Post to Twitter action. Let's look at that now.

Actions and triggers with the Twitter module

Make sure you have enabled the core Drupal Trigger module and the Twitter actions module. First, we'll want to configure the action. Go to **Site configuration** | **Actions** and then scroll down all the way to the bottom of the Actions page and in the **Choose an advanced action** drop down menu, select the **Post a message to Twitter** action:

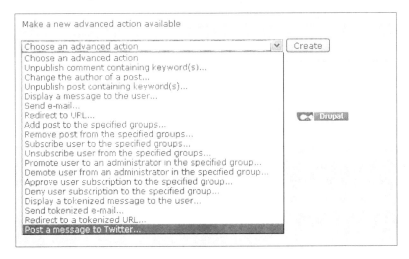

Click on the **Create** button. Now, in order to use this action, you'll also need to add your Twitter account name and password to this action screen as well. Go ahead and do that and add a message that will get posted to your Twitter account page when you post the new Drupal content. The message can include the following tokens: %site_name, %username, %node_url, %node_type, %title, %teaser, %body. Let's go ahead and format the message like this: **New post: %title, %node_url**. This will add the title of our post and a link to its URL. Your action form should look like this:

Configure an advanced action

An advanced action offers additional configuration options which may be filled out below. Changing the *Description* field is recommended, in order better identify the precise action taking place. This description will be displayed in modules such as the trigger module when assigning actions to system events, so it is best if it is as descriptive as possible (for example, "Send e-mail to Moderation Team" rather than simply "Send e-mail").

Description:

Post a message to Twitter

A unique description for this advanced action. This description will be displayed in the interface of modules that integrate with actions, such as Trigger module.

Twitter account name:

jamesweblabs

Twitter password:

•••••••••

Message:

New post: %title, %node_url

The message that should be sent. You may include the following variables: %site_name, %username, %node_url, %node_type, %title, %teaser, %body. Not all variables will be available in all contexts.

Save

Save your action. Now, your action should appear in the main Actions listing at /admin/settings/actions:

system	Post a message to Twitter		configure	delete

You're ready to configure your Trigger now. Now, you can associate your core Triggers with this new action. For example, you can set the Twitter action to happen when you save a new post or update an existing post. Go ahead and assign the **Post a message to Twitter** action to your **Trigger: After saving a new post**:

Click on the **Assign** button. Now, go ahead and create a brand new node on your site. You can leave the 'Announce this post on Twitter' unchecked since you now have a trigger set up in your site to post the announcement automatically when a node is saved. Save your new node. When you save your node, you should go to your Twitter home page and refresh. The new node title and link to its URL should be posted as a tweet:

New post: Drupal 7 update,
http://variantcube.com/node/103
4 minutes ago via Drupal

You have learned how to post tweets from Drupal to your Twitter account and also how to configure these posts to happen automatically using actions and triggers. You can view your site's recent log entries and actually see the actions type posted in your log entries. It should state Action Post a message to Twitter saved. If you click on that log link, you will see the details of the action that ran.

Additionally, for the most recent tweet to appear back in your tweets View block, you'll need to run your cron on the site so that the View updates with the latest tweets from your Twitter account.

This is amazing integration. You have now learned how to post your tweets to your Drupal site and also take Drupal nodes and post announcements about them back to your Twitter home page.

Tweet module

The Tweet module is another contributed module that allows for integration with the Twitter web service API. This module puts a link on your site's nodes to allow for posting node content to Twitter. You can also shorten the URL (to your Drupal node) that gets posted to Twitter using a combination of the Shorten URLs and the Short URL module. You may want to customize your URLs and make them your own formatted short URL instead of relying on the method Twitter uses, which is to automatically shorten any URL that's over 30 characters in length. For example, when we posted nodes to our Twitter site using the Twitter module, you'll notice that the Twitter API automatically created short URLs using the tinyurl format. An example of this is: `http://tinyurl.com/22oy6wf`. We may want more control over these URLs so that we don't have to use the tinyurl formatted link. These modules will enable you to set up your own formatted short URLs to use with your Twitter posts.

We're going to install these three modules and try them out. First, grab the Tweet module from its project page here: `http://drupal.org/project/tweet`. Then, download the Shorten URLs and Short URL modules from their respective project pages here: `http://drupal.org/project/shorten` and `http://drupal.org/project/shorturl`. Install them to your site as you would any contributed module to `/sites/all/modules`.

Go ahead and enable all three modules in your main modules administration page. This will include the Tweet, Shorten, Record Shorten, and Short URL modules. Save your modules configuration.

Configuring short URLs

With our modules enabled, go to your **Site configuration | Shorten** to load the Shorten module configuration page. You'll see the Shorten Web service methods and services listed that you can choose from. The first setting we'll tweak is the **Use "www." Instead of http://**. We're going to uncheck this so that we continue to create links using the http:// protocol. This will open up more flexibility for us because more web services use the HTTP method.

Shorten provides both PHP and cURL methods of retrieving the shortened URL from the Web service of choice. You can also choose a default and backup service from the multiple services listed, including but not limited to: is.gd, short.ie, TinyURL, and so on. For our example, we're going to choose the **Drupal ShortURL module** for the service and **None** for the backup service, for now. We want to leverage the ShortURL contributed module to create our short URLs so that's why we choose that as our service. All other settings on this configuration page can be left as their defaults. You should have a form screen that looks like this:

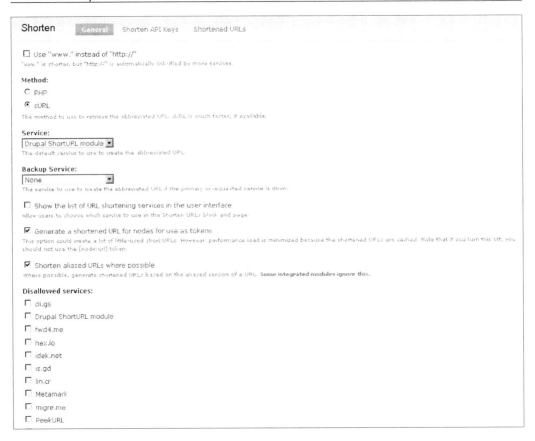

Save your configuration.

Configuring the Tweet module

Now we're going to configure the Tweet module. Go to **Site configuration |
Tweet** to load the Tweet module configuration. For our configuration, let's set
the following:

- **Type of link to show on nodes: icon_text**
- **Type of link to show on teasers: icon_text**
- **Open Twitter: In new window with target="_blank"**
- **Node types on which to display link: blog and page**

You should see a screen that looks like this:

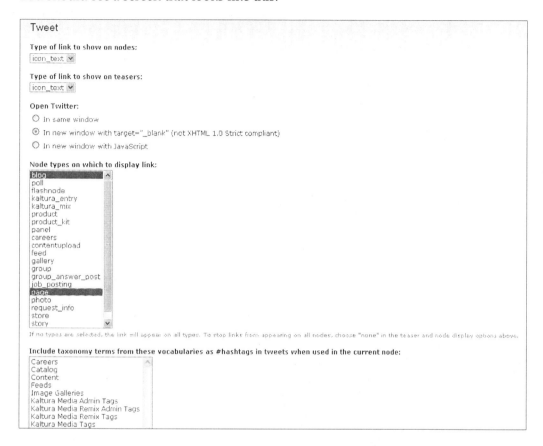

Let's leave the taxonomy terms box blank for now. We'll only use the module with our node types chosen above. Leave the Twitter image set as the default that the module gives you.

Now, scroll down until you see the **Format** and **Text of link** boxes. Here's where we'll set the format of our shortened URL. By default, the shortened URL will be in this format: **[url] [title] [node-tags]**. This means that the node URL will show first, then the title of the node post, then any tags you have associated with the node. Let's delete the node tags token and just leave in the URL and the title tokens. Let's also tweak the **Text of link** field to just read Tweet. This is the link the user will click on to actually post the tweet over to Twitter.

Twitter image:

sites/all/modules/tweet/twitter.png

The location of the icon to use with the "Post to Twitter" link, relative to your Drupal installation. Ex.: sites/all/modules/tweet/twitter.png

Exclude nodes:

Enter the NIDs of nodes which should not have Tweet links, separated by commas.

Format:

[url] [title]

Manipulate the elements of the tweet by changing their order, removing them, or adding them (like hashtags). You can use the case-sensitive tokens [url], [title], [node-tags], and [node-teaser]. The [node-tags] and [node-teaser] tokens only take effect on nodes. Note that some token values may be truncated or left out to fit the tweet into 140 characters.

Text of link:

Tweet

The token [site] will be replaced with the name of the site for which the link is generated. This is only relevant if you picked a display format that uses text.

Save configuration   Reset to defaults

Save your configuration. Now, we can test the module out. Load one of your page or blog nodes and you should now see a new button/link appearing on your node that says **Tweet**. The **Tweet** text should appear next to the Twitter icon. Before clicking on the link, make sure you are logged into your Twitter account:

Let's go ahead and click on the **Tweet** link. If you are not currently logged into your Twitter account, Twitter should open and it will prompt you to log in to your Twitter account. Go ahead and do this. Next you will be redirected to your Twitter home page and the Tweet information will be displayed in the **What's happening?** text box. This will show the shortened URL format for your link and the title of your node. In this example, I have the following format:

www.variantcube.com/lqg Packt presents the e-Pub format

If you are happy with your tweet format, you can go ahead and post this by clicking on the **Twitter Tweet** button. Now, you'll see your new Tweet appear on your home page. The shortened URL is now a link and you can test it to make sure it opens up the correct node:

Testing the link does open the node on your Drupal site. You'll notice that the URL opens on your Drupal site with the `/node/id` URL. Notice on your Twitter home page that the URL is shortened to your site's domain URL followed by the shortened 3-character node URL; in this case it's `1qg`. So, this shortened URL worked for our Twitter configuration and purposes.

If you want to see a listing of all the shortened URLs on your site using the Shortened URL module, you can go to **Site configuration | Shorten | Shortened URLs**. You'll see a table that shows the original URL and the shortened version and the service that provides it, in our case, the Drupal ShortURL contributed module:

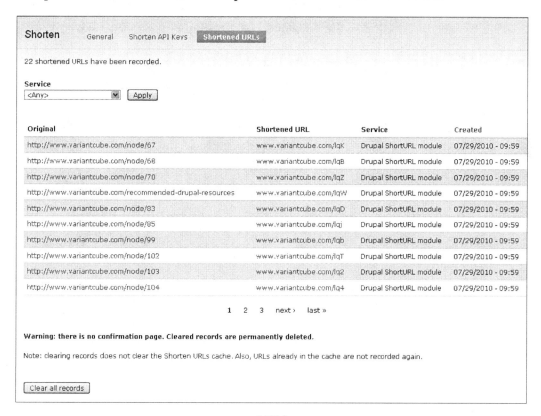

So, we have successfully configured the Tweet module and used our Shortened URL and ShortURL modules to provide short URL services for our Tweet posts to Twitter. We have now expanded our repertoire of methods for getting our Drupal node content over to our Twitter account.

Summary

In this chapter, we looked in detail at setting up web services for integration of Twitter with our Drupal site. This allows us to post Drupal nodes as Tweets to our Twitter account, and also to take tweets and post those back to our Drupal site automatically. We used two main modules including Tweet and Twitter as well as some helper contributed modules in order to provide our node URLS in a shortened format. Here's a brief summary of what we accomplished:

- Enabled the Twitter module and used it to post Twitter account tweets back to our Drupal site and make them appear in View blocks
- Used Twitter module to post our Drupal node content to our Twitter account home page
- Set up automatic actions and triggers to use with our Twitter module
- Enabled the Tweet module to enable easy posting of node content as a Tweet to our Twitter account
- Created shortened URLs for our node URLs so that we can present these in a shorter format on Twitter and so they meet the Twitter requirement of 30 characters or less for hyperlinked URLs

In *Chapter 10, LinkedIn and Drupal*, we'll return to a discussion of Drupal content and how to connect our Drupal site and its nodes and user processes to the popular LinkedIn professional social networking application and Web service using the LinkedIn module.

10
LinkedIn and Drupal

In this chapter we're going to integrate the popular professional and career-based social networking application LinkedIn with our Drupal Web site. If you have a LinkedIn account, you can integrate with your Drupal site using a contributed module called LinkedIn Integration. This allows for authentication of user accounts across the two applications and sharing of LinkedIn statuses on your Drupal site. You can also publish content from Drupal over to your LinkedIn account activity stream as an announcement. We'll look at configuring this integration in detail.

To summarize, in this chapter we will:

- Enable the LinkedIn Integration module and the OAuth module suite and configure each
- Post content to your LinkedIn account activity stream
- Post your LinkedIn profile abstract to your Drupal user profile page and enable a tab in your profile to access your LinkedIn abstract
- Test the authentication and user login process between Drupal and LinkedIn

LinkedIn and Drupal

LinkedIn is a social networking website and application that is geared towards business professionals. You can create an account and post a profile to LinkedIn that describes your professional background including your current jobs, education history, resume, career and job specialties and skills, websites that you have content on, and links to your Twitter account. The LinkedIn site functions as a dynamic social networking community where you can search for colleagues and add them as contacts, communicate with these colleagues via e-mail using the built in LinkedIn Web mail application, join groups of common interests, and post presentations including links to Slideshare presentations you have created.

For example, the site has multiple groups related to Drupal including the Drupal Community Network, Drupal, and Drupal Users Group. You can view the group profile of the Drupal Community Network at: `http://www.LinkedIn.com/ groups?mostPopular=&gid=117056`.

LinkedIn basically functions similar to Facebook, but it serves professionals and your career interests more intensively than Facebook does. The Web application and service has existed since May 2003, and according to the Wikipedia entry, contains more than 70 million registered users from across the globe. The CEO of LinkedIn, Jeff Weiner, worked for Yahoo! before joining LinkedIn. LinkedIn was started by developers who worked at PayPal and Socialnet.com.

In this section, we're going to use two Drupal contributed modules that integrate with the LinkedIn API and allow your Drupal site to interface with your LinkedIn account. LinkedIn provides a detailed description and documents about its public API at the LinkedIn Developer Network: `http://developer.LinkedIn.com/ index.jspa`. You can read documentation on the API via that link including getting up to speed on how the authentication process works when integrating with a LinkedIn account. LinkedIn uses the OAuth Authentication method in order to allow users from a Drupal site to submit API requests to the LinkedIn web service. OAuth is a standard open source protocol that allows for API authorization between desktop software and web applications. There is more on the OAuth protocol at: `http://oauth.net/`.

To review the document explaining all of the details of the LinkedIn OAuth process, go to its official documentation at: `http://developer.LinkedIn.com/docs/ DOC-1008`.

We'll interface with LinkedIn using two contributed modules, the LinkedIn Integration module and the OAuth module. Let's get started.

Installing the LinkedIn Integration and OAuth modules

The LinkedIn Integration module is dependent on the OAuth module, so you'll need to install both. Go ahead and download both modules from their respective project pages: `http://drupal.org/project/LinkedIn` and `http://drupal.org/project/oauth`. Install both modules as normal to your `/sites/all/modules` directory. The LinkedIn Integration module is currently in development, so the latest version you'll be using is **6.x-1.x-dev**. Bear in mind that you'll want to test out the module first in your development environment before implementing it on a production Drupal site.

The OAuth module has dependency modules that you'll need to install in order to enable it. These are the Autoload (`http://drupal.org/project/autoload`) and Inputstream (`http://drupal.org/project/inputstream`) modules. Go ahead and grab modules and upload them to your modules directory.

Go ahead and enable all of the OAuth modules and their dependencies through your modules administration page and save your module configuration:

Enabled	Name	Version	Description
☑	**OAuth**	6.x-3.0-beta2	Provides OAuth functionality Depends on: Autoload (disabled), Input stream helper (disabled), Chaos tools (enabled) Required by: OAuth Consumer UI (disabled), OAuth Provider UI (disabled)
☑	**OAuth Consumer UI**	6.x-3.0-beta2	Provides a UI for when OAuth is acting as a consumer. Depends on: OAuth (disabled), Autoload (disabled), Input stream helper (disabled), Chaos tools (enabled)
☑	**OAuth Provider UI**	6.x-3.0-beta2	Provides a UI for when OAuth is acting as a provider. Depends on: OAuth (disabled), Autoload (disabled), Input stream helper (disabled), Chaos tools (enabled)

The LinkedIn Integration module README file contains all the installation instructions. Go ahead and enable the LinkedIn Integration module once you have enabled the OAuth modules. Save your module configuration.

If you are unable to enable the LinkedIn Integration module because it tells you that OAuth needs to be enabled even when you have OAuth enabled, you'll need to make a tweak to the `.info` file of the LinkedIn module. To do this, open up the `LinkedIn.info` file and change the `dependencies[] = oauth` line to: `dependencies[] = oauth_common`. Your resulting code should look like this:

```
; $Id: LinkedIn.info,v 1.1.2.1 2010/05/13 12:29:36 bellesmanieres
Exp $
name = "LinkedIn"
core = "6.x"
description = "Provides LinkedIn integration."
dependencies[] = oauth_common

; Information added by drupal.org packaging script on 2010-07-11
version = "6.x-1.x-dev"
core = "6.x"
project = "LinkedIn"
datestamp = "1278834742"
```

Upload the updated `LinkedIn.info` file to your server. Now, refresh your modules page and you should now be able to enable the module:

Using the LinkedIn Integration module

In order to use the LinkedIn Integration module, you'll need to sign up for LinkedIn API credentials. This will provide you with a Consumer key and secret code that you'll add to your LinkedIn module configuration. To sign up for the keys, you need to go to the developer site at LinkedIn and request credentials. Also, your site URL will need to match the URL you add to your LinkedIn account information at their developer site. Go to: `https://www.LinkedIn.com/secure/developer` and sign into your LinkedIn account on this page.

This will sign you into the LinkedIn Developer Network. You need to click on the **Add New Application** link or icon to add your site as a Web service application:

Clicking on the **Add New Application** link will launch a form. Complete the form in its entirety and then click on the **Add Application** button. During the sign up process, you can specify whether you want to use the LinkedIn integration in Development or Live status. We'll keep this in Development for now while we test out the status integration, but you can always update your account to move it into Live status.

For the Programming Tools that you'll specify, make sure to select PHP here. For the OAuth Redirect URL, you can also add your site's main root URL.

Once you submit your application, a screen will load showing you your new LinkedIn Developer credentials including your API Key and Secret Key. Make sure to print this out or note down your credentials and keep them in a secure location.

Now, let's go back to our LinkedIn integration form on our Drupal site and add our credentials to the form.

Click on the **Save configuration** button.

Status update and promoting content to LinkedIn

In the Status update section of the LinkedIn module configuration, you can specify what content types on your Drupal site can be posted to a user's LinkedIn account home page as a status update on LinkedIn. So, basically, you can select the node type you want to be able to post over to LinkedIn as a status update/post. Let's go ahead and select the blog entry, page, and story types. You can also specify the Default format string for the actual status post and how that post will appear on your LinkedIn account. This means that the Drupal content will appear on your LinkedIn home page as the following string, for example, for page type content: `Posted "!title" on !site : !url`. Your form should look something like this:

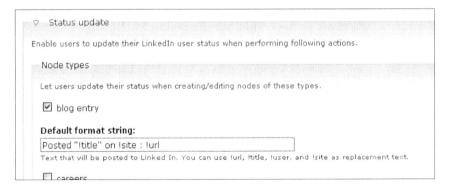

You can also integrate your Drupal site's user profiles with their respective LinkedIn user account if you enable the user profile display. This will let users share their LinkedIn profile information on their Drupal account page. We'll go ahead and enable this for now. There are multiple options for displaying the profile data. Let's set the profile data to be available via a clickable **Tab** button on the user's Drupal profile page:

Now that we have configured our module, we can save our module configuration and then check permissions to make sure our site users can use this LinkedIn Integration module's functionality.

Setting permissions

Check to make sure you have enabled permissions for your users to access the LinkedIn module functionality. You can set this for your authenticated users and make sure they can display their LinkedIn profile, update their LinkedIn status, and use custom status text. Let's enable this for our authenticated users:

Save your permissions.

Posting LinkedIn profile data to Drupal

The first functionality we can test is to bring our LinkedIn profile data over to our Drupal user account. To do this, go to your user account page and click on the Edit tab. Then you'll see a new tab for LinkedIn. Click on this. You may receive the following error immediately when you click on the LinkedIn link:

Fatal error: Class 'OAuthSignatureMethod_HMAC_SHA1' not found in /sites/all/modules/LinkedIn/LinkedIn.inc on line 106

If you do receive this error, here is the fix you'll need to make to the module code to get it working. This fix is derived from a support document on Drupal.org in the LinkedIn Integration module issue queue at: `https://drupal.org/node/848646`. When a user or developer reports an issue for a module to the module's issue queue, another developer will generally provide a method of fixing that bug or issue. This fix was posted in the issue queue on July 13, 2010, after which time, the issue fix will be rolled out to a module patch and submitted to the next official release of the module. At the time this book was put into publication, the issue was still not resolved or patched into the official module release, so we'll provide this fix here based on the support document.

In your `LinkedIn.inc` file, look for the following line of code:

```
$consumer = new OAuthConsumer($consumer_key, $consumer_secret,
NULL);
```

Now, move the following line of code, which should be shown just above, under the above line:

```
$signature = new OAuthSignatureMethod_HMAC_SHA1();
```

You are basically moving the `$signature` line to appear below the `$consumer` line. There are actually two locations in the `.inc` file to add this line of code—around line 20 and line 111 of the `.inc` file. I'm attaching the entire updated `.inc` file to the code files for the book. You'll find the updated code in the attached `LinkedIn.inc` file. The first function, once you edit, should look like this:

```
function LinkedIn_access_token($account) {

   //setting up variables
   $base_url = "https://api.LinkedIn.com/uas/oauth";

   $consumer_key = variable_get('LinkedIn_consumer_key', '');
   $consumer_secret = variable_get('LinkedIn_consumer_secret', '');
   $consumer = new OAuthConsumer($consumer_key, $consumer_secret,
NULL);
   $signature = new OAuthSignatureMethod_HMAC_SHA1();
```

```
$random = md5(rand());
$callback = url('LinkedIn/token/'. $account, array('absolute' =>
TRUE)) .'?action='. $random ; //will be used to discard direct call to
the path
```

The second, around line 106, should now look like this:

```
$consumer_key = variable_get('LinkedIn_consumer_key', '');
$consumer_secret = variable_get('LinkedIn_consumer_secret', '');
$consumer = new OAuthConsumer($consumer_key, $consumer_secret,
NULL);
$signature = new OAuthSignatureMethod_HMAC_SHA1();
$row = db_fetch_array(db_query("SELECT * FROM {LinkedIn_token} WHERE
uid = %d AND type = 'access'", $account));
```

Once you make this fix, go ahead and refresh your /LinkedIn profile page. It should load now. You will see a message telling you that you must first authorize LinkedIn integration to use related features. There is a **Go LinkedIn** button you can click on to take you to the LinkedIn website to complete the integration process. Go ahead and click on that button:

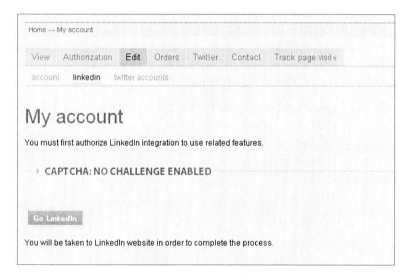

When you click on the **Go LinkedIn** button, you should be redirected to an https authorized URL that contains the name of your LinkedIn application; in our case, I named my application Drupal Integration Test. So, this worked. Now, I need to log in on my application portal page.

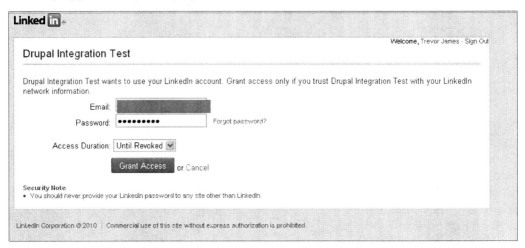

You can choose an **Access Duration** for the length of time you want to grant this session ID. Let's leave it set to **Until Revoked**. Now, click on the **Grant Access** button. If this works, you'll be redirected back to your Drupal profile page, and now you will see two additional checkboxes displayed:

- The first will ask you if you want to display an abstract of your LinkedIn page on your current Drupal user profile page
- In the second checkbox, you can specify whether you want your profile to be automatically updated whenever you post new information to your LinkedIn status. Let's check both of these boxes, as shown here:

Click on the **Save** button. A message will appear notifying you that your LinkedIn preferences have been saved.

Now go to View your user profile main page. You should now see an additional tab in your profile menu that is called LinkedIn. Clicking on this tab will launch the LinkedIn profile page and will display your LinkedIn profile abstract data. You should see something similar to this:

The profile URL should be: /user/%/LinkedIn. The profile abstract and avatar image should be clickable to your full public profile on LinkedIn. Go ahead and test this. When you click on your image or the abstract title you should be redirected to your public profile:

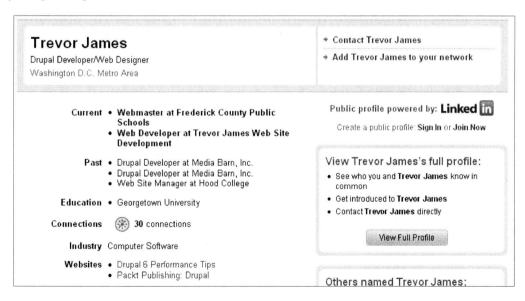

You will also see one of your most recent LinkedIn activity posts appear on your profile abstract page.

Posting Drupal content to LinkedIn

Similar to the Twitter module that we discussed in Chapter 8, the LinkedIn Integration module allows us to announce posts we make to our Drupal site on our LinkedIn activity stream. When we configured the LinkedIn module, we specified that we wanted to announce Page content posts and we also noted the type of format string we want the announcement to post with. Let's go ahead and try this out based on our settings.

Go to post a new page on your site by going to **Create content > Page**. You'll notice on the Page content type form you now have a fieldset titled Post to LinkedIn. You can check the Announce on LinkedIn box if you want to add a link back to the content to your LinkedIn activity stream. Let's make sure the box is checked. Leave the text format string in the field as the following: **Posted "!title" on !site : !url**.

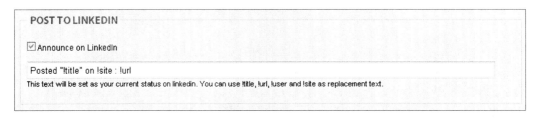

Now, go ahead and save your node. If you get the following error, you'll need to update the `LinkedIn.inc` file again, similar to the fixes we made earlier in the chapter:

Fatal error: Class 'OAuthSignatureMethod_HMAC_SHA1' not found in /public_html/sites/all/modules/LinkedIn/LinkedIn.inc on line 142

We need to swap the following line and make sure it's placed after the `$consumer` line of code around lines 142-144. The line of code you are looking for is:

```
$signature = new OAuthSignatureMethod_HMAC_SHA1();
```

You should end up with something that looks similar to this:

```
function LinkedIn_put_profile_field($account, $field, $body) {
  $base_url = 'https://api.LinkedIn.com/v1/people/~/';
  $url = $base_url . $field ;
  $xml = '<'. $field .'>' . htmlspecialchars($body, ENT_NOQUOTES,
"UTF-8") . '</'. $field .'>';
  $consumer_key = variable_get('LinkedIn_consumer_key', '');
  $consumer_secret = variable_get('LinkedIn_consumer_secret', '');
```

```
    $consumer = new OAuthConsumer($consumer_key, $consumer_secret,
NULL);
    $signature = new OAuthSignatureMethod_HMAC_SHA1();
    $row = db_fetch_array(db_query("SELECT * FROM {LinkedIn_token} WHERE
uid = %d AND type = 'access'", $account));
    $token = new OAuthConsumer($row['token_key'], $row['token_secret'],
1);
    $request = OAuthRequest::from_consumer_and_token($consumer, $token,
'PUT', $url, array());
    $request->sign_request($signature, $consumer, $token);
    $header = $request->to_header();
    $response = _LinkedIn_http_request($url, $header, $xml);
    return $response;
}
```

Once you make this tweak or upload the attached `LinkedIn.inc` file in the book's attached code, you can refresh your error page. The node should post and you will receive a message stating: **Posted to LinkedIn**.

Once saved, head over to your LinkedIn account and you should see the post show up in your LinkedIn activity stream. Confirm that the post has shown up there. One other issue to check and confirm: due to the error we encountered above, you may have accidentally posted this node twice on your Drupal site. Check this and remove one of the duplicates.

When I view my activity on LinkedIn, I see the content posted successfully:

Trevor James Posted "Drupal Views Tutorial of note" on Trevor James - Web Developer : http://lnkd.in/d5x4vE
5 minutes ago • Like • Comment

If you click on the hyperlink provided, formatted as a `/lnkd.in` URL, you should be taken immediately to the node you posted on your Drupal site. Additionally, if you view your LinkedIn home page, you should see your post show in the Network Activity section.

You have successfully taken your Drupal node content and posted it as an announcement to your LinkedIn account activity stream. You have now posted Drupal content to two major social networking applications and websites, Twitter, and LinkedIn. The integration is nearly seamless and flexible and provides a great deal of power as far as duplication of content from one website to another goes. You have also seen the power of web services and their integration with Drupal.

Checking usage statistics for the LinkedIn module

You can check the usage statistics for the LinkedIn Integration module via its drupal. org project page. This is a good practice to engage in when using contributed modules, especially those in development stages. The usage statistics give you a very rough estimate of how many sites are using the module on any given day that is reported out. Statistics only get reported if the site is using the Update Status module. But, this still gives a general statistical overview of how popular the module is. It's interesting to view the usage statistics on the LinkedIn module since they show a steady increase in the amount of sites using the module from February to August of 2010. Hopefully, the module will get patched and submitted back to CVS soon, and with all the bugs worked out (as per our testing in this chapter), we can get this module rolled out as a production level module to the drupal.org community.

Here's a screenshot of the usage statistics for LinkedIn Integration:

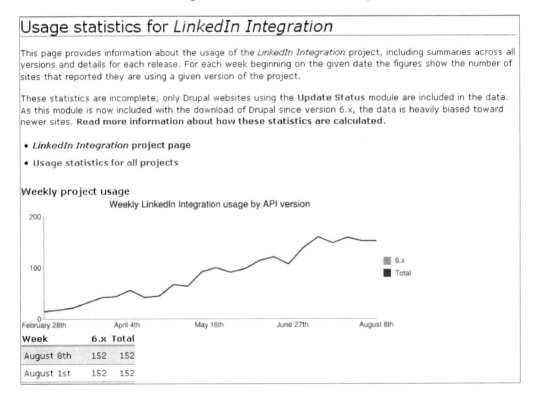

Summary

In this chapter, we looked in detail at setting up web services for integration of the popular professional social networking application LinkedIn with our Drupal site. This allows us to set up user accounts on our Drupal site to authenticate over to the respective user's LinkedIn account.

By doing this, the user can publish their LinkedIn profile abstract to their Drupal user profile page, allowing for easy integration of user content from LinkedIn over to Drupal. This works using the OAuth user account authentication module, which allows us to keep account authentication secure and stable as per the user account on our Drupal site.

We also learned how to post Drupal nodes as announcements over to our LinkedIn account activity stream. We can use any of our Drupal content types to post this content over to LinkedIn. Here's a brief summary of what we accomplished:

- Enabled the LinkedIn Integration and OAuth suite of modules
- Tested authentication of our Drupal user account over to our LinkedIn account using the LinkedIn Integration module configuration
- Posted our LinkedIn profile abstract from our LinkedIn account over to our Drupal user profile page using the authentication methods described above
- Enabled our content types to work with the LinkedIn module
- Created a node on our Drupal site using one of the integrated content types and announced this node automatically to our LinkedIn activity stream at the click of a mouse button

In *Chapter 11, Facebook and Drupal*, we'll return to a discussion of Drupal content and how to connect our Drupal site and its nodes and user process to the popular Facebook social networking application and web service using the Drupal Facebook module.

11
Facebook and Drupal

In this chapter, we're going to explore methods of integrating Drupal with the popular social networking web application, Facebook. If you have a Facebook account, you can easily become a Facebook application developer; you just need to set up an application in your Facebook account, and then connect to this application via your Drupal website. Your Drupal site acts as the server and remote host of the content, and Facebook acts as the web service consuming your Drupal content. This allows you to take your node content from Drupal and automatically post the nodes to your Facebook application. The node content floats into Facebook and retains the Facebook layout and design. Drupal allows this to happen because it integrates with the Facebook layout and specialty markup code by using a customized and specially-designed theme. This Drupal theme integrates with, and supports the Facebook FBML (Facebook Markup language).

The Facebook integration also allows you to integrate your Drupal user base with your Facebook application and your Facebook account users and friends with your Drupal site. In this chapter, we're going to focus on how to post content to Facebook, but you'll also want to be aware of the permissions and user account processes involved, so we'll touch on that as well.

To summarize, in this chapter we will:

- Install the Drupal for Facebook module suite and tweak our Drupal installation and site to support this suite of modules
- Install all of the Facebook client libraries
- Create a developer's account on Facebook and set up a Facebook application environment
- Configure the Drupal for Facebook application settings internally to our Drupal site
- Configure and use the Drupal FBML theme specifically for our Facebook application
- Post content from our Drupal site to our Facebook application home page

What is Facebook?

Facebook is one of the most popular and well-known social networking websites and applications. Facebook allows you to create a profile web page that contains sub-elements including a "Wall", where you can post status updates; an "Info" section that contains your personal user profile data (much like custom fields in a Drupal user profile); and a "Photos" section that allows you to upload photos and create photo galleries to share with your friends.

On Facebook, you can follow friends' accounts and also allow friends to view your content and post to your Wall. It's a similar application to LinkedIn but Facebook leans more towards communication amongst friends than professional colleagues. Facebook was launched in 2004 and by July 2010 it had over 500 million users. For more on the history and timeline of the Facebook web application, go to its Wikipedia entry at `http://en.wikipedia.org/wiki/Facebook`.

Drupal and Facebook

Drupal users and site administrators may want to integrate their Drupal site with Facebook in order to market your Drupal site and open up your site to new users who may visit the site through the Facebook settings. Drupal provides a number of contributed modules that facilitate this integration, including a suite of modules that we'll be looking at in detail in this chapter. The Drupal for Facebook (fb) module suite is a group of modules and themes that allow for user and content integration through Facebook's API; and also paves the way for developers to construct new applications that allow Drupal to talk to Facebook and vice versa. The module developers of the Drupal for Facebook suite want to promote Facebook application development, but they want to make this development happen within the Drupal CMS(Content Management System) framework. This is a powerful set of tools for anyone who wants to bridge the Drupal CMS with the Facebook social networking platform.

There are two basic types of apps you can create to integrate with your Facebook account. These are application types as defined by the Facebook development community. The Facebook Connect application allows you to run a Drupal site on your own domain that integrates with Facebook. More information about Facebook Connect is provided here: `http://developers.facebook.com/docs/guides/web`. Canvas Page apps run inside of your Facebook account. These apps appear in the apps.facebook.com domain. They are web pages that get embedded into Facebook using iFrames or FBML.

The module's project page is available at: `http://drupal.org/project/fb`. The module is currently at version **6.x-2.0-rc2**. There is a detailed documentation provided at: `http://drupal.org/node/195035`.

Drupal also provides a module that integrates Drupal and Facebook user accounts. The Facebook Connect module (`http://drupal.org/project/fbconnect`) allows Facebook users to log in to your Drupal site using their Facebook login information. This happens by way of using the Facebook Connect API. The module provides features that help to tie Facebook and Drupal accounts together and expose data between the two authenticated user accounts. The module is currently in the development phase and version, so it's recommended that you only install and use this module in a development site environment and not on a production-level Drupal site.

This is a huge swath of information to cover and this chapter will not cover all the details and functionality of the Drupal for Facebook module, but will look at it in a general overview and point out some areas of detail. This chapter serves as an introduction to this large suite of modules and integration with the Facebook web service API libraries.

We're going to go ahead and install the Drupal for Facebook suite as well as the Facebook Connect module. We'll enable both sets of modules and look at the functionality of each in detail in the following sections.

Requirements for running Drupal for Facebook

In order to install and use the Drupal for Facebook suite of modules, you will need to make sure you have done the following:

- Sign up for a Facebook account if you do not have one. You can do that here: `http://facebook.com`

- It's suggested that you run the Development (Devel) module on your site while you are developing Facebook applications and integration. The Drupal for Facebook module includes a version of the Devel module that you can enable and that will help you to debug your Facebook apps as you work on them. The Devel (Development) module is a Drupal contributed module suite of helper applications and functions for Drupal developers. You can learn more about the Devel module at: `http://drupal.org/project/devel`.

- The Drupal for Facebook modules require you to be running the JSON extension with your PHP version. If you are running PHP 5.2+, JSON comes bundled with it. You can confirm this by running your PHP info report via Drupal's Status Report page. By checking my site's PHP info, I see that I'm running JSON version 1.2.1, so we're good to go for the following examples.

Installing and enabling Drupal for Facebook

Download the latest version of Drupal for Facebook and upload the suite of modules to your /sites/all/modules directory. You'll see a suite of new modules in your modules admin list that is split up into three sections. Let's enable all the modules in the Drupal for Facebook fieldset. This includes the **Canvas Pages**, **Drupal for Facebook**, **Drupal for Facebook Applications**, **Drupal for Facebook Devel**, **Facebook Connect**, and **User Management** modules:

Enabled	Name	Version	Description
☑	Canvas Pages	6.x-2.0-rc2	For traditional Facebook Apps. Also for Profile Tabs. Depends on: Drupal for Facebook (disabled), Drupal for Facebook Applications (disabled)
☑	Drupal for Facebook	6.x-2.0-rc2	REQUIRED. Imports and uses the Facebook API. You must also download and install the Facebook client libraries, and make manual configuration changes. (See *modules/fb/README.txt*.) Required by: Drupal for Facebook Actions (disabled), Drupal for Facebook Applications (disabled), Canvas Pages (disabled), Facebook Connect (disabled), Drupal for Facebook Devel (disabled), Drupal for Facebook Forms (disabled), Friend Features (disabled), Extended Permissions (disabled), Register Users (disabled), Drupal for Facebook Streams (disabled), User Management (disabled), Drupal for Facebook Views (disabled)
☑	Drupal for Facebook Applications	6.x-2.0-rc2	Allows Drupal to host one or more Facebook Applications. REQUIRED (unless you have implemented a custom replacement). Depends on: Drupal for Facebook (disabled) Required by: Canvas Pages (disabled), Facebook Connect (disabled), Friend Features (disabled), Extended Permissions (disabled), Register Users (disabled), User Management (disabled)
☑	Drupal for Facebook Devel	6.x-2.0-rc2	HIGHLY RECOMMENDED. Displays messages and blocks that help when developing and debugging Apps. Do not even try to get started without this module. Disable it later, on your production server when your site is live. Depends on: Drupal for Facebook (disabled), Devel (disabled), Menu (enabled)
☑	Facebook Connect	6.x-2.0-rc2	For Facebook Connect apps. Allow users to log in using Facebook credentials. Include XFBML and facebook javascript in your website. Depends on: Drupal for Facebook (disabled), Drupal for Facebook Applications (disabled)
☑	User Management	6.x-2.0-rc2	REQUIRED (unless your app is incredibly simple). Create local accounts for users of Facebook Apps. Depends on: Drupal for Facebook (disabled), Drupal for Facebook Applications (disabled)

In the **Drupal for Facebook - contrib** section, enable the **Extended Permissions**, **Friend Features**, and **Register Users** modules. These modules will give us a fine-grained control over how we integrate Facebook users into our Drupal site:

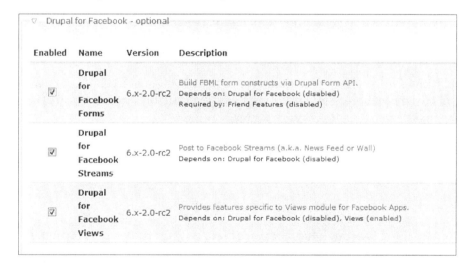

Finally, enable the following modules in the optional fieldset: **Drupal for Facebook Forms**, **Drupal for Facebook Streams**, and **Drupal for Facebook Views**. These modules will provide integration with the Facebook Form construct with the Drupal Form API, and integration with the Drupal Views module:

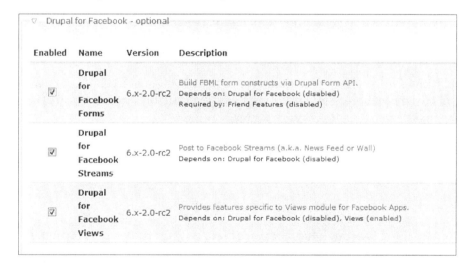

Save your module configuration.

You may be asked to enable the Devel module in order to run the Drupal for Facebook Devel module. Go ahead and do this while we're in development mode and are testing out the Facebook modules.

You will receive the following messages once you save the modules. The first will be in regards to the Facebook libraries. It will state:

> **Facebook client libraries will not work properly if arg_separator.output is not "&". Currently the value is "&". Please change this in settings.php or php.ini.**

> **Drupal for Facebook has been enabled, but not properly installed. Please read the README.txt.**

These two messages warn you that once you have installed the Facebook client libraries (see the following section), you'll need to then make a change to your `settings.php` or `php.ini` file. This requires opening up those file(s) in a text editor and tweaking the `arg_separator.output`. You can go ahead and do this now. You should also make sure to read the Drupal for Facebook's README file to make sure you have completed all the steps of the installation process. This module is a bit more complex to install and enable:

> *** Drupal for Facebook modules enabled. Be sure to install facebook's client libraries and modify your settings.php! Read modules/fb/README. txt and the online documentation for Drupal for Facebook for details.**

> *** Facebook Application module installed. Please grant yourself permissions and then browse to Admin >> Facebook Applications to get started.**

> *** The configuration options have been saved.**

These messages inform you that the modules have been enabled but you also need to install all of the Facebook client libraries. Let's go ahead and install the libraries now and then make the tweak to `settings.php`.

Additionally, once you have installed the libraries, you can then browse to the Drupal for Facebook administrative screen. This module contains its own administrative interface. The interface is: `/admin/build/fb`.

If you launch this admin path now you'll receive the following error:

> **Drupal for Facebook has been enabled, but not properly installed. Please read the README.txt.**

If you launch your status report you'll also get this series of errors now:

> *** Drupal for Facebook has been enabled, but not properly installed. Please read the README.txt.**

* warning: include(facebook-platform/php/facebook.php) [function.include]: failed to open stream: No such file or directory in /home1/variantc/public_html/sites/all/modules/fb/fb.install on line 52.

* warning: include() [function.include]: Failed opening 'facebook-platform/php/facebook.php' for inclusion (include_path='.:/usr/lib/php:/usr/local/lib/php') in /home1/variantc/public_html/sites/all/modules/fb/fb.install on line 52.

Installing the Facebook libraries

These errors are telling us that we need to install the Facebook Platform web service libraries that include the `facebook.php` file. Because we have installed the 2.x version of the Drupal for Facebook module, we will want to download and install the REST version of the Facebook web service libraries. The REST libraries are available at: `http://github.com/facebook/platform/raw/master/clients/packages/facebook-platform.tar.gz`. Go ahead and download the `facebook-platform.tar.gz` archive to your desktop and then unzip it. I have also included this code in the `code` folder for *Chapter 10, LinkedIn and Drupal*, of this book. In this folder—you can locate two folders, `footprints` and `PHP`. The `PHP` folder contains the `facebook.php` file that is appearing in your error message.

Now, we want to upload the `facebook-platform` folder into your Drupal for Facebook module folder that you have already placed in your `/sites/all/modules` directory. Go ahead and do this now.

Now, we need to make a tweak to our site's `settings.php` file to make sure that our main Drupal configuration recognizes where the Drupal for Facebook module is located. To do this, open your `settings.php` file in an editor and add the following line of code to the bottom of your `settings.php` file:

```
require_once "sites/all/modules/fb/fb_settings.inc";
```

In the same `settings.php` file, check to make sure that the `arg_separator.output` does not contain an `&`. The Facebook libraries will not work correctly if you have an `&amp` in that line of code. The correct line of code should have a plain `&`. So, check this and then make sure you have those lines of `arg_separator.output` code looking like this:

```
ini_set('arg_separator.output',     '&');
```

I checked my `settings.php` file and realized this needs to be tweaked, so I'm tweaking it to be `'&'`.

Now, go back to your Drupal site and refresh your status report page. The error messages should have disappeared. On your status report, you should see two green, checked messages stating the following:

> **Drupal for Facebook Settings**Included
> **Facebook Client API**Found**Facebook client API found at facebook-platform/php/facebook.php**

So, you have successfully loaded and configured the Facebook REST-based service APIs. We're now ready to complete our Drupal for Facebook configuration and start using the module.

You can also test to make sure the module is configured correctly by going to your **Administer | Site Building | Facebook Applications** link and that will launch the Facebook Application admin page at /admin/build/fb. You will see various tabbed sections here, including Add Application, Canvas Pages, Facebook Connect, and User Management. We'll come back to look at each of these in detail, but first let's configure our Canvas Pages theme functionality to work with.

Setting up Canvas Pages

To create Canvas Pages for Facebook, you will need to use Facebook's specific markup language called FBML along with iframe, which allows for your markup to be iframed and served from your server. So, your site will be the host that Facebook's web service will consume. To do this, you'll need to use a Drupal theme that supports FBML. The module ships with a starter theme for this called **fb_fbml**. One note to bear in mind is that FBML is now considered by Facebook, so you can start with this theme's code but you might want to pay attention to how the code is upgraded for iframe support with later versions of the Drupal for Facebook module (version 3+). Since we're using version 2.x, we can continue to use the FBML version of the theme.

Let's go ahead and enable the FBML theme, so that we can develop Canvas Pages-driven apps. Go to your FB module themes directory at /sites/all/modules/fb/themes and copy the **fb_fbml** theme directory over to your /sites/all/themes directory. Now, you can enable the **fb_fbml** theme in your themes admin page. Remember here that you can just enable the FBML theme but not make it your default, so you can keep your site's default custom theme running at the same time.

The **fb_fbml** theme on your themes admin page will warn you that you should use this theme on Facebook FBML-driven Canvas Pages only. Obviously, the access to this theme should only be given to your site administrators or developers.

no screenshot	fb_fbml Use on Facebook FBML canvas pages only.	6.x-2.0-rc2	☑	○	configure

Enable the **fb_fbml** theme and then save your themes configuration.

Creating your first Facebook app

Why would you want to create a Facebook app? A Facebook app is basically a space on the Facebook web application site that contains specific types of content you have posted. You may want to create an application on Facebook that hosts your book reviews or music reviews. You can create this app or space on Facebook and then write all of your reviews on your Drupal site. You can then post these reviews and content over to your Facebook app space and that space on Facebook will only contain this type of content. It's a nice method of collecting and organizing similar content on Facebook and keeping this content separate from your main Facebook profile.

As mentioned earlier in the chapter, in order to create a Facebook application, you need to first create a Facebook account if you don't have one already. Once you have your Facebook account, you need to sign up for a developer application. To do this, go to: http://www.facebook.com/developers/createapp.php. If you are currently logged into your Facebook account, you'll be asked to grant the Facebook application access to your Facebook account. Go ahead and allow this access:

You will be redirected to your facebook.com/developers account and see the Developer home page. On this page, you'll see a link to your account and also to your applications. There will also be a button to **Set Up New Application**. Click on this button:

The set up application screen will launch where you'll be asked to name your application. Give your app a simple name in the **Application Name** field. Agree to the Facebook terms of use and then click on the **Create Application** button as shown in the following screenshot:

For this example, I'll call my application **Firehouses and Fire Stations**.

Clicking on the **Add application** button will direct you to a security check page where you'll be required to enter CAPTCHA fields. Do this and then click the **Submit** button. Now, a detailed application profile page will launch, split into multiple tabbed screens including **About, Web Site, Facebook Integration, Mobile and Devices**, and **Advanced,** as shown in the following screenshot. Let's go through each of these.

The **About** screen will ask you for more general details about your Facebook application including the name (as filled out in the previous screenshot), **Description, Icon, Logo, Language, User Support Address** (whether you'll provide a support URL or e-mail address), and any privacy statements or policies that you'll be providing. Go ahead and complete this screen. You can also add other developers to your developer access on this **About** screen if you want other developers who have Facebook developer accounts to access and interact with your account.

Navigate to the **Web Site** tab and a screen will load showing you your application ID and also your app secret key. You can add your site URL and site domain here. In our case, for this example, my site URL is `http://variantcube.com` and my site domain is `variantcube.com`. You can also add a subdomain to the domain field on this screen.

Navigate to the **Facebook Integration** tab and a screen will load. Here, you want to specify the Canvas Page alias for your Facebook app. Here, the Canvas page will be `http://apps.facebook.com/firehouses` and the corresponding Canvas URL on my site and server will be `http://variantcube.com/firehouses/`. Make sure to end your URL with the forward slash /.

Select the FBML Canvas type. You can leave the rest of the settings and configuration set to their defaults.

Save your **About** application changes and Facebook will launch a screen confirming that your application changes have been saved. You will see a synopsis of your application including the number of users, people who like the app, and total users. You will also see your application ID, API Key, Application secret key, site URL, domain, and canvas page that you added in the previous screens. Keep the key information secure as you'll need this API key info to plug into the Drupal side of the application configuration.

You can also re-edit your Facebook application settings via this confirmation screen by clicking on the **Edit Settings** link. You will also get a confirmation that it may take several minutes for your app to propagate across the Web and to all the Facebook servers. In addition, your application will not be listed in the Facebook application directory unless you submit it to the directory. You can click on this link to submit your app.

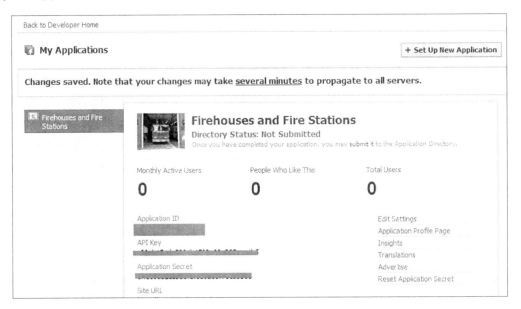

You have now completed the initial configuration and setup of your Facebook application on the Facebook side of the account integration. Now, we'll finish configuring our Drupal site so that we can publish content to Facebook using this app. Congratulations on creating your first Facebook app!

Configuring Drupal to work with your Facebook app

Now that we've set up our Facebook application inside of the Facebook environment and we have our API key, let's complete our integration by setting up the Drupal side of our application.

Go to your Drupal for Facebook administrative page on your Drupal site at **Site building | Facebook Applications** or at `/admin/build/fb`. Click on the **Add Application** button and this will launch the add app form. The form will summarize the instructions that we ran through in the previous section on how to set up your Facebook application in Facebook and get your API key. Now that you have completed that part, we can add the API information to this configuration screen.

First, give your application a **Label**, which is a machine readable name for your app. Add your API key, application secret code, and Facebook App ID to the corresponding fields.

Leave the **Set Application Properties Automatically** box checked:

Leave the **Extended Permissions** and **Register Users** settings on their defaults. Expand the Facebook canvas pages fieldset and make sure that the theme for FBML pages is set to `fb_fbml`.

Go ahead and save your configuration. Once you save your settings, Drupal should show you two confirmation messages:

- **Created Facebook application Firehouses and Fire Stations (firehouses)**
- **Note that it may take several minutes for property changes to propagate to all Facebook servers**

You will also see a table showing your new Facebook application with its label, a link to its About page on Facebook; a link to its canvas page that you originally set up and gave a URL when setting up the app in Facebook earlier; a link to the local version of your application on your Drupal site; an edit link to edit the application and a link to its remote settings on Facebook.

Let's go ahead and test our app.

Testing the Facebook application

To test your application and see if your Drupal site's content has been posted to your Facebook application, click on the link to its path under the Canvas header in the above table. I'll click on the firehouses link and this will launch the Facebook application at: `http://apps.facebook.com/firehouses/`. If the integration has worked successfully per the above instructions, you should see your site's node content posted to your Facebook application page. The canvas page will only show node content that you have posted that can be viewed by anonymous users. It will not show any content that has restricted access. You should see a screen similar to this in layout and design. This is the canvas page that Drupal has created using the FBML theme and integration with Facebook via your API key. You'll also notice that the URLs are the same on Facebook. If your Drupal node is `/node/113`, then it will be posted as `/node/113` on your Facebook application as well:

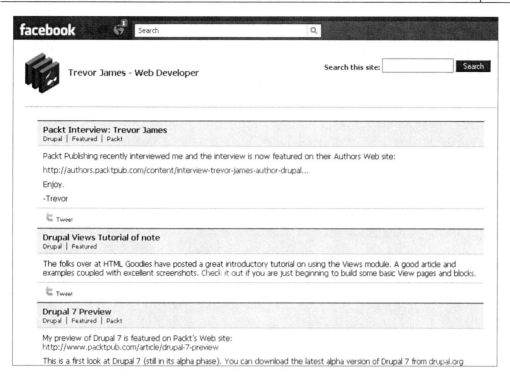

If you try to load a restricted node in your Facebook application, you will receive the following error message:

Application Temporarily Unavailable

Received HTTP error code 403 while loading http://variantcube.com/ node/109

Sorry, the application you were using is experiencing a problem. Please try again later.

You can also test and view all of your Facebook application settings on your Drupal site by clicking on the local **View** link. This will launch a page showing you all of your Facebook application credentials. You'll see a page that looks like this:

You'll see the web service callback URL that your Drupal site is using as well as the Connection URL. Both should be the root URLs to your site. You'll also see **Post-Authorize Callback URL** and **Post-Remove Callback URL**. These URLs are used when a node is posted to Drupal or deleted. These callbacks authorize the post or removal from the Facebook application.

If you click on the **Remote Settings** link, this will launch the original Facebook application settings configuration page that you already completed earlier. This is helpful as you can easily edit your Facebook application settings on Facebook if you need to via this link:

Editing your Facebook application settings

Also remember here that all of my site's posts are showing on the Facebook application canvas page because I have specified that my canvas URL is the root level of my site. If I wanted to only pull nodes from one specific path on my website, I would need to specify this as my canvas URL in my Facebook settings. Go ahead and tweak the canvas URL setting and change it to only pull one node over from your site. For example, I'll change my canvas URL to be: `http://variantcube.com/firehouses`, referring to the earlier /firehouses node I set up specifically for this application. Then, if I go to edit my canvas URL setting via the Remote Settings link in my Facebook application, I can change this URL to the above `http://variantcube.com/firehouses/`. Make sure to enclose the closing "/" in the URL. Click the **Save Changes** button in Facebook.

Now, via your Drupal site, test the link to your Facebook application canvas URL. This time you should only see that node's content but not all of the node content from your website. For example, in this node, I've posted one photo of a firehouse. When I changed my canvas URL in my Facebook application settings and then visited this URL, I now see that only this node is being consumed by Facebook:

So, you have successfully created a custom Facebook application that allows for posting your site's node content over to your Facebook application. Your site is acting as the remote web service server of content here and Facebook is acting as the consumer of that node content. This is pretty amazing integration and sharing of content by two highly robust and popular content management systems and applications. This shows you the power of taking your content from Drupal and automatically serving it out to Facebook so that you can leverage the Facebook community's user base.

There is much more about Facebook applications, including tutorials on how to build complex applications, at the documentation pages for the module on drupal.org:

`http://drupal.org/node/205481.`

Summary

In this chapter, we looked in detail at setting up Drupal web services for integration with the popular social networking application Facebook. This allows us to take our published nodes on our Drupal site and effectively and accurately push them out to our Facebook application so that our content is duplicated in the Facebook environment. This allows our content to be accessible to potentially thousands and thousands of Facebook site users.

We learned how to set up this configuration both on the Facebook side of the web service environment and also in our Drupal site. We learned how to enable the Drupal theme that supports the Facebook markup language and that styles our node content so that it can fit inside the Facebook template. This design and theming also showed us how powerful this Drupal for Facebook module suite is since it takes in both the node content and also how the node content should be styled to match Facebook's style and layout guidelines.

Here's a brief summary of what we accomplished:

- Installed and enabled the Drupal for Facebook suite of modules
- Installed the Facebook libraries on our Drupal server to support the web service integration
- Set up our Facebook application in our Facebook account
- Configured the Facebook application to integrate with our Drupal site by adding the Facebook app API key and our account key to Drupal for Facebook module configuration form in our Drupal site
- Enable the FBML theme for our Facebook content
- Posted nodes from our Drupal site to our Facebook application and viewed it via our app's canvas URL and page

In *Chapter 12, Authentication Services*, we're going to talk in more detail about user permissions and authentication methods and modules that support Drupal web services.

12
Authentication Services

In this chapter, we will explore various authentication web services to use with your Drupal site. First, we'll explore the Open ID protocol and module. This authentication method comes shipped with your Drupal 6.x core, so it's easy to enable and start using. We'll set up OpenID to work with our Google account and see what this integration can do for us.

We'll also look at the OAuth protocol in more detail. We used this module in *Chapter 9, Drupal and Twitter* when we discussed LinkedIn Integration. We're going to return to using OAuth in this chapter and take a look at the additional OAuth modules that can help to expand our repertoire of authentication methods. We'll use the OAuth Connector module to connect to our Twitter account and build a Twitter application using this authentication method.

To summarize, in this chapter we will:

- Enable the OpenID module and configure it on our user accounts
- Set up OpenID to interface with our Google account
- Install and configure the OAuth Connector and Connector modules
- Set up a Twitter application environment
- Connect our Drupal site with our Twitter application using the OAuth Connector module

OpenID and Drupal

OpenID is a web service specifically designed for user logins and authentication. It allows website users to use the same login credentials on multiple websites they visit. This means that they do not need to have a separate username or password on each site but can use the same ones across all the sites they visit if the site supports OpenID.

The OpenID protocol was originally developed in May 2005 by a programmer named Brad Fitzpatrick. Fitzpatrick was working for Six Apart (`http://sixapart.com/`), the company that developed the Movable Type blog software, the TypePad blog hosting service, when he created OpenID. OpenID became quickly popular after blogging sites and services such as LiveJournal implemented the service on their sites. Later in its development timeline, both Symantec and Microsoft announced their support of the service; and then Google, Yahoo!, and PayPal all announced they would utilize the service on their portals. There is much more about the history of OpenID at Wikipedia: `http://en.wikipedia.org/wiki/OpenID`.

You can create an OpenID account through the openid.net web service site. The openid.net site recommends multiple hosts and providers for your OpenID account, including Google, Yahoo!, LiveJournal, Blogger, Flickr, Wordpress, and AOL. Many of these web service applications already provide an OpenID authentication framework that you can use with your Drupal site. You can also host your own OpenID service provider via your Drupal site. We'll look at both the methods in this section. You can learn more about OpenID at the openid.net website at: `http://openid.net/`. The site lists recommended providers of OpenID accounts at: `http://openid.net/get-an-openid`.

Drupal 6 supports the OpenID functionality and OpenID ships as a core module with Drupal 6. If you enable the OpenID module, you will get an additional link on your user login page and block that allows your site users to log in to your site using their OpenID account. This means that new users on your site can create accounts on your site using their OpenID credentials. If a user on your site already has an account, they can still utilize the OpenID module but they will need to edit their account and assign their OpenID identity to their account.

The way the authentication web service works is that when a user visits your site and logs in with their OpenID credentials, your Drupal site communicates with the OpenID host provider to verify the identity of the user. If the user is subsequently logged into their OpenID server, the server communicates back to your Drupal site through the web service and authenticates and approves the login. If the user is not logged into their OpenID server, the OpenID server will ask for the user's credentials first before logging them into their Drupal site.

Let's go ahead and try this out.

Enabling and configuring the OpenID module

To use OpenID, you need to enable the module first. Go to your modules' admin page and enable the OpenID core module. Save your module configuration.

| ☑ | OpenID | 6.18 | Allows users to log into your site using OpenID. |

Once you enable the module, navigate to one of your user accounts. You will notice that there is now an additional tab on your user account page titled OpenID identities. Click on this tab. This will launch the OpenID configuration page for this specific user account. The following message will be shown at the top of the configuration screen as shown below:

This site supports OpenID, a secure way to log into many websites using a single username and password. OpenID can reduce the necessity of managing many usernames and passwords for many websites.

To use OpenID, you must first establish an identity on a public or private OpenID server. If you do not have an OpenID and would like one, look into one of the free public providers. You can find out more about OpenID at the OpenID website at: `http://openid.net/`.

If you already have an OpenID, enter the URL to your OpenID server below (for example, myusername.openidprovider.com). Next time you log in, you will be able to use this URL instead of a regular username and password. You can have multiple OpenID servers if you like.

So, the first thing you'll need to do is establish an OpenID account on one of the listed providers. What I'll do for this example is establish this account with this test user's Gmail account because I know that Google already supports the Open ID framework. So first, let's set up the OpenID server at our provider's location.

Setting up the OpenID server/provider

Let's use Google as our provider for this example. I'm going to set up OpenID for one of my Google Gmail accounts and then use this web service server for my Drupal OpenID authentication. To do this, I'm first going to log in to my Google Gmail account and then browse to my account settings. I'm going to create a Google profile and profile URL if I don't already have one. I can then use this Google profile URL for my authentication method with the OpenID module in Drupal.

To create a profile in Google, first click on the **My Account** link and then look for the **Create a profile** link. Click on that. This will launch the **Google Create your profile** form. Complete the profile form to your liking:

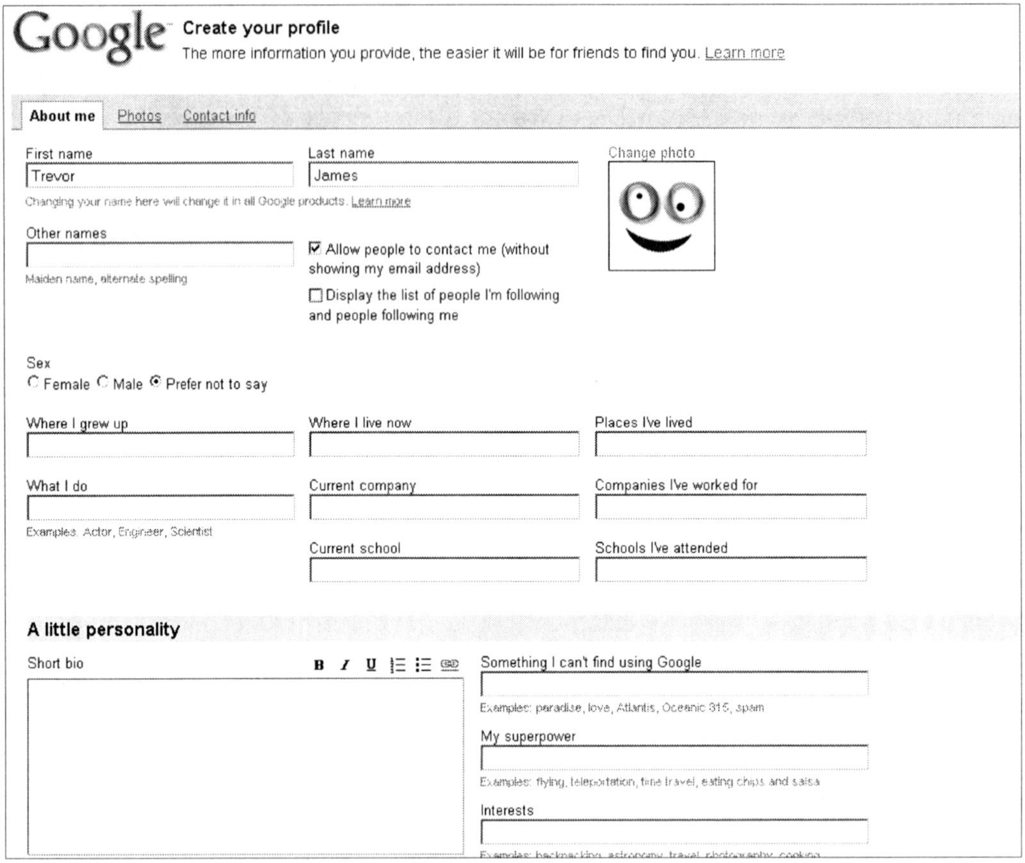

Then, scroll to the bottom of the form and you'll notice that Google will automatically give you a profile URL. This is the most important piece in the configuration because you'll need this profile URL to add to your Drupal OpenID identity on the user account you want to use this profile for. So, make sure to copy this URL now and save it locally. Then, click on the **Create a Google profile** button to create and enable the profile. My Google profile URL is:

```
http://www.google.com/profiles/drupal6performancetips.
```

Once you click on save, Google will launch your profile page at the above URL. You should see something similar to this:

Now, go back to your Drupal site and launch the user account to which you want to add this profile. Edit the OpenID identities for this account, and in the **OpenID** field, paste in the Google profile URL.

Click the **Add an OpenID** button.

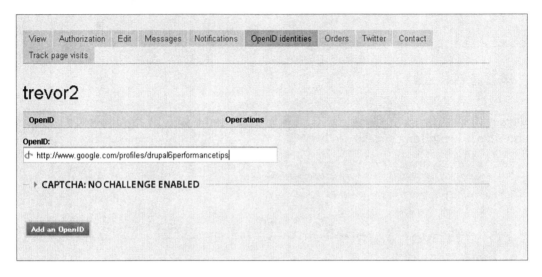

Once you click on the **Add an OpenID** button, your site will try to communicate with the Google profile URL and web service server. You will see a **Google accounts** page launch and ask you to sign in to your profile account and approve the authentication and communication. You should see a screen that looks like this:

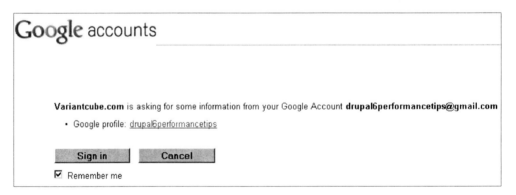

Click on the **Sign in** button and leave the **Remember me** box checked. Once you do this, you will be redirected back to your Drupal site and the following message will appear:

Successfully added http://www.google.com/profiles/drupal6performancetips

You will also see that the profile has been successfully added to the user account in question. Your account screen will look like the following with your saved OpenID profile:

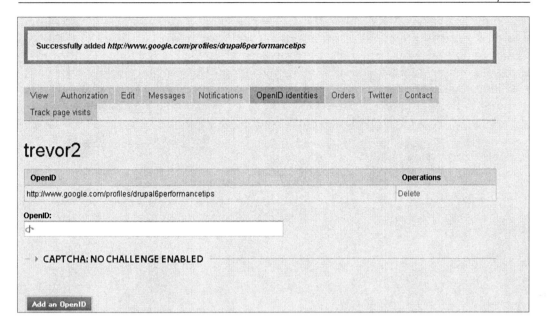

Now you can test the OpenID login for this user account. Log out if you're currently logged in as another admin user. Now, when you launch the user login screen, you should see the **Log in using OpenID** link. You'll want to click on this link to initiate the Open ID authentication process as shown in the following screenshot:

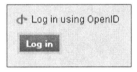

Once you click on this, the Open ID login field will launch. You can now paste in the profile URL. If you are currently logged into your Google account profile, then you should be automatically logged into the Drupal site once you click on the **Log in** button on your Drupal site. Try this first:

The login process will check to make sure you are logged into your Google account and then authenticate back to Drupal and allow the login to occur. You should be logged in and see your Drupal user account screen. If you are not logged into your Google account when you attempt to login via OpenID, you'll get a prompt screen via Google asking you for your Google account credentials. Try it both methods to get used to the login process using OpenID and Google. You'll get a screen similar to this if you're not currently logged into your Google account:

Again, once you log in to your Google account, you'll be automatically redirected back to your Drupal account screen, this time logged in. In addition, if at any time you log out of your Google account, remember that you will not be automatically logged out of your Drupal account because you've already initiated the Drupal account session. So, make sure you log out of Drupal when you complete your account session and work.

Go ahead and try configuring OpenID to work with your Drupal user accounts using a different host provider besides Google. The process should be similar.

OAuth and OAuth Connector

We have already used the OAuth module in *Chapter 9, Twitter and Drupal*, when we looked at the LinkedIn Integration module. LinkedIn Integration uses OAuth as its authentication method. So, you should already have OAuth module installed on your site. If you do not have the module installed, you can download it from its project page at:

```
http://drupal.org/project/oauth.
```

You can also learn more about the OAuth protocol at its main website at:
```
http://oauth.net/.
```

The OAuth module implements OAuth classes on your Drupal site so that you can integrate your Drupal site with other web applications that support the OAuth authentication protocol. The current version of the module is 6.x-3.0-beta2. The OAuth module provides for both web service server functionality and also as a web service consumer functionality. As we saw in the LinkedIn Integration module, the OAuth module allows for our site to act as a content server and to allow node content to be posted to our LinkedIn account which consumes this content.

So, in the case of LinkedIn, the LinkedIn application is a service consumer and allows access to our Drupal site which is acting as the service provider. A user account on our Drupal provider site can take node content and publish it out to the LinkedIn consumer application.

In this section, we're going to hook up our OAuth protocol with additional web services using a new module called OAuth Connector. The OAuth Connector module allows you to sign to third-party applications using your Drupal user account credentials. We've already seen this using the LinkedIn Integration module with that specific application. Now, we're going to enable this module and test the process with other applications including Twitter and Digg.

Using OAuth Connector

First, to confirm our OAuth installation from the previous chapter, I'm checking the modules admin list and making sure that I have enabled the **OAuth**, **OAuth Consumer UI**, and **OAuth Provider UI** modules:

Enabled	Name	Version	Description
✓	OAuth	6.x-3.0-beta2	Provides OAuth functionality Depends on: Autoload (enabled), Input stream helper (enabled), Chaos tools (enabled) Required by: LinkedIn (enabled), OAuth Consumer UI (enabled), OAuth Provider UI (enabled)
✓	OAuth Consumer UI	6.x-3.0-beta2	Provides a UI for when OAuth is acting as a consumer. Depends on: OAuth (enabled), Autoload (enabled), Input stream helper (enabled), Chaos tools (enabled)
✓	OAuth Provider UI	6.x-3.0-beta2	Provides a UI for when OAuth is acting as a provider. Depends on: OAuth (enabled), Autoload (enabled), Input stream helper (enabled), Chaos tools (enabled)

Now, I need to install the OAuth Connector module, the Connector module, and the HTTP Client module. You'll also need to make sure you have installed Chaos Tools. Get the modules from the following project pages:

- Connector: http://drupal.org/project/connector
- OAuth Connector: http://drupal.org/project/oauthconnector
- HTTP Client: http://drupal.org/project/http_client
- Chaos Tools: http://drupal.org/project/ctools

Connector, HTTP Client, and Chaos Tools Suite modules are all required modules for the OAuth Connector module to work. OAuth Connector relies on each of these three additional modules to be installed. Chaos Tools suite is a set of APIs and tools that assist the Drupal developer. The module contains helper utilities that other modules rely on and use. Also, bear in mind here that the Connector and OAuth Connector modules are both in their infancy and development versions. So, you will want to make sure to test these modules out on your development site before implementing them in production.

Go ahead and install and enable all of the above modules. Once installed, enable all of the above modules through your modules admin page. You should enable the following modules: Under **Services - clients** fieldset, enable the **Http Client** and **Http Client OAuth**:

Under the **Connector** fieldset, enable the **Connector** and **OAuth Connector** modules:

Save your module configuration.

Once you have enabled the modules, you can access your OAuth Connector configuration at **Site building | OAuth Connector** or here:

```
/admin/build/oauthconnector.
```

The table will be empty by default. Here, you can add a provider by clicking on the **Add provider** link:

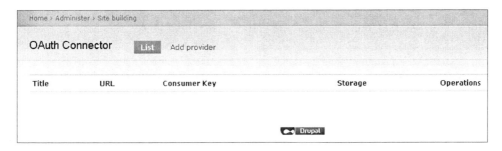

Let's go ahead and click on the **Add provider** link and start to configure our connection.

Configuring a provider connection for Twitter

Once you click on the **Add provider** link, you'll launch the **Add provider** configuration form where you can add your provider application data including any OAuth consumer key and secret ID that the provider gives you to make the connection using OAuth. As an example, we're going to connect to a Twitter application using OAuth. To run the Twitter configuration, we'll need to do two things:

First, we'll need to apply for a Twitter developer account so that we can set up a Twitter application and get OAuth credentials from Twitter as the provider.

Then, we'll also need to configure our Drupal OAuth Connector to recognize and communicate with this Twitter application. The OAuth Connector module developers provide us with some code to get us started with this configuration. If you visit the OAuth Connector module's project page and click on the Example export link, next to the Twitter API example, you will get a page of PHP code that shows you how the connection is made with a Twitter app. The code is available at:

```
http://gist.github.com/545469.
```

I've also added the code here for your reference and it's in the attached code files for the book:

```php
<?php
$provider = new stdClass;
$provider->disabled = FALSE; /* Edit this to true to make a default
provider disabled initially */
$provider->name = 'twitter';
$provider->title = 'Twitter';
$provider->url = 'http://api.twitter.com';
$provider->consumer_advanced = array(
  'signature method' => 'HMAC-SHA1',
  'request token endpoint' => '/oauth/request_token',
```

```
    'authorization endpoint' => '/oauth/authenticate',
    'access token endpoint' => '/oauth/access_token',
);
$provider->mapping = array(
  'fields' => array(
    'uid' => array(
      'resource' => 'http://api.twitter.com/1/account/verify_
credentials.json',
      'method post' => 0,
      'field' => 'id',
    ),
    'real name' => array(
      'resource' => 'http://api.twitter.com/1/account/verify_
credentials.json',
      'method post' => 0,
      'field' => 'name',
    ),
    'avatar' => array(
      'resource' => 'http://api.twitter.com/1/account/verify_
credentials.json',
      'method post' => 0,
      'field' => 'profile_image_url',
    ),
  ),
  'format' => 'json',
);
```

If we examine this code, we'll see that it corresponds to the OAuth Connector frontend configuration page. The application is named twitter and titled Twitter. The base URL for the application is the URL of the OAuth provider, in this case http://api.twitter.com. Then, we see the array for the API fields including the **User ID** fieldset, **Name** fieldset, and **Avatar** fieldset.

We should also notice that the **OAuth Consumer Advanced Settings** includes a Signature method called **HMAC-SHA1**, and that this advanced setting also includes an array with **Request token endpoint**, **Authorization endpoint**, and **Access token endpoint**.

So, we can take this code and insert it into our frontend OAuth Connector **Add provider** form. We should have a form that resembles the following screenshot based on the code we provide:

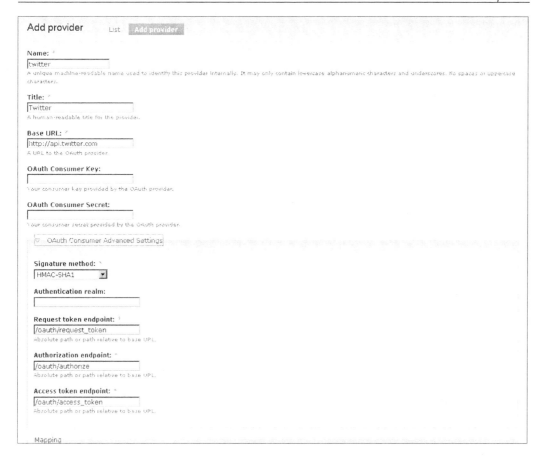

We have not applied for the Twitter developer account yet, so we don't have our Twitter OAuth Consumer key or Consumer Secret yet, but we can fill out the other information here.

In the Mapping section of our OAuth Connector configuration page, we can add the Resource URLs from the code to our **User ID Resource** field, **Name Resource** field, and **Avatar Resource** field. The field names for all of these respectively are: id; name; profile_image_url.

The method we're using is a POST request and we're using the JSON format for all three:

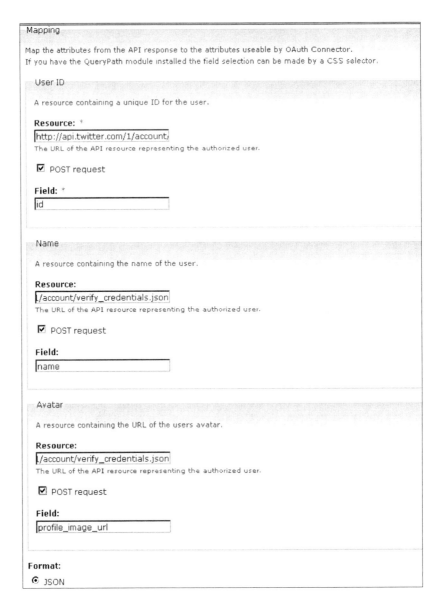

Once you have added this data, go ahead and click the **Save and proceed** button. When you save, you'll get redirected to your OAuth Connector list page and you'll see your new provider in the table. You'll receive the following message:

Your new provider Twitter has been saved.

You'll also see a warning that tells you that the **Consumer Key** is **Missing** and provides a link to **Add** one:

That's what we'll do next.

Setting up the Twitter developer application account

In order to complete the OAuth Connector configuration and ultimately test our Drupal account login and access with our Twitter application, we first need to configure an application and developer account via our Twitter account. So, first log in to Twitter and once logged into your Twitter account, click on the **Settings** link in the top right header menu area. Then, once your settings configuration loads, click on the **Connections** link in the top menu bar:

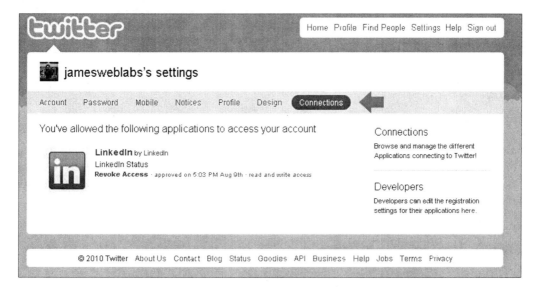

You'll notice the Developers right side bar block and info. Click on the link in that block to set up the application. That will launch a screen that will look like this:

Now, click on the **Register a new application** link. This will launch the application form. Go ahead and complete the form with the pertinent data. Your application home page can be the root home page of your Drupal site or a specific node on your site. Keep the application type selected to the Browser type. This will use a Callback URL to return to your application after successfully authenticated to Twitter. Type in the Callback URL. This can be the same URL as your application URL. Leave the Default Access Type set to Read-only, and check the Twitter login box if you want to set up your application so it uses your Twitter account for log in and authentication purposes before logging into your Drupal site. If you want to log in directly to your Twitter application using your Drupal account, you can leave this box unchecked.

Register an Application

Application Icon:

	Browse...

Maximum size of 700k. JPG, GIF, PNG.

Application Name: Firehouses

Description:
```
This is a test application to
integrate with my Drupal Web site.
```

Application Website: http://variantcube.com/firehouses

Where's your application's home page, where users can go to download or use it?

Organization:

Website: http://variantcube.com

The home page of your company or organization.

Application Type: ○ Client ● Browser

Does your application run in a Web Browser or a Desktop Client?

- Browser uses a Callback URL to return to your App after successfully authentication.
- Client prompts your user to return to your application after approving access.

Callback URL: http://variantcube.com/firehouses

Where should we return to after successfully authentication?

Fill out the CAPTCHA and then click the **SAVE** button. Once you click the SAVE button you'll be redirected to an applications details page where you'll see your **Consumer key, Consumer secret, Request token URL, Access token URL,** and **Authorize URL**. You'll need all five of these settings for your OAuth Connector configuration so make sure to print out this page and then go back to your OAuth Connector page on your Drupal site.

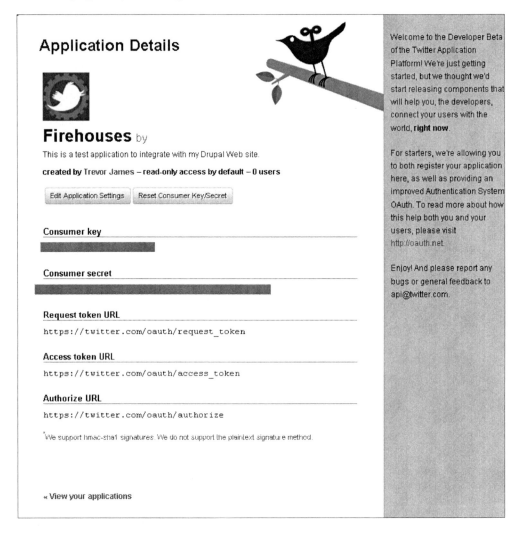

Notice here that the token URLs match the `consumer_advanced` array token paths in your Drupal OAuth Connector code. Your Authorization URL should also match your Drupal Authorization endpoint.

Open up your OAuth Connector configuration page in Drupal and then click on the Add link under the Consumer Key heading in the table. Copy your consumer key and secret code into the fields in your configuration settings.

Save your OAuth configuration once more and you should receive a successful updated table page with your Consumer key listed. Congratulations! You have completed the authorization configuration for OAuth Connector with your Twitter application. Now, it's time to test the connection.

Summary

In this chapter, we looked in detail at setting up a number of authentication protocols to work with our Drupal web services. We enabled the OpenID module and tested this integration with our Google Account so that when we log in to Drupal, we can use our Google credentials.

We also learned how to set up a Twitter application and use this application to integrate with our Drupal site using the OAuth connector and connector contributed modules. We then tested this connection. You now know how to set up various authentication protocols to work with your Drupal site and to make it easier for your site's users to access and log in to your Drupal website and their corresponding web service applications.

Here's a brief summary of what we accomplished:

- Enabled the OpenID module and configured it on our user accounts
- Set up OpenID to interface with our Google account
- Installed and configured the OAuth Connector and Connector modules
- Set up a Twitter application environment
- Connected our Drupal site with our Twitter application using the OAuth Connector module

A
Modules Used in the Book

In this appendix, we're going to summarize the contributed modules we've used in the book and present a listing of modules that allow for integration between Drupal and web service applications and servers. This chapter will present a concise and organized listing of modules that access remote servers and services, and that integrate and install with the Drupal content management framework. This chapter will serve as a cheat sheet and summary for you to use during your Drupal-based projects. All modules used in the book are listed and summarized here.

For more information about using Drupal modules, you can visit the main drupal. org Modules repository at: http://drupal.org/project/Modules. Modules are listed by popularity, category, and compatibility. There is a search box that allows you to search for specific modules by keyword and also a sort filter that allows you to search by relevance, most installed, author, and more. Here, you will find modules listed with a summary of what the module does, and a table showing the versions, date of last update, status, and links to download the module. There is also a link provided that points you to a full index of all Drupal modules available at: http://drupal.org/project/modules/index. This index lists all 6,000+ modules in alphabetical order.

Another good Drupal module resource is Drupal Modules at drupalmodules.com. This site is an open source community-driven project that lists, rates, and reviews all Drupal modules. This site allows you to search for modules and restrict your search to Drupal versions. It highlights new modules and contains a blog that posts interesting modules, related news, and case studies. It presents links to the highest rated and most downloaded modules. For example, in September 2010, the most downloaded module according to Drupal Modules was the Administration menu module, closely followed by CCK. If we do a search on Drupal Modules for the Twitter module, we get a page that shows the detailed ratings for the module, a module overview, and download links.

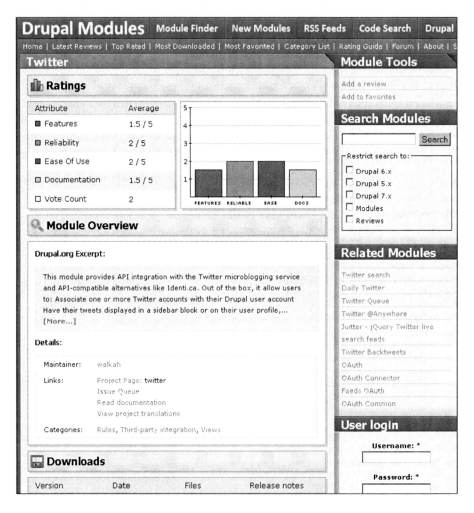

I'm also including a link to the usage statistics page for each module via Drupal.org. Usage statistics show how often the module is being used on a weekly basis. You can see the number of downloads for the module in both the 5.x and 6.x versions for each week since the module was released and also stats on the usage per module release version. This is interesting data in that it shows that the majority of modules are seeing steady growth in usage and downloads over time. Here's an example of what a usage statistics graph for the Amazon module looks like:

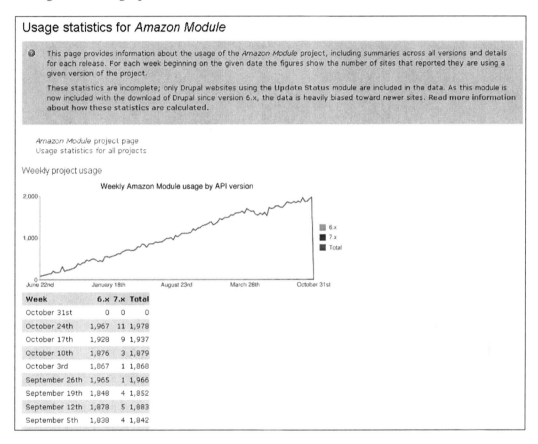

To summarize, in this chapter we will:

- List and summarize all the modules used in the book
- Provide a brief summary of the module and why we used it
- Provide module project page links and downloads for each module used

Modules used in Chapter 1

In *Chapter 1, About Drupal Web Services,* we introduced web services and explored the various web service frameworks and protocols including XML, RSS, SOAP, and REST. We introduced various contributed modules that allow for integration of popular web service applications with Drupal. Where applicable, I've noted the project page, maintainers, usage statistics, Drupal Modules page, and current version. All versions are production site ready unless otherwise noted.

CCK

To run many of the modules and follow along with all of the examples in this book, you definitely need to install the CCK (Content Construction Kit) module on your Drupal site. CCK, simply put, allows you to create your own content types and add custom data fields to these content types. This module extends and expands the default core Drupal content types of Page, Story, and Blog. With CCK, you can create and customize content types to work with all of the web service modules that we use in the book.

- Project page and URL: `http://drupal.org/project/cck`
- Maintainers: KarentS, markus_petrux, fago, yched
- Usage statistics: `http://drupal.org/project/usage/cck`
- Drupal modules page: `http://drupalmodules.com/module/content-construction-kit-cck`
- Current version: 6.x-2.8

Mollom

Mollom is a web service that provides spam prevention and spam blocking. The service is smart in that it responds and learns dynamically from the types of spam that are being submitted and generated to your Drupal website. Drupal integrates with the Mollom web service using the contributed Mollom module. The Mollom web service was developed and designed originally by Dries Buytaert, Drupal's founder. Mollom provides various spam prevention functionality including its own CAPTCHAs. It allows for blocking comment spam, contact form spam, and can protect the user registration process by using CAPTCHA elements.

- Project page and URL: `http://drupal.org/project/mollom`
- Maintainers: sun, Dries Buytaert, Dave Reid
- Usage statistics: `http://drupal.org/project/usage/mollom`
- Drupal modules page: `http://drupalmodules.com/module/mollom`
- Current version: 6.x-1.13

Auto Tagging

The Auto Tagging module allows for integration of your Drupal's taxonomy and tag vocabs with popular tagging web services including OpenCalais, Yahoo! Terms Extraction, and tagthe.net. We installed this module and then signed up for an API key account on the OpenCalais web application. We integrated the module and our Drupal site with the OpenCalais tagging framework.

- Project page and URL: `http://drupal.org/project/autotagging`
- OpenCalais application URL: `http://www.opencalais.com/APIkey`
- Maintainers: acstewart
- Usage statistics: `http://drupal.org/project/usage/autotagging`
- Drupal modules page: `http://drupalmodules.com/module/auto-tagging`
- Current version: 6.x-1.4-beta3

AMFPHP

The AMFPHP module integrates with the Drupal Services module to provide support and integration for the AMFPHP protocol and format with Drupal sites. This can allow for the integration of Flash, FLEX, and Air Web client applications to interact with Drupal's PHP backend and Services. You'll need to install the Drupal Services module to integrate the AMFPHP module.

- Project page and URL: `http://drupal.org/project/amfphp`
- Maintainers: snelson
- Usage statistics: `http://drupal.org/project/usage/amfphp`
- Drupal modules page: `http://drupalmodules.com/module/amfphp`
- Current version: 6.x-1.0-beta2
- Requirements: Services module and AMFPHP 1.9 beta 2

Modules used in Chapter 2

In *Chapter 2, Consuming Web Services in Drupal*, we looked at how Drupal sites can act as web services consumers. A Drupal site can connect to a web service application using a contributed module and then consume content from that externally hosted web application and service. We explored the SOAP protocol that allows this integration to occur. For an example of this functionality, we installed the FedEx API module with an installation of Ubercart. We connected to the FedEx web service to return real time shipping quotes to our Drupal site The FedEx API module allows for this integration with the FedEx web service.

SOAP Client

The SOAP Client module is required by Drupal to integrate your Drupal site with the PHP SOAP client and server extensions. First, you need to enable these PHP extensions and then install the SOAP Client module. This module allows your Drupal site to communicate with the PHP 5.x SOAP or nuSOAP extensions.

- Project page and URL: `http://drupal.org/project/soapclient`
- Maintainers: ilo, ebizondrupalservices, BoogieBug
- Usage statistics: `http://drupal.org/project/usage/soapclient`
- Drupal modules page: `http://drupalmodules.com/module/soap-client`
- Current version: 6.x-1.0-beta2
- Requirements: the PHP 5.x SOAP extensions or nuSOAP extensions need to be installed and enabled on your server

FedEx web services

FedEx provides a web service API that you can use to integrate with your Drupal and Ubercart site. You need to sign up for a FedEx API service account at the following URL: `http://fedex.com/us/developer/`.

FedEx shipping quotes for Ubercart

In order to get real time shipping quotes from FedEx, we need to install and integrate the FedEx Shipping quote module. This module gets installed into our Ubercart module folder and then enabled in Drupal. The module communicates with our FedEx developer API account to return real time shipping quotes, both domestic and international, in response to our site shopper's shipping information that they add to the Ubercart checkout form.

- Project page and URL: `http://drupal.org/project/uc_fedex`
- Maintainers: TR
- Usage statistics: `http://drupal.org/project/usage/uc_fedex`
- Drupal modules page: `http://drupalmodules.com/module/fedex-shipping-quotes-for-ubercart`
- Current version: 6.x-2.0
- Requirements: Ubercart and Token modules

Ubercart

We need to install the Ubercart module and configure an online shopping cart in order to use the FedEx Shipping Quotes module.

- Project page and URL: http://drupal.org/project/ubercart
- Maintainers: Island Usurper, TR, rszrama
- Usage statistics: http://drupal.org/project/usage/ubercart
- Drupal modules page: http://drupalmodules.com/module/ubercart-conditional-actions-sms-integration
- Current version: 6.x-2.4
- Requirements: Token

Token

The Token module is required by both the Ubercart and the FedEx Shipping Quotes modules.

- Project page and URL: http://drupal.org/project/token
- Maintainers: Dave Reid, greggles, fago, eaton
- Usage statistics: http://drupal.org/project/usage/token
- Drupal modules page: http://drupalmodules.com/module/token
- Current version: 6.x-1.14

Modules used in Chapter 3

In *Chapter 3, Drupal and Flickr*, we continued our discussion of Drupal's interaction and integration with external web services and applications. We looked in detail at how Drupal consumes web data from these external hosts. Here, we turned our attention to using the Flickr modules to enable integration with the popular photo-sharing web application Flickr.

Flickr account and API key

To follow along with examples in *Chapter 3, Drupal and Flickr*, it's a good idea to set up a Flickr account and create some galleries and sets that you can work with. You can sign up for a Flickr account at: http://flickr.com/

You will also need to sign up for a Flickr API key and developer account at:

http://flickr.com/services/api/

Flickr module

We installed and enabled the Flickr module so we can integrate our Flickr photo galleries with our Drupal site. The Flickr suite of modules includes Flickr Block, Flickr Filter, Flickr Sets, and Flickr Tags.

- Project page and URL: `http://drupal.org/project/flickr`
- Maintainers: paulbooker, ksenzee, KarenS, drewish
- Usage statistics: `http://drupal.org/project/usage/flickr`
- Drupal modules page: `http://drupalmodules.com/module/flickr`
- Current version: 6.x-1.2

idGettr

This tool allows us to get the Flickr ID # of a user's photostream or Group pool if it's publicly available.

- idGettr application page: `http://idgettr.com/`

Modules used in Chapter 4

In *Chapter 4, Drupal and Amazon*, we integrated our Drupal site with Amazon's web service API by installing and enabling the Amazon module suite.

Amazon web service and API key

To integrate your Drupal site with the Amazon Web Services, we first need to sign up for an Amazon API key and web service account at:

`http://aws.amazon.com/`

Amazon module

The Amazon module includes the following suite of sub-modules: Amazon API, Amazon Examples, Amazon Field, Amazon Filter, Amazon legacy importer, Amazon media, and Amazon Search.

- Project page and URL: `http://drupal.org/project/amazon`
- Maintainers: rfay, eaton
- Usage statistics: `http://drupal.org/project/usage/amazon`

- Drupal modules page: http://drupalmodules.com/module/amazon-module
- Current version: 6.x-1.1
- Requirements: Amazon Examples module requires the Drupal Features module

Features

This is a helper module for Drupal that is required if you want to enable and use the Amazon Examples module of the Amazon module suite.

- Project page and URL: http://drupal.org/project/features
- Maintainers: yhahn, jmiccolis, Adrian
- Usage statistics: http://drupal.org/project/usage/features
- Drupal modules page: http://drupalmodules.com/module/features
- Current version: 6.x-1.0

Views

To use the Amazon Examples module and develop dynamic lists of Amazon products displayed in table or grid format on your site, you'll want to install and enable the Drupal Views module.

- Project page and URL: http://drupal.org/project/views
- Maintainers: dereine, merlinofchaos, chx, dww
- Usage statistics: http://drupal.org/project/usage/views
- Drupal modules page: http://drupalmodules.com/module/views
- Current version: 6.x-2.11

Amazon store module

This module extends the functionality of the Amazon module, allowing you to integrate a full Amazon marketplace of products and a shopping cart into your Drupal site. Site visitors can then add Amazon products to their shopping cart on your Drupal site and purchase them via their Amazon account.

- Project page and URL: http://drupal.org/project/amazon_store
- Maintainers: rfay
- Usage statistics: http://drupal.org/project/usage/amazon_store

- Drupal modules page: `http://drupalmodules.com/module/amazon-store`
- Current version: 6.x-2.1-rc2
- Requirements: Amazon module, PHP 5.2+

Modules used in Chapter 5

In *Chapter 5, Drupal and Multimedia Web Services,* we continued our discussion of how Drupal interacts and integrates with external web services and applications, and consumes web data from these external hosts. Here, we turn our attention to using multimedia-based web services and modules, including modules that integrate video-based web services including CDN2, Kaltura, and the Media: Flickr module. These modules allow our site users to upload video and host the uploaded video via the web service server, and also to add more multimedia and dynamic components to our Flickr module, allowing us to map entire photosets into our Drupal site and present our site visitors with interactive Flickr-based slideshows and videos.

CDN2 web service

The CDN2 web service is available here. You need to sign up for an account before you integrate and use the CDN2 video module: `http://www.workhabit.com/products/cdn2`. WorkHabit also provides documentation on how to use the CDN2 web service at: `http://www.workhabit.com/products/cdn2/guide`. To use CDN2, you need to make sure you are using PHP 5.2+ and that you have the SOAP extension enabled. You also need the Drupal CCK module installed and enabled as well as various PEAR libraries mentioned in detail in *Chapter 4, Drupal and Amazon.*

CDN2 video module

The CDN2 module allows for integration with your CDN2 web service account. The CDN2 suite of modules comes with CDN2 Dash Player and Flowplayer integrations and the main CDN2 video module.

- Project page and URL: `http://drupal.org/project/cdn2`
- Maintainers: kylebrowing, acstewart, akalsey
- Usage statistics: `http://drupal.org/project/usage/cdn2`
- Drupal modules page: `http://drupalmodules.com/module/cdn2-video`
- Current version: 6.x-1.10

Kaltura web service

The Kaltura open source video web service and application allows you to purchase hosting space on Kaltura's servers to upload and stream your video and multimedia and then present this video via your Drupal site using the Kaltura module. You can learn more about and sign up for the Kaltura web service at: `http://corp.kaltura.com/`.

Kaltura module

The Kaltura module allows for integration of the Kaltura web service with your Drupal site and also enables you to integrate your video with Drupal modules including CCK and Views. The suite of Kaltura modules includes: Kaltura as CCK Field, Kaltura Media Comments, Kaltura Media Node, Kaltura Media Remix Node, and Kaltura Media Views.

- Project page and URL: `http://drupal.org/project/kaltura`
- Maintainers: grobot, univate
- Usage statistics: `http://drupal.org/project/usage/kaltura`
- Drupal modules page: `http://drupalmodules.com/module/kaltura`
- Current version: 6.x-1.5

Media: Flickr

This module allows us to map our Flickr photosets into an embedded media field in a CCK-powered custom field. So, you'll need both the CCK and the Embedded Media Field modules to use this module.

- Project page and URL: `http://drupal.org/project/media_flickr`
- Maintainers: aaron
- Usage statistics: `http://drupal.org/project/usage/media_flickr`
- Drupal modules page: `http://drupalmodules.com/module/media-flickr`
- Current version: 6.x-1.11

Embedded media field

This module adds a custom media field to support audio and video content to your custom content types using CCK. This module supports images, audio, and video and offers the following support in its suite of modules: image field, video field, audio field, media thumbnail, inline media, and media import. You need this module in order to integrate the Media: Flickr functionality.

- Project page and URL: http://drupal.org/project/emfield
- Maintainers: aaron, Alex UA, Rob Loach, kleinmp
- Usage statistics: http://drupal.org/project/usage/emfield
- Drupal modules page: http://drupalmodules.com/module/embedded-media-field
- Current version: 6.x-1.24

Modules used in Chapter 6

In *Chapter 6, Drupal Web Services the Easy Way: The Services Module*, we looked in detail at using the Drupal Services module suite. The module provides a standardized API method of integrating multiple external web services and applications with internal modules to your Drupal site. This includes integration with the following web server applications and protocols: JSON server, JSONRPC server, REST and SOAP servers, and AMFPHP.

Services module

- Project page and URL: http://drupal.org/project/services
- Maintainers: heyrocker, skyredwang, marcingy, Hugo Wetterberg
- Usage statistics: http://drupal.org/project/usage/services
- Drupal modules page: http://drupalmodules.com/module/services
- Current version: 6.x-2.2

Modules used in Chapter 7

In *Chapter 7, Drupal, Spam, and Web Services*, we looked in detail at using contributed modules that help to prevent and block spam submissions to your Drupal site. This included examples using the CAPTCHA and reCAPTCHA modules; the Antispam module; and a return to our earlier discussion in *Chapter 1, About Drupal Web Services* of using the Mollom spam service and module.

CAPTCHA

This module adds a CAPTCHA field to your Drupal forms including the contact form, user registration process, and your custom content types to help prevent spam submissions from machine-based visitors to your Drupal site.

- Project page and URL: http://drupal.org/project/captcha
- Maintainers: soxofaan, Rob Loach, wundo
- Usage statistics: http://drupal.org/project/usage/captcha
- Drupal modules page: http://drupalmodules.com/module/captcha
- Current version: 6.x-2.2

reCAPTCHA

The reCAPTCHA module extends the functionality of the CAPTCHA module by providing an integration of your Drupal site with the reCAPTCHA web service. To use this module, you'll need to sign up for an API key and account at the reCAPTCHA service application at: https://www.google.com/recaptcha/admin/create.

- Project page and URL: http://drupal.org/project/recaptcha
- Maintainers: Rob Loach, kthagen
- Usage statistics: http://drupal.org/project/usage/recaptcha
- Drupal modules page: http://drupal.org/project/usage/recaptcha
- Current version: 6.x-1.4

AntiSpam

The AntiSpam module allows for integration with multiple spam prevention web services including Akismet, TypePad, and Defensio. All three of these web service applications are accessible here:

- Akismet: http://akismet.com
- TypePad AntiSpam: http://antispam.typepad.com
- Defensio: http://defensio.com
- Project page and URL: http://drupal.org/project/antispam
- Maintainers: pixture
- Usage statistics: http://drupal.org/project/usage/antispam

- Drupal modules page: `http://drupalmodules.com/module/antispam`
- Current version: 6.x-1.2

We looked at the Mollom module and its project page and information in the *Modules used in Chapter 1* section of this appendix.

Modules used in Chapter 8

In *Chapter 8, Using XML-RPC*, we explored how Drupal uses the XML-RPC protocol for integrating XML-RPC-based web services with Drupal. This included examples of taking a Google Document and integrating that document to your Drupal site as a node. We also looked at how to set up an auto-sync of content between two Drupal sites using the Deployment module with the Services module.

BlogAPI module

The BlogAPI module is a core module that ships with Drupal 6. We need this module in order to integrate with our Google Docs account. It does not come enabled by default, so you need to enable it in your modules admin page:

- Drupal modules page: `http://drupalmodules.com/module/blog-api`

Google Documents

You need to sign up for a Google account in order to use Google Documents at: `https://www.google.com/accounts`.

Deployment module

The Deployment module is a module under active development that allows for site managers to deploy content from a staging or development version of their website over to the production version of their site. So, it allows you to move and migrate Drupal nodes automatically from one Drupal site to another across one server or from one to another Drupal server.

- Project page and URL: `http://drupal.org/project/deploy`
- Maintainers: dixon, heyrocker
- Usage statistics: `http://drupal.org/project/usage/deploy`
- Drupal modules page: `http://drupalmodules.com/module/deployment`
- Current development version: 6.x-1.x-dev

This module relies on the Services module to be installed and enabled and specifically the Key Authentication and XMLRPC Server modules that come shipped with the Services module suite. The Deployment module comes with the following suite of submodules that will need to be enabled: Deploy Comments, Deploy Content Type, Deploy Dates, Deploy Files, Deploy Nodereferences, Deploy System settings, Deploy Userreferences, Deployment, Node Deployment, and more.

Modules used in Chapter 9

In *Chapter 9, Twitter and Drupal*, we integrated the popular social networking application Twitter with our Drupal site using multiple contributed modules. This allows us to post our Drupal nodes and content out to Twitter using our Drupal site as a web service; and also taking our Twitter content and automatically consuming that content into our Drupal site.

To follow along with the examples in this chapter, you need to sign up for a Twitter account at: `http://twitter.com/`.

Twitter module

- Project page and URL: `http://drupal.org/project/twitter`
- Maintainers: eaton, walkah
- Usage statistics: `http://drupal.org/project/usage/twitter`
- Drupal modules page: `http://drupalmodules.com/module/twitter`
- Current version: 6.x-2.6

Tweet

The Tweet module also allows for posting Drupal content to your Twitter account.

- Project page and URL: `http://drupal.org/project/tweet`
- Maintainers: IceCreamYou
- Usage statistics: `http://drupal.org/project/usage/tweet`
- Drupal modules page: `http://drupalmodules.com/module/tweet`
- Current version: 6.x-4.0

In order to use shortened URLs with the Tweet module and format your URLs specifically to your liking, you'll also want to install and enable the Shorten URLs and Short URL modules.

Shorten URLs

- Project page and URL: http://drupal.org/project/shorten
- Maintainers: IceCreamYou
- Usage statistics: http://drupal.org/project/usage/shorten
- Drupal modules page: http://drupalmodules.com/module/shorten-urls
- Current version: 6.x-1.9

Short URL

- Project page and URL: http://drupal.org/project/shorturl
- Maintainers: irakli
- Usage statistics: http://drupal.org/project/usage/shorturl
- Drupal modules page: http://drupalmodules.com/module/short-url
- Current version: 6.x-1.2

Modules used in Chapter 10

In *Chapter 10, LinkedIn and Drupal,* we integrated the popular career and professional-based social networking application LinkedIn with our Drupal site using multiple contributed modules. This allows us to post our Drupal nodes and content out to our LinkedIn profile page as status posts and also to integrate our LinkedIn content with our Drupal site.

LinkedIn integration with Drupal relies on OAuth authentication and so you need to install and enable the OAuth suite of modules to make this integration work. You will also need to sign up for a LinkedIn account at: http://www.linkedin.com/.

OAuth module

- Project page and URL: http://drupal.org/project/oauth
- Maintainers: voxpelli, Hugo Wetterberg
- Usage statistics: http://drupal.org/project/usage/oauth
- Drupal modules page: http://drupalmodules.com/module/oauth
- Current version: 6.x-3.0-beta2
- Requirements: Autoload and Inputstream

Autoload

- Project page and URL: http://drupal.org/project/autoload
- Maintainers: Crell
- Usage statistics: http://drupal.org/project/usage/autoload
- Drupal modules page: http://drupalmodules.com/module/autoload
- Current version: 6.x-1.4

Input Stream

- Project page and URL: http://drupal.org/project/inputstream
- Maintainers: Hugo Wetterberg
- Usage statistics: http://drupal.org/project/usage/inputstream
- Drupal modules page: http://drupalmodules.com/module/input-stream
- Current version: 6.x-1.0

LinkedIn Integration

- Project page and URL: http://drupal.org/project/linkedin
- Maintainers: bellesmanieres, greg.harvey
- Usage statistics: http://drupal.org/project/usage/linkedin
- Drupal modules page: http://drupalmodules.com/search/node/linkedin
- Current development version: 6.x-1.x-dev

To use the LinkedIn Integration module, you will need to sign up for a LinkedIn Developer network account at: https://www.linkedin.com/secure/developer.

Modules used in Chapter 11

In *Chapter 11, Facebook and Drupal*, we integrated the popular social networking application Facebook with our Drupal site using multiple contributed modules. This allows us to post our Drupal nodes and content out to our Facebook profile page as status posts and also to integrate our Facebook content with our Drupal site. The Drupal for Facebook suite of modules enables you as a Drupal developer also to write applications for integration with Facebook. You can also integrate your Facebook users and user account credentials with your Drupal account system and user base.

Drupal for Facebook

The Drupal for Facebook suite of modules provides you as a Drupal developer with methods for writing custom applications for integration of Facebook with Drupal.

- Project Page and URL: `http://drupal.org/project/fb`
- Maintainers: Dave Cohen
- Usage statistics: `http://drupal.org/project/usage/fb`
- Drupal modules page: `http://drupalmodules.com/module/drupal-for-facebook`
- Current version: 6.x-2.0-rc2

This suite of modules includes: Canvas Pages, Drupal for Facebook, Drupal for Facebook Devel, User Management, Drupal for Facebook Applications, Extended Permissions, Friend Features, Register Users, Drupal for Facebook Forms, Streams, and Views.

Facebook Connect

The Facebook Connect module allows your site's users to log in to your Drupal site using their Facebook login credentials. This happens by connecting your Drupal site using this module with the Facebook API.

- Project page and URL: `http://drupal.org/project/fbconnect`
- Maintainers: vectoroc, LaNets, budda
- Usage statistics: `http://drupal.org/project/usage/fbconnect`
- Drupal modules page: `http://drupalmodules.com/module/facebook-connect`
- Current version: 6.x-2.0-alpha2

Facebook—Auth

- Project page and URL: `http://drupal.org/project/facebook_auth`
- Maintainers: halkeye
- Usage statistics: `http://drupal.org/project/usage/facebook_auth`
- Drupal modules page: `http://drupalmodules.com/module/facebook-auth`
- Current version: 6.x-1.1

Modules used in Chapter 12

In *Chapter 12, Authentication services,* we looked in detail at various Drupal web service authentication processes and protocols. Modules explored in this chapter included OAuth (previously installed and used in this book) as well as other authentication modules including the following:

Google Apps authentication

- Project page and URL: `http://drupal.org/project/googleauth`

- Maintainers: ssnider

- Usage statistics: `http://drupal.org/project/usage/googleauth`

- Drupal modules page: `http://drupalmodules.com/module/google-apps-authentication`

- Current version: the module is available in production status for Drupal 5.x sites but does have a patch to allow it to work with Drupal 6 at: `http://drupal.org/node/250260`.

Summary

In this appendix, we reviewed all of the core and contributed modules we have used throughout the book that allow for integration and functionality with various web services and external applications including Flickr, Amazon, Mollom, LinkedIn, Facebook, and Twitter.

Index

Symbols

--enable-soap 27
<m:GetShippingQuote> 26
<soapenv-Envelope> tags 46
<SOAP-ENV:Envelope> tags 45

A

Access Key ID 73
Active SOAP Library section 29
Add to Cart buttons 87
Akismet web service module 150
Amazon
    accessing 72
    Amazon Web Services (AWS) account,
        signing up for 73
    configuration, testing 76-78
    module, installing 74
    modules, enabling 75
Amazon API 74
Amazon API account
    signing up for 72
Amazon associate tools module
    URL 72
Amazon content type
    using, with views 80
Amazon Example content type
    testing 78
Amazon Examples 74
Amazon field 74
Amazon filter
    using 83, 84
Amazon Filter 74
Amazon input filter
    testing 84

Amazon legacy importer 74
Amazon media 74
Amazon module
    about 72, 273, 278
    Amazon API 74
    Amazon API keys 76
    Amazon content type with views,
        using 80-82
    Amazon Example content type, testing 78
    Amazon Examples 74
    Amazon field 74
    Amazon Filter 74
    Amazon filters, using 83, 84
    Amazon input filter, testing 84
    Amazon legacy importer 74
    Amazon media 74
    usage statistic graph 273
    Amazon search 74
    enabling 75
    URL, for downloading 72
    URL, for installing 72
    using 78
Amazon search 74
Amazon Standard Identification Number
    (ASIN) 73
Amazon Store module
    about 85, 279
    configuring 87, 88
    installing 85
    testing 90
    using 85-87
Amazon Web Services (AWS)
    about 71
    account, signing up for 73
AMFPHP
    about 20

F

Thank you for buying
Drupal Web Services

About Packt Publishing

Packt, pronounced 'packed', published its first book "*Mastering phpMyAdmin for Effective MySQL Management*" in April 2004 and subsequently continued to specialize in publishing highly focused books on specific technologies and solutions.

Our books and publications share the experiences of your fellow IT professionals in adapting and customizing today's systems, applications, and frameworks. Our solution based books give you the knowledge and power to customize the software and technologies you're using to get the job done. Packt books are more specific and less general than the IT books you have seen in the past. Our unique business model allows us to bring you more focused information, giving you more of what you need to know, and less of what you don't.

Packt is a modern, yet unique publishing company, which focuses on producing quality, cutting-edge books for communities of developers, administrators, and newbies alike. For more information, please visit our website: www.packtpub.com.

About Packt Open Source

In 2010, Packt launched two new brands, Packt Open Source and Packt Enterprise, in order to continue its focus on specialization. This book is part of the Packt Open Source brand, home to books published on software built around Open Source licences, and offering information to anybody from advanced developers to budding web designers. The Open Source brand also runs Packt's Open Source Royalty Scheme, by which Packt gives a royalty to each Open Source project about whose software a book is sold.

Writing for Packt

We welcome all inquiries from people who are interested in authoring. Book proposals should be sent to author@packtpub.com. If your book idea is still at an early stage and you would like to discuss it first before writing a formal book proposal, contact us; one of our commissioning editors will get in touch with you.

We're not just looking for published authors; if you have strong technical skills but no writing experience, our experienced editors can help you develop a writing career, or simply get some additional reward for your expertise.

Drupal e-commerce with
Ubercart 2.x

Build, administer, and customize an online store using Drupal
with Ubercart

George Papadongonas   Ylannis Doxaras   [PACKT]

Drupal E-commerce with Ubercart 2.x

ISBN: 978-1-847199-20-1   Paperback: 364 pages

Build, administer, and customize an online store
using Drupal with Ubercart

1. Create a powerful e-shop using the
   award-winning CMS Drupal and the
   robust e-commerce module Ubercart

2. Create and manage the product catalog and
   insert products in manual or batch mode

3. Apply SEO (search engine optimization)
   to your e-shop and adopt turn-key internet
   marketing techniques

Drupal 6
Social Networking

Build a social or community web site with friends lists, groups,
custom user profiles, and much more

Michael Peacock   [PACKT]

Drupal 6 Social Networking

ISBN: 978-1-847196-10-1   Paperback: 312 pages

Build a social or community web site, with friends
lists, groups, custom user profiles, and much more

1. Step-by-step instructions for putting together a
   social networking site with Drupal 6

2. Customize your Drupal installation with
   modules and themes to match the needs of
   almost any social networking site

3. Allow users to collaborate and interact with
   each other on your site

Please check **www.PacktPub.com** for information on our titles

Drupal 6 Performance Tips

ISBN: 978-1-847195-84-5   Paperback: 240 pages

Learn how to maximize and optimize your Drupal framework using Drupal 6 best practice performance solutions and tools

1. Monitor the performance of your Drupal website and improve it

2. Configure a Drupal multisite environment for best performance

3. Lot of examples with clear explanations

4. Choose and use the best Drupal modules for improving your site's performance

Drupal 6 Site Builder Solutions

ISBN: 978-1-847196-40-8   Paperback: 352 pages

Build powerful website features for your business and connect to your customers through blogs, product catalogs, newsletters, and maps

1. Implement the essential features of a business or non-profit website using Drupal

2. Integrate with other "web 2.0" sites such as Google Maps, Digg, Flickr, and YouTube to drive traffic, build a community, and increase your website's effectiveness

3. No website development knowledge required

Please check **www.PacktPub.com** for information on our titles

Drupal 6 JavaScript and jQuery

ISBN: 978-1-847196-16-3   Paperback: 340 pages

Putting jQuery, AJAX, and JavaScript effects into your Drupal 6 modules and themes

1. Learn about JavaScript support in Drupal 6

2. Packed with example code ready for you to use

3. Harness the popular jQuery library to enhance your Drupal sites

4. Make the most of Drupal's built-in JavaScript libraries

Drupal 6 Search Engine Optimization

ISBN: 978-1-847198-22-8   Paperback: 280 pages

Rank high in search engines with professional SEO tips, modules, and best practices for Drupal web sites

1. Concise, actionable steps for increasing traffic to your Drupal site

2. Learn which modules to install and how to configure them for maximum SEO results

3. Create search engine friendly and optimized title tags, paths, sitemaps, headings, navigation, and more

Please check **www.PacktPub.com** for information on our titles

Drupal 6 Panels Cookbook

ISBN: 978-1-849511-18-6   Paperback: 220 pages

Over 40 recipes to harness the power of Panels for building attractive Drupal websites

1. Build complex site layouts quickly with panels

2. Combine Panels with other Drupal modules to create dynamic social media websites

3. Get solutions to the most common 'Panels' problems

4. A practical approach packed with real-world examples to enrich understanding

Drupal 6 Themes

ISBN: 978-1-847195-66-1   Paperback: 312 pages

Create new themes for your Drupal 6 site with clean layout and powerful CSS styling

1. Learn to create new Drupal 6 themes

2. No experience of Drupal theming required

3. Techniques and tools for creating and modifying themes

4. A complete guide to the system's themable element

Please check **www.PacktPub.com** for information on our titles

LaVergne, TN USA
26 March 2011

221698LV00003B/32/P